The
HOUSE
of
AWADH

PRAISE FOR *THE HOUSE OF AWADH*

'Abhimanyu Kumar and Aletta Andre have brought Malcha Mahal and the lost house of Awadh back to vivid, poignant life, in this sweeping saga that is, by turns, both melancholy and fascinating.'

—Narayani Basu

'*The House of Awadh* delves into the life of the enigmatic Begum Wilayat who claimed descent from the Nawab of Awadh and lived with her children in a fourteenth-century hunting lodge in the heart of Delhi. Was she a true descendant of nobility or merely an imposter? This intriguing book takes us on a journey to discover the truth behind her storied past.'

—Rana Safvi

The
HOUSE
of
AWADH

A HIDDEN TRAGEDY

ALETTA ANDRÉ
ABHIMANYU KUMAR

HarperCollins *Publishers* India

First published in India by HarperCollins *Publishers* 2025
4th Floor, Tower A, Building No. 10, DLF Cyber City,
DLF Phase II, Gurugram, Haryana – 122002
www.harpercollins.co.in

2 4 6 8 10 9 7 5 3 1

Copyright © Aletta André and Abhimanyu Kumar 2025

P-ISBN: 978-93-6569-369-0
E-ISBN: 978-93-6569-705-6

The views and opinions expressed in this book are the authors' own and the facts are as reported by them, and the publishers are not in any way liable for the same.

Aletta André and Abhimanyu Kumar assert the moral right to be identified as the authors of this work.

All rights reserved. No part of this publication may be reproduced, stored in a retrieval system, or transmitted, in any form or by any means, electronic, mechanical, photocopying, recording or otherwise, without the prior permission of the publishers.

Typeset in 11/15 Adobe Caslon Pro at
HarperCollins *Publishers* India

Printed and bound at
Replika Press Pvt. Ltd.

This book is produced from independently certified FSC® paper to ensure responsible forest management.

To our parents,
V.P.N. Singh, Punam Singh, Lex André and Froukje André

The detailed notes pertaining to this book are available on the HarperCollins *Publishers* India website. Scan this QR code to access the same.

CONTENTS

Introduction ix

Part I: Memory

1. Malcha Mahal 3
2. City of Nawabs 25
3. The Family Retainer 57
4. The Princess's Diary 74

Part II: History

5. The Looted Begums 101
6. Rebel Queen 117
7. The Real House of Awadh 140

Part III: Identity

8. Paradise Lost 179
9. Kashmiri Citizens 201
10. Transformation 223

| 11. | Royal After All? | 267 |
| 12. | Beyond Truth and Lies | 289 |

Epilogue: History Repeats Itself   305
Acknowledgements   311
Notes   313
Index   315

Introduction

'They would all occupy a separate corner in the Mahal, sitting away from each other. They seemed consumed by disappointment.'[1]

It's hard to pinpoint exactly what it was that attracted us to the story of Begum Wilayat Mahal and her children, Princess Sakina and Prince Ali Raza.

Was it their seemingly eccentric behaviour highlighted by the international and Indian press? Their claims of centuries of injustice towards the rulers of Awadh, a former kingdom annexed—unfairly— by the British in 1856? Their self-inflicted solitude or, rather, exile in degrading circumstances? Or was it just the mystery about their origins and ancestry?

The self-proclaimed royals of Awadh had inhabited an overgrown and dilapidated Tughlaq-era hunting lodge in New Delhi's Ridge Forest for decades, refusing to mingle with 'commoners' and demanding 'their' palaces in Lucknow be returned to them. Indian and foreign journalists had followed the family since their dramatic arrival at the New Delhi Railway Station in 1975, where they squatted for a decade before being given the centuries-old monument Malcha Mahal to live in.

Despite the extensive coverage of the family in mainstream press, we always had the sense that there was something missing. It was hard not to be intrigued and even captivated by it, like many others. The more we came to know, the more it seemed as if the family's history was tied to the story of India itself—from British rule to Partition, post-Independence nation-building, identity politics and the rise of Hindu nationalism.

In a way, this book took root in 2015, when Abhimanyu wrote a short article on the family in a weekly newspaper he was working with at the time.[2] He recalled, in another, longer article published a few years later:

> Years ago, I had heard from a heritage enthusiast that Princess Sakina had died. The rumour was that Prince Ali Raza was keeping the corpse in the Malcha Mahal without burying it. (…)
> I was then able to get the prince's landline phone number from a guard at the Indian Space Research Organisation (ISRO) Earth Station next to the Mahal. A prim gentleman's voice answered the call on the other end, betraying a slight trace of annoyance. I remember telling him that I was an admirer of his ancestor, the king Wajid Ali Shah, for his secular views, and that I wished to meet him for a story. I knew he was not keen on meeting Indian journalists, but took a chance. He refused to meet or talk any more, only telling me cryptically that princess Sakina was 'very much around'. Of course, this did not answer my query if she were alive or not.
> I tried again [the] next day and got the same reply. 'If you are a gentleman, you will not press further.' I did not try to meet him

after that. For a while, I had the idea to wait for him standing on the long and winding road that connects Malcha Mahal to Sardar Patel Marg outside, with its rows of state bhawans and behind them, the Malcha Marg residential area. But, busy with other assignments, I couldn't pursue the story further.[3]

After the prince died, approximately in the last week of September 2017,[4] there was a flurry of stories in the newspapers, and we began looking into the family again. Shortly after the news broke, we hiked up to Malcha Mahal to see what could be found there—anything that would tell us a bit more about the extraordinary lives that Ali Raza, Sakina and Wilayat had lived. We found paintbrushes, colours and an easel; handwritten essays on Awadh's history—on thick handmade paper embossed with the emblem of two fishes, the symbol of the House of Awadh—proclaiming the family as the last inheritors of Wajid Ali Shah and Hazrat Mahal; dog magazines in Dutch; envelopes with stamps from all over the world, addressing them as His or Her Highness, among the senders were academics, artists, journalists and members of royalty; a photocopy of Ali Raza's voter ID; names and phone numbers scribbled on numerous pieces of paper; bank passbooks; telephone bills; clothes. All these discoveries were akin to puzzle pieces that we have tried to put together in this book.

Towards the end of 2019, the family made international news once again. The *New York Times* published an article titled 'The Jungle Prince of Delhi', citing relatives scattered in England, Pakistan and the United States who dismissed the royal claims.[5] The publication presented—what seemed like—an altogether different narrative: that the family, including Wilayat, were Kashmiris who had adopted the royal personae after the death of her husband, a Mr Butt from Kashmir. That they were from Pakistan and had no actual connection to Lucknow or royalty. Everything they had told the press, the *New York Times* claimed, was a blatant lie, a fraud, in essence. The article relied heavily on an interview with a dying brother of Ali Raza, who dismissed all claims of royalty. Despite several other leads that pointed to hitherto unexplored aspects of the family and its members, the lengthy article chose to focus on the most sensational aspect—the royal status. A set of documents shared by the home ministry with the newspaper, discussed in a follow-up article in 2020, buttressed the claims about them being Kashmiris, to the exclusion of any links with Lucknow.[6]

Publications in India and abroad ran with it, with articles employing words and phrases such as 'frauds', 'the fake queen', 'web of lies', 'imposters' and 'mentally ill'.[7]

If royal descent could not be proved, the articles seemed to conclude, Wilayat Mahal must have been either completely out of her mind or a fraudulent imposter, and not much in between. Ellen Barry, the writer of the *New York Times* article, concluded that she had finally uncovered the truth. 'I have plundered their secret,' she remarked towards the end of the article. 'I must admit, it offends me a little when people think they can lie to reporters.'[8]

So, was it a lie, a secret or, as Barry wrote elsewhere in her article, a 'family business'? These were words that implied an intentional deceit. Barry's take on the family subtly elided over the question of power as well. The Malcha Mahal residents had no power in any sense of the word. It would have been apposite and perfectly understandable had she been offended by the falsehoods of a figure in power, for example. But she chose to employ her substantial journalistic resources over a family that had been cast away from society and had been contemptuously mocked for decades by the mainstream media, especially in the last years of their lives. Journalism is supposed to speak truth to power, not humiliate the powerless.

Over the course of our investigation, we found that Wilayat's claims were actually not completely removed from the truth—though we had no idea about this at the start. We set out with the thought that there were other ways of interpreting the same circumstances without compromising with the truth in any way. Ultimately, claims of 'truth' in a case like this appear to us as somewhat overstated; it will be far more honest to say that the best anyone—including us—can do is present a version of it.

As early reports on the family show, they did not hide their pre-Partition past. The identity of Wilayat's husband, who had a prestigious job at the Lucknow University; their move to Pakistan after Partition; their falling-out with the political elite there; their stay in Kashmir in the 1960s—all of these facts were shared with Indian journalists and published after their arrival in Delhi in 1975.[9] In their mind, this did not contradict their claims of royal descent, which they later laid emphasis on as interest from international media in their story grew.

Such disputes over lineage, in any case, form part of the narrative around royal families in India and even abroad. For example, in the 1970s, a controversy raged in Delhi and the national press about Bahadur Shah Zafar's official heir. Two sides contended for the title, but no one could prove their claim conclusively. The story was reported in *Hindustan Times* in 1975, the same year Wilayat entered the stage, with headlines such as 'Five Year Fuss for "Mogul" in Penury' and 'Zafar's Real Descendant Stakes His Claims'. While both these stories were published in October, in November the newspaper published a long letter from one of the descendants staking his claim. Nothing came off it.[10]

In Wilayat's case, other claimants to the Awadh royal heritage started to dismiss her statements as soon as she appeared in Delhi in 1975.[11] Prince Anjum Quder,[12] descendant of Wajid Ali Shah and Hazrat Mahal's son Birjis Qadr, regularly sought the attention of the media and government with his counterclaims.

Hazrat Mahal was one of Shah's hundreds of wives, but she became the most well-known of them, as she played a major role in the 1857 Revolt. Wilayat claimed to be Hazrat Mahal's descendant, a possibility dismissed by Anjum Quder. But his protests were rarely picked up or mentioned by journalists writing on Wilayat, whether consciously or not. The story as told by her was perhaps just too intriguing and exciting. Outlandish statements by Wilayat and her children—'Ordinariness is not only a crime, it is a sin'[13]—and their eccentricities such as Wilayat's wish to be photographed only on moonlit nights[14] were sure to cause enough of a sensation in the press. And they did.

But there is much more to this tale. Among other things, Wilayat internalized and lived her 'role' to such an extent—with royal insignia, extensive historical knowledge and negotiations with the Indian government for justice—that her persona merged with the legacy of the House of Awadh.

While the mainstream press became increasingly hostile, some writers have taken a more sympathetic stance in recent years. Alejandra Moreno-Álvarez of the University of Oviedo, for example, gives prominence to the traumatic history of Partition in Wilayat's story in the academic journal *Revista Canaria de Estudios Ingleses*. She argues that Wilayat's identity may (or may not) have been imagined, but that this would not make it 'fake'—quoting Urvashi Butalia from her book about Partition, *The Other Side of Silence*: 'The way people choose to remember their history is as important as what we may consider historical facts'; and James Young from his book *Writing and Rewriting the Holocaust*: 'Whatever "fiction" emerge from the survivors' accounts are not deviations from the "truth" but are part of the truth in any particular version.'[15]

This line of thought also corresponds with that of Leonie Broekstra, a Dutch photographer who was asked by Ali Raza to digitalize his photo archive in the years before he died. 'He felt the same urge to archive his life, his history, just like his sister had,' she recollects from their first meeting in an interview with the South Asian photography journal *Pix*.[16]

Broekstra's reference to Sakina concerns a memoir she wrote and self-published, which is a combination of Awadh history, personal experiences and poetry. It had been sadly dismissed as 'incoherent' by the few foreign journalists who were given a copy. Barry called it 'almost unreadable',[17] but we see it as an important document in the family's story, as did Broekstra, who argues: 'How did the Royals of Oudh archive themselves? What does it say about their search for meaning and selfhood, their claim to fame, holiness, and a place in the history of India? Their story lives on and could not be more relevant in a country riven by questions of identity and belonging.'

What got obscured in the magnetic pull of Wilayat's interpretation of the culmination of the historic events leading to the 1857 Revolt and subsequent developments was that the House of Awadh never really ceased to exist. Wilayat Mahal was more a symbol of its past; her tragic life and her pride in destitution can be seen as a stand-in for the tragic fate of the House of Awadh and its demands for justice, which were ignored for centuries by the British as well as successive Indian governments.

Many descendants of the House of Awadh have continued to live in Kolkata and Lucknow, receiving pensions till date from the government, although the amounts are minuscule. However, their properties were never returned, while many other erstwhile royal families in India have continued to own palaces, some turning them into successful businesses. Government papers accessed in the National Archives reveal the reason behind the government's refusal to compensate the royal descendants of the House of Awadh; the papers also demonstrate that the government of independent India was as censorious about the last king of Awadh as the British, who saw Wajid Ali Shah as a debauched ruler who needed to be stopped;

we discuss this in the chapter dealing with the Kolkata-based descendants of Hazrat Mahal.

Some critics believe that the neglect of nawabi architecture in the decades since reflect this attitude, which has carried over from the time of Independence. In the state of Uttar Pradesh this seems to have become more pronounced in recent years under the regional Hindu nationalist government.

The Bharatiya Janata Party-led government set the tone shortly after coming to power in March 2017. Chief Minister Yogi Adityanath said that the Taj Mahal, one of the most famous monuments in the world, was not representative of Indian heritage, and in July of that year it was left out of the annual budget's heritage plan and a booklet highlighting the main heritage sites of Uttar Pradesh.[18] Member of the legislative assembly, Sangeet Som, went on to say that the Taj Mahal was built by traitors—it was built by Mughal Emperor Shah Jahan as a monument to his deceased wife. Adityanath was forced to do damage control, by visiting the Taj Mahal, becoming the first BJP chief minister of the state to ever do so; he declared during his visit that it was an important part of India's heritage, after all.[19] The booklet, the government explained later, was meant to highlight new projects and focus areas.[20]

This booklet, however, also made no mention of the Bara Imambara in Lucknow, built by the fourth nawab, Asaf-ud-Daula. It is Uttar Pradesh's second best visited monument, but in dire need of basic upkeep and restauration work.[21] Such an approach to monuments with a Muslim heritage has created an impression among some of Lucknow's Muslims that the selection of what not to include was made based on the Hindu-nationalist ideology of the party. One descendant of Asaf-ud-Daula wrote a letter to the chief minister, which was reported to have stated that 'it appeared that the Imambara was being denied the glory it deserved just because it had religious significance for the Muslims'.²² Lucknow-based journalist Kulsum Mustafa wrote that the Imambara was 'the epitome of good governance'. 'It embodies a ruler's love and concern for his subjects during difficult times. The Nawab provided work and food through the construction of the Imambara.'²³

That's not how the current rulers of Uttar Pradesh view the nawabs of Awadh, however. In February 2023, for example, deputy chief minister of the state, Brajesh Pathak, said he demanded the name of Lucknow to be changed to Lakhanpur or Laxmanpur. He said he considered the name Lucknow a symbol of slavery, because he believed this name was introduced by Nawab Asaf-ud-Daula. 'It seems completely wrong to give a signal of slavery by telling stories of luxury and wastefulness of the Nawabs of Lucknow to our future generation,' said Pathak, followed by a statement of approval regarding the annexation of Awadh by the British.²⁴

What Wilayat Mahal did, in essence, was stage a decades-long protest: against the annexation of the House of Awadh, the loot of the kingdom's wealth by the British East India Company and the unfair aftermath of these events in independent India. It could even be said that she was ahead of her time in this particular aspect, considering the recent growth of a wider international movement for apologies and reparations for historical injustices of the colonial period. Though significant, Wilayat's protest to draw attention to Awadh and the historical injustice is, in our view, just one layer. The outer layer.

This book seeks to use history, documents, cross-border reportage and interviews to explore the other layers of experiences and traumas of the family of Wilayat Mahal and how they ultimately connected to Awadh and its discontents. It also seeks to establish her and her family as part of a wider milieu of Muslim citizens of pre-Partition India who were forced to make certain choices during the tragic event of the country being torn asunder in two. For some, these choices did not pay off and ended up destroying their lives, like in the case of Wilayat and her children.

Part I, 'Memory', deals with the selective and subjective parts of the family's history, tracing it from different perspectives—the places where they lived; the people they encountered in the final decades of their lives; and the letters and photos they left behind.

Part II, 'History', goes into historical events that were intertwined with their personal memory—the conduct of British Governor-General Warren Hastings in Awadh and the question of historical justice; Wilayat's claim of ancestry from a long line of brave and strong royal women; and the legacy of Awadh in Kolkata.

Part III, 'Identity', addresses the forgotten histories and conspiracies in the first decades after Partition; questions regarding the family's roots in Kashmir and Pakistan; and Wilayat's place among the Awadh royalty.

Part I
Memory

'Your history gets in the way of my memory.'

—Agha Shahid Ali[1]

Malcha Mahal[1]

'It has no doors or windows. It is stark open to all the four seasons of nature in complete dilapidated ruination. It has the honour of being nearly 700 years old.'[2]

With these words, Sakina poetically described the mixed feelings she had about the monument she moved into with her brother, Ali Raza, and her mother, Wilayat Mahal, on 28 March 1985.[3] It was not what they had hoped for when they started their protest at the New Delhi Railway Station a decade earlier. But Malcha Mahal, a hunting lodge built in the fourteenth century, turned out to be the best deal they could get. After all, the lodge had been in the possession of the nawab of Awadh until the kingdom was annexed by the British in 1856. He reportedly visited it regularly to hunt deer and leopards in the Ridge Forest.[4] Never mind that there was no running water, no electricity and no protection from bats and snakes. It was a former royal abode, now restored to them, self-proclaimed claimants to the throne of Awadh.

Soon, the family formalized the status they accorded to the lodge. Large signboards appeared at the entry, stating it to be the residence of the 'Rulers of Oudh'—Oudh being the anglicized spelling of Awadh, which Wilayat preferred. She used the same spelling in a gold-printed letterhead on thick, handmade paper for her correspondence and on metal trunks, both of which we first saw when we entered Malcha Mahal for the first time after Ali Raza's death in 2017. By that time, the trunks were already empty, looted of whatever valuables may have been kept inside. Papers were scattered on the hard, uneven floor that was littered with bat faeces, along with old clothes, magazines and tubes of oil paint, offering a peek into the lives that were lived here.

For decades, Wilayat, till her death in 1993, Ali Raza and Sakina lived extremely secluded lives, offering entry and an interview only to the occasional foreign correspondent. The resulting articles contributed to the mysterious air around them, describing servants carrying handwritten notes on silver platters, chained dogs and arrogant siblings.

We first walked the forest path up to the 'Rulers of Oudh' signboard in 2015, not daring to go beyond it as it warned in clear language that intruders would be gunned down or attacked by hound dogs. It was hard to imagine how an old prince and princess could live there, somewhere behind the dense and hostile-looking greenery, full of cacti and keekar trees, and why. Their invisible presence defined the location, and its meaning, in an overwhelming way.

But with the last inhabitants dead and most of their possessions removed—a little bit more every time we visited—their decades of existence here has become merely one of the many layers of the past concealed in the monument's bricks.

∼

To reach Malcha Mahal, you enter the Central Ridge Forest, a surprisingly dense stretch of greenery at the edge of the affluent diplomatic enclave of Chanakyapuri. The area has some of the city's most luxurious hotels and residences of the rich and the well-connected, in the heart of India's capital.

The same forest houses the crumbling boundary walls of an ancient water well and an 800-year-old dargah surrounded by dozens of earthen pots said to imprison the spirits of bad souls and djinns. The pir, caretaker, of the dargah still holds regular exorcisms to add to the collection.[5]

When we met the pir after the prince's death in 2017, he said the latter would visit him occasionally. 'I advised him to be less reclusive as he was alone and getting on in years, but he paid me no heed,' the pir lamented. The pir's last pressing concern was that the Municipal Corporation of Delhi had cut off his water supply and he requested us to help him with it.

Passing by the dargah, and going up the road whose sides are full of garbage, monkeys and jackals, we come to a dead end at the entry gate to the Delhi Earth Station run by India's space agency, ISRO. Nothing here indicates the presence of a monument. No signboards exist. But those who know what they are looking for can climb over a yellow police barricade and follow a narrow, slightly uphill path lined by broken barbed wire and tall, thorny plants. Not long after, an imposing building with arched gateways and high ceilings appears. The structure is elevated with a stone plinth; the main entry above a staircase of seven steps which you can climb from two sides. From there, one enters a central hall that connects to three different bays, one on each side, except where the entry is. Both at the back and at the front entry, there are narrow staircases to the flat rooftop.

Currently, no one administers Malcha Mahal, and the Archaeological Survey of India (ASI) has shown no interest in managing it after failing to get it back from Wilayat in 1986. A non-profit called the Indian National Trust for Art and Cultural Heritage (INTACH) filed a proposal in October 2019 to conserve it on behalf of the Delhi government, which never materialized. In July 2022, the Delhi government announced that its archaeology department would carry out restoration work. A year later, thirty-six trees that were deemed dangerous for the monument were removed, but no other work has been done yet. Plans for a boundary wall with an iron grill and the construction of toilets for visitors were stopped by the High Court, which said that the forest was too important for Delhi's air quality, and the monument should be protected without adding new structures.[6]

So, for now, the walls are occupied by bees and the ceilings by bats. Trees grow wild through the windows and staircases that lead to the flat roof, which offers stunning views of the forest and central Delhi. Centuries after it was built, the monument has become almost one with its surroundings.

Malcha Mahal was most likely built by Firoz Shah Tughlaq, who reigned over the Sultanate of Delhi from 1351 to 1388. One story, narrated by the noted Delhi chronicler the late R.V. Smith, is that the sultan lost his way during one of his hunting trips in the area and was taken care of by a gypsy girl. He built the lodge in gratitude to her.[7] It is unknown who named the monument Malcha Mahal, or whether the lodge predates the village of Malcha that once stood around the monument or the other way around.

When it was first built, the lodge's surroundings must have been dense forest. According to Pradip Krishen, an expert on Delhi and the Ridge Forest who lives in neighbouring Chanakyapuri, hunters would certainly have encountered leopards and deer, and possibly even tigers. 'The villagers were pastoral people, who lived inside the forest,' says Krishen, who walks his dog in the forest every day. 'The monument may have been used by them for protection in the last days of Mughal rule, as this was a common practice in those days when power was loose and many bandits active.'[8]

The great Mughal empire, which once extended from Lahore (now in Pakistan) to Dhaka (now in Bangladesh), formally met its end in 1858 when the British exiled the last emperor, Bahadur Shah Zafar, to Burma—though his power had already been extremely limited.

It can be said now—with the benefit of hindsight—that his fate had been sealed two years earlier, with the annexation of Awadh, a wealthy kingdom, at the beginning of 1856.

The annexation would lead to the so-called Sepoy Mutiny in 1857, also called the First War of Indian Independence or the 1857 Revolt[9]—which, in turn, would motivate the British government to abolish the East India Company and take direct charge of India, finally bringing the curtains down on the Mughal empire.

Awadh was one of the kingdoms that came up in the autumn of the Mughal empire, which began to crumble from the eighteenth century onwards. It is generally believed that the downfall started in 1707 after the death of Aurangzeb, the ruthless emperor known for a southwards expansion. Others mark the Persian invasion of Delhi in 1739 as the beginning of the end. Whatever the tipping point was, those who had been waiting on the sidelines seized their chance as the centre weakened.

Among them were the nawabs or governors of Awadh, a fertile province of the Mughal empire, adjacent to its capital of Delhi, roughly corresponding to the present-day state of Uttar Pradesh. In the book *Begums of Awadh*, K.S. Santha writes:

> The limits of the province roughly were the Himalayas on the North, Bihar in the East, Manikpur (in the province of Allahabad) in the South and Kanouj in the West. The length of the province was about 270 miles and the breadth was about 230 miles. The province was unevenly divided into five

districts: Haveli Awadh (Faizabad), Gorakhpur, Bahraich, Lucknow and Khairabad.[10]

It was said to be a wife's taunt upon which the House of Awadh was founded. Ashirbadi Lal Srivastava writes in his book *The First Two Nawabs of Awadh*: 'One day ... Mir Muhammad Amin's wife taunted him for being a hanger-on in her father's house.' In a fit of anger, Amin, whose early life is lost to history, and who would later be known as Sadat Khan, left his hometown of Nishapur in today's Iran. His father and brother had already left for India, where they lived on state patronage in Azimabad, today's Patna, in the early years of the eighteenth century. Srivastava adds that the story of the wife's taunt may have been an invention of the historian who first chronicled Sadat Khan's life, as it was written more than a century after his death. 'In Indian folk-lore we find the same romantic story ascribed to every ambitious youth,' he adds in a footnote.[11]

From Patna, Khan went to Gujarat to serve a feudal lord, Sarbuland Khan, but left when he was accused by his master of being too haughty for his position; according to Srivastava, who describes him as 'the proud and sensitive child from Iran', he was employed as a camp supervisor and had not taken enough care one windy evening to make sure Sarbuland Khan's tents were pitched properly.[12]

Sadat Khan ended up in Delhi, where he rose through the ranks over time. His fortunes shifted with a change in patrons, and slowly he became adept at court intrigue. The Mughal claim of being the central authority in India was by then in free fall. The Marathas were winning territories and becoming stronger in Central India. Mughal emperors ascended to and departed from the throne in short intervals, dependent on powerful factions operational in the court, and always fearing a foreign invasion.

Sadat Khan, described as a cultured man with military skills and clout, thrived in this atmosphere. He allied himself with whichever political faction was powerful at any given period in the emperor's court and which could help him achieve his ambitious goals.

He had already become the governor of Agra when in 1722 he was asked to take over as the governor of Awadh. The task was difficult, as Awadh was then ruled by a group of nobility called the Sheikhzadas, who resisted him with all their might. But Khan persevered and managed to subdue them before establishing a dynasty that would make Awadh a place of wonder and splendour in the next 130-odd years. Amaresh Mishra writes in *Lucknow: Fire of Grace*:

> In A.D. 1722 he was neck deep in a sea of revolts and instability and had to virtually fight his way to the heart of Lucknow. Resisted stoutly by the Sheikhs, he won the battle by a combination of diplomacy and military strength.[13]

After the demise of Sadat Khan, his son-in-law, Safdarjung, came to power. About him, the historian Ravi Bhatt writes in his book *The Life and Times of the Nawabs of Awadh*: 'Nawab Safdar Jung was an ambitious ruler and played his cards very well in the game of power.'[14]

He was succeeded by his son, Shuja-ud-Daula. His 'reign was marked by a combination of violence, subterfuge and suffering', writes Amaresh Mishra.[15]

The two powers, the East India Company and Awadh, met on the battlefield in 1764, in Buxar, now in Bihar. The former's troops defeated the armies of the latter, resulting in the permanent stationing of Company troops and British interference in Awadh.

Subsequent injustices committed by British officials, in particular Warren Hastings, left a deep impression on Wilayat Mahal, and we will look into these in more detail in Chapter 5. For now it suffices to say that the British managed to exercise their influence and extract large sums of money from the nawabs.

Rosie Llewellyn-Jones, in her book *The Last King in India*, calls it a 'classic example of divide and rule',[16] when the Company in 1819 offered Ghazi-ud-Din, who was the nawab of Awadh at the time, the title of king of Awadh if he declared his independence from the Mughals. The nawab jumped at the opportunity, even though the title was merely ceremonial and mostly helped the Company in weakening the authority of the Mughals. He got a festive coronation but was treated by the British as a mere puppet.

With the anointment of Wajid Ali Shah as the king in 1847, the British grew alarmed. Shah was too grand a personality to be anyone's puppet. Even when he was only the heir apparent, as Llewellyn-Jones writes, the British were worried about his 'character', which they did not find to be suitable for a king.

Shah was a poet, musician, dancer, dramatist, connoisseur of the fine arts and a bon vivant in general. At the same time, he was also a competent administrator. Despite being a Muslim king, he enjoyed the loyalty of his majority Hindu subjects, perhaps partly because the kings of Awadh had a long tradition of appointing Hindus in important positions in their court, among other things.

Shah was also an aficionado of Hindu culture, as well as a practitioner of the classical Hindu arts. The thumris he composed are sung till date, for example. He was a devotee of Lord Krishna, and wrote and acted in plays about Him.

For the British, such behaviour was not worthy even of a man, much less a king. They thought Shah 'effeminate' and found his artistic endeavours nothing more than a cover for his 'debauchery'. The ultimate annexation of Awadh and Shah's exile to Calcutta in early 1856 seemed to have been predetermined pretty much from the moment Shah ascended the throne.

∼

Shah's mother, Malika Kishwar, refused to give up without a fight. Soon after the annexation, she decided to set sail from India to

London seeking redress for what she perceived as a great wrong, believing in the British sense of fair play. England was then under the crown of Queen Victoria, who had ruled for almost two decades. The Queen Mother's delegation had prepared an appeal to Queen Victoria to reverse the annexation, but it was doomed to fail.

In most articles, it is mentioned that Wilayat claimed to be a descendant of Wajid Ali Shah. Interestingly, she hardly referred to him in public. Wilayat, as reflected by Sakina's book and interviews the family gave over the years, preferred to see herself as part of a long line of women who fought back. Not just the Queen Mother, but also, in particular, Hazrat Mahal, one of Shah's mut'ah or temporary wives, who became a heroine of the 1857 Revolt, and about whom we will write more in Chapter 6. She had stayed back in Lucknow after Shah accepted a generous pension—Rs 1 lakh per month—and moved his entire court to exile in Calcutta (present-day Kolkata), where he continued to live in splendour. While he distanced himself from the Revolt—which was concentrated in Delhi and parts of Awadh and is widely believed to have been sparked by the latter's annexation—Hazrat Mahal led an army against the British.

Residents of the village of Malcha, too, played their part. 'Historical accounts suggest that the villages of the area had played host to mutineers during the 1857 revolt and provided them with supplies during the march to Red Fort in the old city of Shahjahanabad,' wrote the late journalist Arpit Parashar in 2012 in a well-researched article for the magazine *Fountain Ink*.[17] Parashar further describes a Jat soldier from Malcha village, Gulab Singh, who fought the British. He 'later came to be known for his bravery in the villages of the area as *Kaaleghodewala* (one who rode a black horse)'.

The Revolt broke out during the Queen Mother's failed delegation to London, where it got a lot of media attention, but no serious response to its main demand: the restoration of the kingdom of Awadh. The delegation consisted of princes, their wives and children, servants and other officials, who all lived in style in London, renting out an entire hotel for their use for no less than thirteen months. The press had a field day speculating on the fate of the exotic delegation and mocking the royals for being vain—including the Queen Mother, who kept a strict purdah, which was reported as a curiosity, while the satirical magazine *Punch* delighted in her loss and desperation.

By the time the Queen Mother finally got an audience with Queen Victoria in July 1857, the Revolt had started, crushing whatever chance she may have had of a sympathetic ear. So, the delegation left. During a stopover in Paris, the Queen Mother died. Her funeral, at the famous Père Lachaise cemetery where artistes such as Frédéric Chopin and Oscar Wilde are buried, reportedly had the ambassadors of Turkey and Iran in attendance.[18] This illustrates the respect Awadh had at the time in the Islamic world—though it was quickly forgotten in the following decades of imperialism, war and the struggle for independence.

∽

In the 1970s, the spectre of the House of Awadh came back to haunt the Government of India, then under the prime ministership of Indira Gandhi.

Begum Wilayat Mahal, claiming to be the last heir of the House of Awadh, moved into the first-class waiting room of the New Delhi Railway Station. Along with her were three children—although one of them seems to have joined her later, remaining in the shadows throughout—a retinue of servants, a pack of ferocious pedigreed dogs, expensive carpets and antique china.

One of the first articles about her appeared in *Hindustan Times* on 21 March 1975. We found it in the Nehru Memorial Library[19] in central Delhi, after days of painstakingly going through old newspapers preserved on microfilm. Some details we later discovered to be incorrect, but the gist of the family's background story is remarkably complete. Written by reporter Promilla Kalhan, who at the time already had a biography of Kamala Nehru to her name, it opens with Wilayat's claims of descent from Hazrat Mahal and Wajid Ali Shah. It goes on to narrate how Wilayat and her husband crossed over to Pakistan at the time of Partition, where he died, after which she returned to India in the early 1960s, where she was allotted a bungalow in Kashmir and given a monthly maintenance allowance.[20] It is remarkable that this entire back story was almost immediately forgotten. We never read about it in any other articles about the family in the following decades. Perhaps it was all just too complicated to fit into the sensational story of the homeless queen.

Like the Queen Mother in London over a century earlier, Wilayat had ambitious demands just short of 'her kingdom' being restored to her. She wanted some of the erstwhile kingdom's property back, such as a palace in Lucknow that India's first Prime Minister, Jawaharlal Nehru, had converted into a scientific drug research institute.

Like the Queen Mother, Wilayat fought for what she saw as rightfully hers until her death. And much like the Queen Mother, Wilayat and her 'delegation' were met with a combination of curiosity, fascination and ridicule.

At the same time, Wilayat perhaps accomplished more than the Queen Mother ever could. To be sure, it took her more than ten years at the New Delhi Railway Station, rather than thirteen months in a hotel—and we will explore those railway years in more detail in the following chapters—but in those years she met government officials, was offered monies and multiple residences and ultimately a palace in 1985, which she accepted, though it was dilapidated and infested with bats and snakes. It also happened to be in Delhi, rather than in Lucknow.

In the 128 years since the 1857 Revolt, Malcha Mahal and its surroundings had lived multiple lives by the time Wilayat, Sakina and Ali Raza moved in. For starters, the village of Malcha and a large part of the forest around it had disappeared as a consequence of the British moving their capital in the vicinity in 1911.

Malcha and other villages, such as Raisina, had to make space for the new capital of New Delhi. All that remains of Malcha village now is the area called Malcha Marg in Chanakyapuri, the address of many diplomats and expats, the nearby Malcha Marg market and a temple that used to belong to the village. What remained of the forest—the area around Malcha Mahal—was developed for horse riding.

The villages did not, however, go down without a fight. 'Village panchayats were held and it was decided by Jats of at least seven villages—Malcha, Palam, Prahladpur, Sultanpuri, Manglapuri, Motibagh and Gothda—that they would fight for their lands,' wrote Parashar in *Fountain Ink*. The farmers prepared for battle, fortifying the boundaries of Raisina and Malcha villages, led by village head Amar Singh. Coincidentally, Singh was the grandson of Gulab Singh, the local rebel who had fought in the 1857 Revolt, whose family had gained in status due to their ancestor's heroism.

The British handled the situation with colonial might, killing thirty-three people including Amar Singh, and leaving the villages in ruins. Survivors moved northwestwards and settled in what is today the Sonipat district of Haryana, where they formed a new village, which they named Malcha Patti.

∼

Standing on the flat roof of Malcha Mahal, one can feel the perfect isolation of the place. About 2 kilometres away are the Parliament House and Rashtrapati Bhavan, the latter having originally been built as the Viceroy's House in the decade that followed the destruction of Malcha village. The grand buildings look small in comparison to the significant stretch of the dense, green and peaceful forest that lies in between. The sound of debates, protests, rallies and pens signing treaties does not reach here. When the symbols of colonial power became symbols of independent India at midnight, 15 August 1947, the view from Malcha Mahal remained unchanged.

'It was beautiful, surrounded only by nature,' recalls painter Shanti Dave, who is eighty-nine when we speak to him in late 2019. He was one of the first residents of Malcha Mahal after Independence, and though it was only for a few years, he remembers it well. Dave, along with three sculptors, used it as an art studio. At the time he was an internationally established painter known for his large murals, including one that he painted in 1964 at the JFK Airport in New York. Photos of him standing in front of Malcha Mahal in the late 1960s show a monument not yet overgrown with brush and vegetation. There was space to stand back and take a picture of the entire structure—something that's impossible today.

It was Prime Minister Jawaharlal Nehru who in 1962 gave the old hunting lodge in the care of the Lalit Kala Akademi, the central organization responsible for the promotion of arts in the country. Before that, some had proposed that it be renovated as a boutique hotel or a tourist destination, but, as per a *Times of India* article, it was Nehru who preferred the idea of an art studio there. In 1961, the Akademi had submitted a proposal for this to the government.[21] The actual handing over of the monument to the academy happened after Nehru's death, around 1966. By that time, the *Times of India* wrote a few years later, 'anti-social elements had taken over the neglected monument as an ideal hide-out' and had to be 'flushed out'.[22]

It is not clear when Malcha Mahal got its current name. Dave knew it as Bistedari Mahal or Bistedari Malcha, a name that according to INTACH refers to the columns used in the structure. When the journalist from *Times of India* visited the art studio in the late 1960s, they did not refer to it by any name. It was described in pretty much the same state as Wilayat and her children would find it two decades later. 'There is no electricity. No water-supply. No tea-snack-and cigarette-stall around. But the artists have stuck tenaciously to the spot. They know they will not get a better studio site in the Capital.'[23]

Dave confirms this. 'We were young artists, trying to find out who we were after Independence,' says Dave, now partially blind and hard of hearing. He did not live in the monument, but drove there every morning, carrying water, milk, food and petroleum lamps for the evenings. His fond memories of the space included a ceiling-high artwork he painted, a jackal that once occupied his studio for days, wood-fired lunches and moonlit performances on the roof by the famous Indian classical dancer Uma Sharma. At the time of the *Times of India* visit, he was organizing an exhibition of his art there, expecting only 'true art lovers' to show up at the remote location.

One of the artists who frequented Dave's studio was Jagdish Swaminathan, a painter, poet and writer who was also an active member of the Communist Party of India. In a 2006 article in *India Today*, Swaminathan's son, S. Kalidas, writes:

> I vividly remember visiting Shanti-bhai's magnificent high-domed workspace with my painter father for extended day-long picnics where artists would make merry with beer or rum. Sushila-ben, Shanti-bhai's wife, would serve us delicious lunch or dinner cooked over wood fire.[24]

The dream ended soon after, when the artists had to vacate the space because the site next to it had been marked for the Delhi Earth Station—a structure used for satellite observations by ISRO—which was officially inaugurated in 1977. Plans by the New Delhi Municipal Committee to start an open-air museum of sculptures, including a garden and piped water connection for sanitary facilities, never materialized. Guards of the Earth Station started using the monument's roof as a badminton court during breaks.[25] The only trace of the artists' presence that remained were rolling steel shutters on all the outer gates that had been installed to keep the monkeys out and lock the place up at night.

Today, those shutters are broken or hanging from nearby trees. But for years they proved useful to Wilayat and her children, who lived there under spartan conditions.

∽

From the moment the family moved into Malcha Mahal till her death, Wilayat never appeared in public again. She only met a handful of foreign journalists until she passed away in 1993, as did Sakina, while Ali Raza would venture out to sell jewellery for cash or to buy food. Indian journalists were not given access—perhaps because the international media had been more sympathetic to them during the railway years, writing about their claims, the questionable annexation of Awadh and the appallingly neglected palaces of Lucknow.

After the move into their new home, this sympathy slowly faded. Regardless of the question of their lineage—to which less and less attention was given—visiting journalists clearly did not believe the family was really heir to the Awadh palaces. Moreover, there was no sign of empathy towards them. A 1998 *New York Times* article described Wilayat as 'obstinate' and Sakina's talk of the past as 'bemoaning' and 'lamenting'. To be fair, Sakina is quoted to have said that they would 'not accept the demonic democracy of any country that has deprived royalty of their proper position'.[26]

Most who visited just described the exotic appearance of the family, their peculiar use of language, and their 'strange' habits. In a way, Wilayat and her children were dehumanized. They were far from happy with the coverage, often writing long letters of protest to the organizations that had run stories on them, in TV or print.

The Swiss diplomat Bernard Imhasly, who later became the South Asia correspondent for the newspaper *Neue Zürcher Zeitung*, remembers visiting the family in the 1980s. During that time, Imhasly writes, the President's Bodyguard had a practice area in the Ridge Forest, which also served as a polo field. 'Back then, thanks to the presidential cavalry, we expats got cheap polo ponies and a playing field,' he writes in an obituary after Ali Raza's death.[27] He recalls Ali Raza coming to the field to make a connection with the expats, and notes he had a particular interest in women. 'I had noticed the young man without thinking anything about it. He stayed back between the trees and watched us. He was obviously very shy, but the real reason no one spoke to him was the smell of his unwashed body, smelling from a distance of several meters.'

Later, Ali Raza invited Imhasly's American colleague, a woman, to Malcha Mahal, and according to him 'reluctantly agreed' when she insisted Imhasly and another male friend come along.

It was the first of several meetings and phone calls that Imhasly had with Ali Raza, whom he calls 'the strangest friend I have ever had'. He describes Wilayat as 'taciturn'. 'Even when she spoke, she forced the words out of her half-closed lips.'

Ali Raza was anxious about the world outside Malcha Mahal, suspecting his dog food supplier of poisoning the meat and fearing that he was being followed by the secret service. But Imhasly also got the impression that he was a young man with 'normal human needs'. 'That's why he drew us into his chilly, tense closeness. Once he spoke to me in his tight staccato and with piercing eyes: "Bernard, get me a wife ... I need a woman. But she has to be white, and blond, like my nanny used to be." And then his face melted into a soft, hopeless childishness: "Oh, how I miss her!"'

~

Over the years, the sound of dogs howling from behind the thorny bushes stopped, and foreign journalists who wished to go inside were no longer greeted by submissive servants with handwritten notes on silver platters. It was clear that the siblings had become increasingly isolated and vulnerable.

When we first visited in 2015 to find out whether Sakina had indeed passed away, we could not hear any dogs nor see any signs of life. As most Indian journalists who took an interest, we spoke to the guards of the Earth Station. They gave us some insights into how the premises of Malcha Mahal got connected to their water supply and telephone network. Pradip Krishen later told us that he had also played his part. 'This man approached me and asked me if I could help him with a telephone line,' Krishen recalled their first meeting, sometime in the early 2000s, while he was walking his dog. 'So I did that. After that I ran into him about twice a year. One of the last times I did, he seemed very unhinged. He talked about an attack and wanted to meet the police.'

Ali Raza might have been talking about a police raid in early 2015, organized by a reporter of the populist channel India TV. It was revealed by heritage activist Vikramjit Singh Rooprai on his blog that an India TV journalist had jumped the fence and barged inside in May 2015. When Sakina screamed and called Ali Raza to unleash their dogs and pull out a gun, the journalist and his photographer ran outside and called the police to report 'suspicious activity' and, in the words of the journalist—who had narrated his act proudly to Rooprai—'have the place raided'. The journalist accompanied the police, who later complained about the false alarm. They searched the entire property and found nothing. But the whole episode left a clear message: that in present-day India, there is not much respect left for the once-mighty House of Awadh with its diplomatic links to Persia and Turkey.

Rooprai was appalled by the story and wrote on his blog that he had vowed to never give an interview to India TV. As a heritage expert who conducts regular photography walks in the Ridge Forest, he says he has been receiving questions about the Malcha Mahal residents for years. Once, his group encountered Ali Raza and tried to have a conversation with him, but the prince had 'quickly jumped into the bushes and disappeared'.

Trying to find out more, Rooprai spoke to forest officials for a blog entry he posted in 2012—later updated with the India TV incident and the news of Ali Raza's death.[28] This conversation mostly reveals how much mystery surrounded the place. The forest officials said that in the initial days of the family moving to the monument, they could hear 'the sound of music and dance' emanating from it. In 2012, they somehow suspected the family of 'illegal activities'. Without mentioning any names, they claimed one or two reporters once went inside Malcha Mahal, and never returned. Of course, there are no such missing reporters, but it clearly illustrates that there was little knowledge about or sympathy for the family.

Rooprai himself showed more empathy and understanding in his blog than any of the journalists who met them over the years. He briefly described the royal claims of Wilayat as well as the opposing claims of Prince Anjum Quder, stating that he did not know which version was true. But regardless of the 'truth', he showed respect for Wilayat's children, sensing that there was a much deeper story to be told beyond its mere exotic and eccentric aspects. 'All I know is that Princess Sakina and Prince Raza deserve a peaceful life. They have had enough torture and pain in all these years. We cannot estimate their loss.'

It is hard to imagine the extent of loneliness that must have engulfed Ali Raza after the death of his sister. Initially, he could not even admit that she had passed away—telling us on the phone that she was 'very much around'. To Ellen Barry, who first visited him in the spring of 2016, he said that Sakina was travelling out of Delhi. A few months later he admitted to her that Sakina had, in fact, died seven months earlier and that he had told nobody.

A small group of regular dog-walkers, like Pradip Krishen, describe a man who was increasingly confused and helpless—though nobody saw him frequently. He no longer actively sought human contact, like the Ali Raza of the 1980s described by Imhasly—the man in his thirties who watched expat polo games and still had dreams of marriage. When Ali Raza died in 2017, it took about a month for the news to become known. The BBC correspondent who had been a regular visitor found the place abandoned and spoke to the police, who said his body had been discovered a month earlier. The Earth Station guards later told journalists that it appeared he had been ill with dengue fever for about a week and had refused to be taken to a hospital. They made sure someone checked up on him daily. His body was found lifeless on the cold stone floor.

∼

Fast-forward six years, to the summer of 2023. The Tourism Department of the Delhi government announces a series of 'Haunted Walks'. The first destination: Malcha Mahal. Again, Wilayat and her children were back in the news, more dehumanized than ever: this time as ghosts to entertain tourists. 'People can also make reels, take selfies,' said one official to the *Indian Express* at the announcement, promising a 'chilling experience'.[29] In another article, a staff reporter says that 'locals' believe that Wilayat's spirit still lives in the monument—not specifying who these locals are.[30] *India Today* journalist Tiasa Bhowal signed up for the 'Haunted Walk' and reported how the stories of the occupants of Malcha Mahal 'sent a chill' down her spine.[31] To add to the excitement, the guide told her that a participant in the same walk, on another date, had heard 'the sound of anklets'. 'This place does have a spooky and eerie ambience. It's the story of the occupants that add to the uncanny factor. Let me be very frank, I was holding on to a small Hanuman Chalisa booklet during my visit to the Malcha Mahal.'

Other descriptions of the walk are similarly sensational. It seems that the last residents of Malcha Mahal are not to be remembered as humans of flesh and blood.

The 'Haunted Walks' follow what the government said is popular demand. It is not surprising, given the many blogs and media items we came across over the previous years claiming the monument to be haunted.

In September 2019, for example, a team of the Indian TV channel News24 visited Malcha Mahal, looking for ghosts. In the resulting video, two journalists discover an old fridge covered in red powder and speculate about its origins, wondering whether they've found the site of a Tantric ritual.

What they had found were the remnants of a performance by a young artist called Ajay Sharma from a few months earlier, making Malcha Mahal once again an artists' studio space, though informally this time around.[32]

In a video that Sharma produced of his performance,[33] which was shown at a festival of performance art in South Korea, he is seen fully naked, sitting on some of the furniture in Malcha Mahal, his face covered with a huge piece of meat. Later, as he stands under the arched gates inside the monument, his face is covered by a cow's skull.

The work, he explains, is an artistic commentary on the growing intolerance towards Muslims in today's India—currently governed by the Hindu-nationalist BJP—and directly inspired by a brutal, heavily publicized mob-lynching incident in 2015. Around the time Sakina and Ali Raza were raided by the police and India TV, a Muslim ironsmith named Mohammad Akhlaq was killed by an angry mob in the village of Dadri, Uttar Pradesh, on suspicion of having slaughtered a cow and eaten its beef. The meat of a cow was allegedly stored in his fridge. Whilst some of Akhlaq's Hindu neighbours tried in vain to protect him, others were actually part of the mob that killed him.[34, 35]

With its 'layers of history', says Sharma, Malcha Mahal was a perfect venue for the video. The site already had an abandoned fridge. At the end of the video, Sharma covers his whole body with red powder, symbolizing blood. He tucks himself, and the meat, into the fridge, still naked and in a foetal position.

∼

The fridge is one of the objects that stands out during our first visit inside Malcha Mahal, a few months after Ali Raza's death is reported in the news. It is a Frigidaire, a famous brand of its time, though rusted and broken down from disuse over the years.

On the floor are broken plates, clothes beside an empty trunk and papers. There are empty packets of expensive perfumes and flyers of art galleries—probably because Ali Raza was an artist. We find his easel, paint bottles and brushes, caked with disuse, and later learn that he had even received some art lessons at the railway station. In one of the rooms is a dining table, ornate but covered with dust. There are glass plates with designs and motifs laid out on the table. Bats scurry across the rooms, making ululating sounds. The atmosphere is surreal. We feel like we are transgressing a boundary. The air seems to be heavy with years of disappointments and suffering.

It is hard to imagine that someone had been living here just some months earlier, let alone had lived there for years. More than three decades of life had been looted and ravaged. Who knows what happened to the carpets, the souvenirs, the paintings and the signboards?

Not all the treasures are gone, though. Among the papers we find clues of who Ali Raza, Sakina and Wilayat were as people. They loved dogs and read magazines in Dutch about how to care for them. They were interested in art and international news. They corresponded with embassies, journalists and academics. They also communicated with the royal family of Udaipur and appear to have been in touch with the royal family of Nepal. Ali Raza had a voter ID card, in the name of Ali Raza Mahal, and his father's name listed as 'Raja Hussain'—King Hussain. His age was listed as forty-eight in 2007, which was most likely a bit younger than his real age.

Also in evidence are piles of business cards and loose pieces of paper with landline numbers and mobile phone numbers written on them. Most of these numbers no longer exist. But after trying a dozen of them without result, something unexpected happens on dialling one number. A man named Mohammad Kasim picks up. And he says he knew the family far more intimately than possibly any other living person: he had been their servant at the New Delhi Railway Station and in Malcha Mahal.

It takes months of pursuing Kasim before he agrees to meet us. In the meantime, we decide to visit the prince's lost kingdom.

City of Nawabs

The train to Lucknow is already waiting at platform 16 of the New Delhi Railway Station. It is a sunny afternoon in February 2022, almost two years after the world was ravaged by the Covid-19 pandemic. The morning papers suggest that the virus is not spreading so fast and virulently anymore. This has encouraged the Delhi government to open schools for older children.

The second-class AC coach is further down the platform with its multiple chai and magazine stands. One of the news magazines features the finance minister on the cover, defending the current state of India's economy. Another one's cover features the chief minister of Uttar Pradesh, Yogi Adityanath. Elections for the Uttar Pradesh assembly are due to start in a couple of days and will last for an entire month, given the size of the state.

When the train starts moving, the sky is blue as it can be. The February sun is bright, but not too warm. A monkey eyes the passengers, sitting on top of the iron grill that acts as the boundary of platform 16, nibbling on something.

On the side-lower berth, two women joke to someone on the phone that they have missed their train.

The train crosses the Yamuna: a dark, swampy and wide swathe of the river, with small cultivated fields on its banks, alongside a forested wilderness.

A stocky man in a grey sweater and blue jeans has turned up to occupy one of the side-lower seats, next to the only other window in the compartment. He has earphones plugged in, and is talking loudly about computers and internet connections. Suddenly, he exclaims: 'Don't worry about Lucknow. It is the city of nawabs! We will also act like nawabs when we get there.'

As the train enters the wide plains of Uttar Pradesh, yellow mustard fields spring up, hinting at the approaching spring.

~

The Charbagh station has a dreamy air, as if conjured by a magician on a whim. Its tall canopies with pointy domes are spread out over a large area. Fluted columns and Corinthian pillars bear the weight of the endlessly stretching roof, reminiscent of the architecture of Chattar Manzil, one of the palaces that Wilayat Mahal demanded as her inheritance. The unusually symmetrical style of the station suggests a Palladian influence.

Our pre-booked hotel is only a cycle-rickshaw ride away, but it takes some effort to find it, as it is tucked in between several similar-looking, bland concrete structures. The balcony in the small, second-floor corner room, where previous guests have scribbled on the walls and where paint has peeled off in multiple places, opens out to the main road. Right in front is a building called Lifestyle Mall, but it seems to be permanently closed. Next to it is a juvenile reformation centre. On its other side are restaurants that offer only vegetarian fare. The loud, tuneless singing of bhajans from a nearby temple dominates the airwaves, giving ample indications of a new Lucknow in the making.

But the old is never far away in Lucknow, which is enveloped in layers of history, just like Malcha Mahal. After a quick bucket bath and tea brought in a plastic bag and consumed in earthen cups, it is time to go out in search for Wilayat Mahal in her city; the one she considered her ancestral home.

~

Although since Independence, Awadh and the former North-Western Provinces have been called by the unimaginative appellation of Uttar Pradesh, its former name derived from the town of Ayodhya, the birthplace of Ram where a contentious Ram temple was recently built. Ram, in the ancient Sanskrit epic Ramayana, was the prince of Ayodhya, and Lucknow, the myth suggests, was ruled by his brother, Lakshman.[1] There are other versions too regarding its founding, and at least one credits a lower-caste mason called Lakhna with it.[2]

Ruled by various regional dynasties till Humayun conquered it and made it part of the Mughal empire around 1555, Awadh and its nawabs began to acquire prominence when the Mughal empire began to disintegrate. It was a fertile and affluent kingdom, with many small and big towns that had developed as places of economic activity and were well-connected to trade routes. The opulent tomb of Safdarjung—who became the second nawab in 1739—at the intersection of Lodhi Road and Aurobindo Marg in New Delhi bears testimony to the influence Lucknow's nawabs held in the Mughal capital.

Today's Uttar Pradesh is larger than the erstwhile kingdom of Awadh, as it includes Agra, Varanasi and Allahabad, which used to be separate principalities or administrative regions. Lucknow, in parts razed to the ground by the British in 1857, still retains an old-world charm in some pockets, having undergone a sea change in every other respect. The older parts of Lucknow, such as Chowk, Aminabad, Charbagh and Kaiserbagh, with their jumbled lanes and crowds, coexist with the more modern and well-laid-out parts of the city, such as the university area, and Vikramaditya Marg, where the city's rich and powerful reside. The Gomti flows through Lucknow, dividing it neatly into two parts, as Amaresh Mishra has written in his book *Lucknow: Fire of Grace*. Now, there is a metro train that connects the different parts, another powerful symbol of modern development and progress.

The palaces Wilayat claimed as hers are in a terrible state. Of particular interest to her was Chattar Manzil on the banks of the Gomti, which was built by Nawab Ghazi-ud-Din, who became Awadh's first king in 1818. It later became a stronghold of Hazrat Mahal and her revolutionary army during the Revolt of 1857. The British victors of the war, who partially destroyed the palace to win it back, gave it away to an American organization, which used it as a recreational club. After Independence, the building was repurposed as a government drug research institute, officially inaugurated in 1950 by Prime Minister Nehru.

The building now lies abandoned. Most windows are broken and the doors locked. One opens to a hall with a black-and-white checked floor and lowered ceilings that are partially broken, revealing the arched gates that were hidden behind it. There are loose wires, beehives and stains from multiple leakages everywhere, and it does not seem safe to explore the rooms beyond this hall.

In 1989, heritage experts had advised the government that Chattar Manzil should be vacated, and the government had agreed, though it took till 2010 for the last occupants to leave. 'There is an official plan to renovate it and conserve it as a museum, but we are still waiting for this dream to come true,' says Roshan Taqui, an authority on Lucknow's history and heritage who has penned many books on the city. We meet in his sparsely decorated living room in the old part of the city. He serves tea and biscuits while we discuss Wilayat and her claims.

Trained as an engineer, Taqui has been an activist for the restoration and conservation of Lucknow's rich heritage and was part of the group of experts advising the government in 1989. Speaking passionately on the subject, he says that some maintenance work had started after 2012, but that the results are not visible. 'It was abruptly stopped when the government changed in 2017, citing a lack of funding.'

The state archaeological department did report several rounds of excavation work next to the palace since 2017, in which underground rooms, a royal boat and two waterways were unearthed. But when we visit there is no work going on and Taqui says it is just not enough. 'The present government never spent a penny. You cannot see any change.'

It is a fair observation, given the state of the building in which even blackboard notes remain intact over a decade since the institute vacated it. We refer to the debate in recent years, with some commentators accusing the present government of favouring Hindu heritage over Islamic heritage, and ask if he suspects the same.[3] Taqui is unwilling to give a direct answer, but hints that he agrees. 'The answer is very obvious,' he says, and 'you can understand', giving the example of Lucknow's most prominent monument, the Bara Imambara, of which a portion had collapsed in heavy rain just the week before our meeting.

～

The Bara Imambara, a Shia place of mourning built by the fourth nawab, Asaf-ud-Daula, is Uttar Pradesh's second-largest revenue-making monument, next only to the world-famous Taj Mahal in Agra. It receives on an average 8,000 visitors per day, who through loudspeakers are continuously warned that it is a religious place and not suitable for the recording of videos for social media. At a stone's throw away stand several other landmarks. The smaller Chhota Imambara, the Rumi Darwaza, the Husainabad Clock Tower and the Picture Gallery, which was built in 1838 as the summer home of the royals and where portraits of all the nawabs who ruled Lucknow are now displayed.

The area behind the Picture Gallery is known as Sheesh Mahal. Some of the old nobility of Lucknow still lives here, and Wilayat and her children also stayed for a short while in 1976. They had been invited by the chief minister of Uttar Pradesh, says Ammar Rizvi, a prominent politician in the state who was then with the Congress. In his long political career, Rizvi has been a minister several times and twice the acting chief minister of Uttar Pradesh. In 2019, he moved to the ruling BJP, accusing the Congress of neglecting its senior leaders. During our first visit to Lucknow, he was busy campaigning outside Lucknow for his new party, which, a month later, was declared the winner of the elections. We met him twice later in that year during our follow-up visits to Lucknow.

Rizvi lives in a spacious apartment in the posh locality of Park Road in Lucknow. His photos with leaders like George W. Bush, Rajnath Singh and Yogi Adityanath hang on the walls of the living room, where we sit. There are framed photographs of Jawaharlal Nehru and Indira Gandhi. On one wall, an ornately carved dagger is kept in an enclosed cupboard. Another painting has verses from the Quran in beautiful calligraphy.

'I was a cabinet minister in Hemwati Nandan Bahuguna's government in UP,' he tells us. 'Bahuguna had read in some newspapers about Hazrat Mahal's great-granddaughter living at the New Delhi Railway Station. This was in March or April 1975.'

This seems to refer to Promilla Kalhan's article in *Hindustan Times* in March 1975, three months after Wilayat and her children first arrived at the New Delhi Railway Station. Apparently, they had initially travelled lightly. Kalhan makes no mention of the Nepali servants, the doberman dogs and the Persian carpets that foreign correspondents would later begin their articles with. Instead, Kalhan describes an ordinary family that happened to be of royal descent. 'A mother (45), her daughter (19) and son (17). She is Wilayat Mahal, who claims to be a great-grand-daughter of Hazrat Mahal, wife of Wajid Ali Shah, the last Nawab of Oudh.'[4] Kalhan also mentions a third child: 'The elder son is holding the fort in Srinagar, keeping watch over the family's remaining possessions.'

The elder son was Asad, whose life and death were a mystery left as it was by earlier publications, including the 2019 article in *New York Times*; it took us considerable effort to slowly glean information about him—which we will present in a later chapter.

About the two children she met, Kalhan writes: 'Her elder son, now 20 and a fine cricketer, studied up to the Intermediate, her daughter, Sakeena, up to pre-medical and her younger son, Ali Raza, up to Higher Secondary.' Further down: 'Sakeena and Ali Raza want to become doctors.' This is interesting, as they were later quoted saying that as royals, they would never consider holding ordinary jobs. It seems as if, as the years went by, they grew into their roles. The article also mentions Wilayat's late husband, their time in Pakistan and a shocking rumour, which we will discuss later in more detail: that he was involved in the assassination of Pakistan's first Prime Minister, Liaquat Ali Khan, in 1951.[5]

This information apparently did not scare off Chief Minister Bahuguna, whose focus was the claim of royal descent. Rizvi continues his story: 'He told me: she belongs in Lucknow.'

On behalf of Bahuguna, Rizvi travelled to Delhi and met Wilayat. He remembers her as 'rude', and uses the description several times when he narrates their first dialogue:

'She said: The CM is my servant.

'I said: Madam, India is a democracy. The CM is the elected leader. We don't have servants.

'She then asked a very blunt question: *Mere liye kya kar sakte hain?* What can he do for me? This is a rude way of talking.'

Rizvi says he suggested that she come to Lucknow at the expense of the CM's office to discuss her demands: the palaces.

'She said: I don't want to come to Lucknow.

'I said: I'll take your leave, then.

'She then said, rudely: *Baith jao*. Sit. And: All right, I'll go to Lucknow.'

This was followed by a dramatic scene. Rizvi took out an envelope with Rs 10,000 for her travels, a significant amount. But Wilayat threw it in the air, saying it was not enough.

'Then I spoke harshly,' Rizvi says. 'I told my colleague: Let's go. I will tell the CM that she is not interested. After that she became polite. *Baithiye*, she said, using the formal form. She took the money, and five or six days later I got to know that she was coming.'

Wilayat's first stay in Lucknow, which materialized some months later, was brief. Wilayat had refused a guesthouse, says Rizvi, as she preferred to stay in the waiting room of the Charbagh Railway Station. 'But while meetings were being arranged, there was a political change. Chief Minister Bahuguna was being replaced. So she went back.' The episode reminds of the Queen Mother of Awadh, who also had to abandon her mission in London due to similar political upheavals.

∼

It was a period of political turmoil for Uttar Pradesh and the entire country. On 25 June 1975, citing threats to national security and facing massive strikes and protests, Prime Minister Indira Gandhi declared a state of Emergency—a flirtation with authoritarian rule that was going to last for twenty-one months. This was in keeping with Indira's socialist turn. She was backed strongly by the Communist Party of India in those days. The Opposition was led by the conservative Jana Sangh and the nominally socialist Janata Party.

Those were turbulent times, and violence against the State was on the rise—an article in *Hindustan Times* in December 1974 mentioned that a sadhu casually lobbed a bomb in South Block, which houses the PMO, as he was upset over the Khosla Commission report on Netaji.[6] The same month, student protests were also reported. It was, hence, no surprise that the State resorted to extra-Constitutional means to curb such activities. It is remarkable, if one truly considers the scenario in its entirety, that Wilayat had the gumption to occupy prime space on the railway platform meant for VIPs in Delhi, protesting against the government, when political opponents of Indira were being imprisoned without trial.

The situation in the rest of the world was also grim. The oil crisis was far from being resolved. In June 1975, the Watergate scandal in the US reached its crescendo as aides of President Nixon were convicted for snooping on their opponents.

Bahuguna later said he came to know about the Emergency decision at breakfast the next morning. In any case, he and Indira Gandhi had not been the best of friends. ThePrint, in a profile of Bahuguna published on his thirtieth death anniversary in 2019, quoted from an interview he once gave:

> As soon as I took an oath for the CM's position, I had a fight with Indira Gandhi on a foundational issue. She felt that I should consult her for every work. My stand was that 'back seat driving' was not possible.[7]

ThePrint also quotes from the book *An Indian Political Life: Charan Singh and Congress Politics, 1967 to 1987* by Paul R. Brass, who wrote that Bahuguna worked in favour of minorities such as Dalits and Muslims and acted boldly to suppress anti-Muslim rioting. 'Indira Gandhi had no interest in such issues as she moved steadily toward total power by installing political lackeys.'[8]

Indira Gandhi, together with her influential younger son, Sanjay, found a more suitable candidate in Narayan Dutt Tiwari, a former Indian Youth Congress leader. Bahuguna was in trouble for a while. In December 1974, *Hindustan Times* reported that he faced corruption charges. This was followed by a report saying he had offered to quit. In April, the newspaper reported about the political crisis he faced, especially opposition from dissidents in the party. Incidentally, he had come to power after the chief minister before him, Kamalapati Tripathi, had been removed under similar circumstances. He had later become railways minister in February 1975. In November, Bahuguna was forced to resign and after about two months of President's Rule, Tiwari replaced him in January 1976.

Tiwari went on to have a long and successful political career, with ministerial posts and two more stints as Uttar Pradesh chief minister, until a sex scandal forced him to resign as governor of the southern state of Andhra Pradesh in 2009, when he was well into his eighties.[9]

The local political turmoil is likely why nothing much came of an adjournment motion filed in the Uttar Pradesh legislative assembly in April 1975, asking the assembly to sympathize with Wilayat. It was filed by MLA Satya Pal Malik of the Bharatiya Kranti Dal, a Congress breakaway party whose leader, Charan Singh, would later serve as the country's home minister and also the Prime Minister for a short stint post the Emergency. Malik was soon jailed along with other political opponents of Indira Gandhi when she declared the Emergency. A few months later, the assembly was dissolved and President's Rule declared in the state.

∽

During President's Rule, shortly before Tiwari's appointment as chief minister, Wilayat made her second appearance in Lucknow, again staying at the Charbagh Railway Station, this time with children and dogs in tow. And this time, she made sure to leave an impression. 'She caused inconvenience to passengers,' remembers Rizvi, who was once again sent to meet her. 'Half the first-class waiting room was occupied with her paraphernalia. Dogs, prince and princess ... and then Muharram came.'

Rizvi recalls how Wilayat was presiding over the bloody ritual in which Shia men cut themselves with swords and knives. This is usually done on the Day of Ashura, which marks the tenth day of the holy month of Muharram, which was in January in 1976. This is the month of mourning for Shia Muslims, and the Day of Ashura is when they commemorate the death of Prophet Mohammad's grandson Imam Hussain in 680 AD during the Battle of Karbala. The cutting of their bodies is a ritual of mourning.

'Wilayat was reciting verses, meanwhile,' Rizvi says. Finally, about four weeks into her stay, the Union Railway Minister Kamalapati Tripathi called him. 'He asked me: Ammar, do something. Ensure she shifts from there.' Bahuguna, before his resignation, had actually allotted a house to Wilayat, says Rizvi. 'This was in Mahanagar Colony in Lucknow, at that time the biggest type of house as far as government construction is concerned. I took her to see it. But she said it was too small for her family, including her dogs.' She even mentioned horses, says Rizvi, though it is unclear where she kept these horses if any were indeed in her possession.

Wilayat instead demanded Chattar Manzil. 'I told her that this is impossible, as it houses a prestigious research institute.' She then made the decision to live at Sheesh Mahal, says Rizvi. 'There is a house there that belongs to the secretary of the Husainabad Trust. One night, without telling us, she packed up all of her belongings and arrived at that house. And then she broke all the locks.'

The Husainabad and Allied Trust was founded as a charity for the Muslim community in 1839 by King Mohammad Ali Shah, Wajid Ali Shah's father, with a starting capital of reportedly Rs 12 lakh. Besides providing welfare such as scholarships, it is the custodian of mosques and heritage buildings built under the nawabs, such as the Bara Imambara. All income from those monuments goes to the trust, though the ASI is now responsible for the protection and upkeep of those listed as protected monuments.

The trust has also provided funds for religious functions, in particular the public processions during Muharram. This, according to scholar Aishwarya Pandit, helps to explain how and why Lucknow re-emerged after Independence as the heartland of the Shias of India, and arguably of South Asia.[10] But it also provoked conflict within the Shia community about how to manage the funds. In the 1960s, Ali Zaheer, independent India's first ambassador to Iran, then law minister of Uttar Pradesh, reorganized the trust and introduced multiple government representatives as trustees. The district magistrate of Lucknow, a senior bureaucrat, always functions as its chairman. There are still two families with royal ancestors who are represented, but it has been decades since the last elections for the top functions were held.

Meanwhile, the number of royal descendants kept growing. The trust is also responsible for the distribution of the wasiqa or royal pension to the nawabs and their descendants, operating from an office in the Picture Gallery. At the time of the trust deed the king made with the British East India Company in 1839, the initial sum of Rs 12,00,000 would bring in an annual interest of Rs 48,000. Out of this amount, Rs 18,000 was set aside to pay the wasiqa to the nawab's descendants. At that time, he had only twenty-one immediate family members. By now the group of eligible pensioners is about 3,500, though for some the pension is hardly a few rupees per year. According to an official working at the trust, many come to collect their pension only when the amounts become substantial, which takes a few years.

In 2011, after a legal battle launched by an organization called the Royal Families of Awadh (RFA), the pensions were increased thirtyfold.

The Husainabad Trust keeps diligent records of the names of the descendants who are getting a pension. Wilayat's name is not, and never was, in this record. This can be explained: Wilayat claimed royal lineage through a female line, which would not be reflected. Still, her absence in the trust's records is the main reason why those who are on the list dispute her claim and have done so ever since she set foot in Sheesh Mahal the night she broke the locks of the trust's secretary's house. Though, as we were to find out, some of them fiercely dispute each other's claims too.

'Her credentials were suspicious,' says Ibrahim Ali Khan, an elderly gentleman who is said to be one of the last surviving nawabs in Lucknow with links to the House of Awadh. 'She did not have proof. You must have a family tree.'

Newspaper and magazine reports suggest Khan is active in keeping alive the legacy of nawab-era Lucknow. He serves as president of the RFA, the organization that fought for the royal pensions to be increased. Nevertheless, his house in Sheesh Mahal is not easy to find.

Sheesh Mahal means a palace of mirrors. It was once part of the Daulat Khana complex that was built by Asaf-ud-Daula, who as the fourth nawab ruled in the final quarter of the eighteenth century. He was the first to rule from Lucknow. He is credited with building most of the nawabi Lucknow, as the kings before him had their capital at Faizabad. Not much of the old grandeur remains today, and the area called Sheesh Mahal largely consists of small, modern houses.

An arched gate with the ubiquitous symbol of two fishes engraved on top stands at the entry of the neighbourhood. The same symbol was also used by Wilayat Mahal on her letterhead and on the 'Rulers of Oudh' signboard she placed at the entry to Malcha Mahal. It refers to a legendary story about Awadh's first nawab Sadat Khan's journey to Lucknow after having been appointed the governor. While crossing the Ganga river, two fishes are said to have jumped into his lap, staying with him for the remainder of the journey. It was considered a good omen. As a symbol, it became more prominent after it was included in the design for the royal insignia for the coronation of Awadh's first king in 1819.

We ask around for Ibrahim Ali Khan's house but cannot locate it, despite getting specific directions—which lead us to a house belonging to someone else with the same name. Frustrated, we ask a passerby if he has heard of Nawab Ibrahim Ali Khan. He turns out to be a servant working at his house, luckily, and offers to lead the way, crisscrossing several lanes.

The present-day nawab's living room seems straight out of another world. It is full of old paintings, artefacts and plaques that cover the walls and fill the cupboards. He is thin and frail; his eyes are deep-set in his face, giving it a gaunt look. His manner is courteous.

In Khan's memory, it was his uncle, Abid Ali Khan, also called Dara Nawab, who convinced Wilayat to leave the railway station and come to Sheesh Mahal—although it was never his intention for her to inhabit the trust's secretary's house. 'My uncle got a call from the district magistrate's office—that there is a lady claiming royal descent staying at the station. Out of sympathy, he went to see her, on the DM's request, as she would not see or deal with commoners,' he says.

The night she arrived and broke the locks of the secretary's house, Dara Nawab intervened and offered Wilayat one of his properties to stay at, a dilapidated palace nearby. Khan remembers visiting the family there. 'I was just curious, as there were so many stories about her. She did not allow us to spend much time there. We would just get a glass of water and nothing else. The children were not allowed to speak to visitors.'

Though Khan says that among the descendants there is a prevalent sentiment of the injustice done to Awadh, they did not support Wilayat's demands for the great palaces of Lucknow. 'Everyone had their own property, and nobody could claim that these palaces belonged to them. They were all taken over by the government. Whatever happened a hundred years ago, everything had been settled. India was a republic now, a democracy.'

Describing Wilayat, he carefully chooses his words. 'I would not say she was mentally disturbed, but she was not stable. Quite eccentric.' In the end, he echoes Rizvi: 'She was rude to everyone who came knocking.'

∼

All considered, it was not exactly a sympathetic political climate to arrive in for an erstwhile princess in need of a palace. In 1971, just four years before Wilayat arrived in Lucknow, Prime Minister Indira Gandhi had stripped Indian royalty of their last special privilege: the Privy Purse.

Until Independence, hundreds of princely states in India had survived with minimal political power and some tax-collecting rights by entering into subsidiary allegiances with the British colonial powers who retained paramountcy. When the British left in 1947, independent India offered them little in terms of political power or revenues, even as it claimed the paramountcy. By signing instruments of accession, their lands were integrated into the newly independent India. Princely states who tried to opt for independence, like Hyderabad, were annexed soon enough, while the circumstances of Jammu and Kashmir's accession to India remains contested till date, by Pakistan[11] as well as some Indian political leaders.[12] But in all cases, the royal families immediately lost all remaining political power and soon after were stripped of their feudal landholdings, too.

They were offered, however, a generous allowance ranging from a few thousand rupees per year to 2.6 million, depending on how large and powerful their princely state had been. Sardar Vallabhbhai Patel, who is credited with forging Indian unity by bringing all the princely states within the ambit of the Indian Union, had defended this Privy Purse as a fair compensation for all that they had given up, in terms of land, cash balances and control. But after over two decades, the support for this position had faded. In line with the idea that all citizens should be equal, as well as the need to cut government spending, the Privy Purse was abolished.

Though it had never applied to the royalty of Awadh, as the kingdom had been annexed by the British long before Independence, the fact that all royal allowances were cancelled just a few years before Wilayat appeared on the scene is relevant. Royalty had just been made a thing of the past quite conclusively—or so it seemed. In the year 1975 other developments involving the royalty were afoot. In March, *Hindustan Times* reported tax raids on the Jaipur Palace, which were discussed in the Parliament on 5 March. Later in the same year, the newspaper reported that the palace of Hyderabad's nizam could be acquired by the government.

~

The so-called palace that Wilayat, Sakina and Ali Raza lived in for a few months can be better described as a mansion in ruins. It has the same Palladian architecture as Chattar Manzil and was likely part of the eighteenth-century Daulat Khana complex. Tall Corinthian pillars support the roof and a large passageway winds around it in a semi-circle, giving it the look of an amphitheatre. There is wild grass growing on most of the open space in the front, and the walls are mouldy, their colour completely faded. The roof has fallen away almost totally.

A family stays in one corner of the ruin. Its members squat on the floor, or on the ground in the front, where some goats are tied. They do not want to say anything, only stating that they pay rent to the owner of the property who lives nearby. They point to a medicine shop a few steps behind the ruins. The owner of the shop is a young man in his thirties called Tabrez Raza. He is diligently carving into shape a column of a miniature ivory palace in front of him; it is to be used as a backscratcher.

Raza claims to be connected to the royal family of Awadh, giving a complicated description involving doubtful paternity, a running theme in the history of the House of Awadh. The Mahal was granted to his family by Nawab Amjad Ali Khan in 1862, he says. Now, the seventh generation of the family is in possession of it. Two hundred members of the family live in the area.

Raza is a keen student of Lucknow and his family's history and maintains a Pinterest account full of pictures of Lucknow's historical landmarks. The mansion also features there, identified as Asafi Kothi. After Wilayat's stay, Raza says his grandfather gave it on rent to the government, and it was used to run an institute to train officials from the finance and revenue departments till 2005. 'The government still owes us money, and the court gave orders in 2012 for the arrears to be cleared,' he says.

Even in 1976, the mansion was in a bad state. Without running water or a working kitchen, Wilayat and her children depended on the kindness of outsiders for their food and baths, the latter not being a luxury, considering that during their stay the hot Indian summer kicked in. In particular Akhtar, a well-liked housewife and tailor who lived opposite the mansion in a simple two-room house, welcomed them. 'She had many friends that were all like her sisters,' her daughter Asmat Aru recalls her mother, who was of African descent from her mother's side. Aru spoke to a journalist once before, she says, who had wanted to know everything about her African roots.

Today, there are around 50,000 people of African descent in India. They trace their ancestors from Ethiopia, many of whom included merchants, mercenaries and slaves. In Lucknow, they are said to have served the court of Awadh's second king, Naseer-ud-Din, as devotees reciting poems of mourning.[13] Interestingly, both men and women from the community fought against the British during the 1857 Revolt.

Aru does not know whether her great-grandparents also fought the British and how they came to live in the Sheesh Mahal neighbourhood. She is now seventy-five and lives in Delhi, where she ended up in 1989 with her four children after running away from her husband. In Lucknow, she worked for an Urdu newspaper and also wrote novels. 'But the doctor advised me to quit writing, as I had too much on my mind and developed high blood pressure.'

Aru's small house is in a congested area in east Delhi. Her son, Rais, guides us there on his motorbike, which we follow on a cycle rickshaw through a maze of narrow lanes. Aru sits in the front room, which is covered almost entirely by a day bed, which she occupies along with other women from her family and neighbourhood. All are excited to meet a couple of strange visitors, and multiple selfies are taken. With knowledge of Aru's African roots, one might notice them in her facial features, but they could easily go unnoticed as she blends in with the other women, dressed in salwar kameez and sipping chai.

To Aru, there is no doubt that Wilayat must have been royalty, and she remembers the short period fondly. 'It seems like a novel ... that a queen once lived among us.' She still refers to Wilayat as 'rani', queen. 'Everyone in Sheesh Mahal came to meet them, telling each other that a begum had come.'

Soon, Aru would begin seeing Wilayat and her children daily, as her mother started cooking their meals, which Aru on occasion brought to the palace. 'One of the rooms was used by them, but there was nothing there. No carpets, no stuff, no crockery.'

The family also came to their small house, to use the bathroom and wash themselves. Akhtar's husband was a kite-rope salesman and travelled around India during kite-flying festivals, which meant Akhtar was mostly home alone with her children. There was not much conversation between them, but Aru remembers that they spoke excellent Urdu, though they preferred English amongst each other. Asked if she thought them to be rude or eccentric, like Rizvi and Khan, Aru protests. 'They were very respectful to my mum,' she says. 'The begum was very tall and beautiful,' she adds, and describes how she usually wore a sari. 'The kids were also beautiful. I don't think they were lying. But the nawabs did not trust them. They did not like their arrival.'

Aru's younger brother, Abrar Hussain, echoes her words. He, too, is till date convinced of their royal status, no matter what information has come out in the media. Hussain, now sixty-five, says he has a lot to thank Wilayat for. He still lives in Lucknow and earns a living as a dog trainer, a career that started with Wilayat. 'They had two doberman dogs, called Himalaya and Kagra, one labrador called Pentra, and the labrador had six puppies. I had never seen such dogs in my life. But I had a special interest in animals and Rani Sahiba trained me.'

Kagra, one of the dobermans, would later attack and kill a policeman near the railway station, Hussain says, though we have not been able to find anything to verify this.

Wilayat told them she was from Kathmandu, says Hussain. She said nothing about Kashmir or Pakistan, indicating she had by then started to change the narrative from the time she first spoke to Indian journalists a year earlier. Kathmandu is where Hazrat Mahal, whom

Wilayat claimed to be her ancestor, lived during her final years and died.

Like his sister, Hussain remembers that the family had caused a sensation in Sheesh Mahal, where he still lives and owns a small pet shop, which he runs with his daughter. He meets us in the evening in front of the shop and arranges two plastic chairs and some chai from a nearby stall. Passersby continually stop to look at the Persian cats, bunnies and small dogs on display.

'They looked royal,' Hussain says, while shooing away a young boy who is trying to sell us balloons. Sakina, whom he refers to as shehzadi, Urdu for princess, always wore jeans, T-shirts and boots. But the attention was not always positive. 'The wall of our home, where the bathroom was, was low. People used to come and try to look over the wall during their baths. Once someone made a lewd comment. Rani responded fiercely: I have been fighting the Indian government, so I could skewer you on a stick.' Hussain smiles. 'She also told the media to not harass them.'

When we finish our chai, he shows us his house. The low wall has been replaced by a proper wall. Other rooms have been renovated since Wilayat's stay as well.

Hussain recalls the response to Wilayat by the nawabs of the area. He mostly refers to Jafar Mir Abdullah, the estranged brother-in-law of Ibrahim Ali Khan, and a sort of patron to Hussain. Abdullah's mother-in-law was a close childhood friend of Hussain's mother, Akhtar, but Hussain says he shares a less equitable relationship with Abdullah.

His voice acquires an angry edge when he recalls how the nawab's family treated Wilayat and her children. 'They used to cover their noses when they came close, saying she smelled bad,' he says. 'Nobody helped them. Nobody supported them.'

One day, Abdullah's mother-in-law suggested to Akhtar that she and her children stay with her for a few days to escape the crowds that came to see Wilayat. It was in those few days that Wilayat left, says Hussain. 'In our absence, they were left without any support.' Asked if he felt sad when they left, he says, visibly emotional, 'Yes. Even today I feel sad.'

∼

Jafar Mir Abdullah lives in the same building as his estranged brother-in-law, Ibrahim Ali Khan.[14] Outside the house, there is a marble statue of a scowling old man. A child goes by, putting a pair of broken sunglasses on it.

The door to the house is painted ochre; made of wood, it has thick panels. Just above the door, the two fishes of Awadh's insignia are painted on the wall. Across a courtyard, there are stairs to the first floor, where a partially open roof leads to a semi-lit corridor. One section is partitioned off with pink curtains to serve as another room. The room that opens next to it is where Nawab Jafar Mir Abdullah lives.

It is only after our meeting that we learn the details of his internecine feud with his brother-in-law. The bare bones of the matter are thus: Khan and Abdullah are the two main claimants to the title of the last nawab of Lucknow. Both have connections to the House of Awadh through long-deceased relatives. Khan's ancestors served as prime ministers or wazirs to the kings of Awadh. Abdullah, whose younger sister is married to Khan, has a connection to Awadh's royalty through his maternal side—his grandfather married a second cousin of Khan's father. He also claims that his father is a direct ancestor of Awadh's third king, Muhammad Ali Shah, through his great-great-grandmother—although the family belongs to Patna, in Bihar.

The squabble got worse after the establishment of the RFA. The organization, with Khan as its president, accused Abdullah of monetizing his claims of being a nawab by working with travel agencies and others. 'The time has come to expose the impostor who has been indulging in cultural fraud and fleecing foreign tourists openly,' an angry Khan told *India Today* in 2008.[15]

Abdullah, who is quite a fixture in Lucknow's social life, often attends Page Three parties but denies his social activities are for money-making. He does admit having an arrangement with a local travel agency that lets people spend an hour with him, with stories of nawab-era Lucknow thrown in, for a fee of Rs 1,500. The agency calls this novel idea 'Tea with Nawab'.[16] It shows how much India is still in awe of its royalty, decades after it was legally abolished.

Moreover, the two nawabs' feud demonstrates how fragile the claims of belonging to the House of Awadh are. Claims can be made by anyone with tenuous connections to Awadh's royalty, since there is hardly anyone left to prove or disprove them conclusively.

This has, indeed, been done. Many recall a French woman who claimed she was married to a descendant of Wajid Ali Shah and tried to visit Lucknow in 2009 with the purpose of cleaning up slums. Then, too, the RFA of Khan had objected, saying she had no proof. Historian Taqi mentions another example, of a lady who claimed to be a begum and started living under a bridge in Lucknow. 'She was living like a beggar. Was she really a begum? Nobody knows, but people went to see her anyway, out of curiosity.'

What all this suggests is that those in Lucknow who claim to be direct descendants of the nawabs are themselves hard-pressed to defend their claims, and this leaves them with little scope or even credibility to validate claims made by others, such as Wilayat.

~

Jafar Mir Abdullah's largish room is adorned with colourful chandeliers hanging from the roof and old, sepia-tinted photographs. In one of the photos he is with former Prime

Minister Atal Bihari Vajpayee of the BJP, a favourite amongst Shia Muslims, who would get elected to the Parliament from the Lucknow constituency. There is also one with Akhilesh Yadav, former chief minister of Uttar Pradesh, giving him an award. In another photograph on the other side of the room, he sits reclining on a diwan, with a hookah behind him. On the other end of the diwan is another man. A chess board is placed in between them. The scene seems straight out of the film *Shatranj Ke Khilari*, directed by Satyajit Ray, which depicted the last days of Awadh and its royalty just before the Revolt of 1857.

Another photo shows him surrounded by curios and antiques. A former executive for a pharmaceutical company, he is now a dealer of antiques, he says. His family has been living here—a former palace that was added to the Daulat Khana complex in the nineteenth century—since 1862. Abdullah quit his job and moved in here in 1994, after his father took ill. He has three daughters, one of whom is based abroad.

We sit around an oblong table that covers a third of the room; the huge bed covers the rest of it. There are books and papers on the table and a beautifully carved tumbler of water with a cover on top. Behind the table, there is a small TV and a refrigerator. On one wall there are paintings of his ancestors. Awards and trophies line the multiple shelves on the walls. Abdullah is wearing an emerald blue knitted cap, an embroidered, half-sleeve waistcoat and a dark-coloured shirt underneath it. Behind him, there is a cupboard with a stack of books in Urdu, Hindi and English.

The nawab has an expansive air and clearly likes to talk about his family history. He starts by launching into an introduction to Lucknow, repeating the belief that the city was ruled by Lakshman. He mentions Abdul Rahim, the nobleman who ruled Lucknow during the early Mughal period, and from whom the ruling class of Sheikhzadas was descended.

Talking of the Shia influence on Lucknow, he narrates in detail the history of the Battle of Karbala, in which the Prophet's grandson Hussain was killed with his seventy-two companions, a story held in reverence by Shias all over the world.

Only then the conversation veers towards Wilayat Mahal. He remembers her stay in Sheesh Mahal, Abdullah says. A young man in those days, he was curious to know more about her. 'I visited her with a friend. I posed as a journalist, and he posed as my cameraman. I asked her about details to her connection with the royalty. She said she had papers to prove it, but did not show us any.'

Not long after that, he says one of his aunts recognized Wilayat from before Partition. 'Are you not the wife of Mr Butt?' the aunt had asked, to which he claims Wilayat's answer was: 'Shut up.'

∽

To journalist Promilla Kalhan of *Hindustan Times*, who had visited Wilayat at the New Delhi Railway Station before she went to Lucknow, Wilayat had said that her late husband's name was Inayat Hussain and that he had been the acting vice chancellor of Lucknow University before Partition.[17] The name Hussain matches Ali Raza's ID card, which we found after his death in Malcha Mahal, and had his father's name listed as 'Raja Hussain'.

But Abdullah is pretty sure that his surname had been Butt— which is interesting, because it is generally known to be a Sunni name. And Wilayat was, by all accounts, Shia. Not just because of the heritage she claimed, of the famously Shia House of Awadh, but also because of the rituals she followed. Then again, what's in a name? There are numerous exceptions to the typical Shia and typical Sunni names, and their usage.

In the records of Lucknow University, there is indeed one I.U. Butt who was the registrar in the pre-Partition years, but there is no record of any Inayat Hussain. In the university's library, we find an advertisement in the *Times of India* of 3 August 1929. The short ad, asking for a 'demonstrator in physics' and a 'lecturer in physics', was signed by I.U. Butt, officiating registrar. On a wooden board in the administration's building his name is the third in a chronological list of registrars since the founding of the university in 1921. The years listed before I.U. Butt are 1944–1948. Any other information on Butt, such as his father's name, place of birth or educational record, is not available in the university. When we checked in the administration's building, we were only given the minutes of meetings in the 1940s, mentioning the comments of the registrar without his name. Sachin Tripathi, a journalist who researched the university's history for a book celebrating its hundredth anniversary, also said that he could find no more information on I.U. Butt in the archives.

Abdullah had heard some tales of them from when they had lived in the city before leaving for Pakistan. His brother-in-law's father, Syed Mohammad Yusuf, knew them. He was a senior advocate at the Lucknow High Court and a friend of Butt's.

'They used to move amongst the royal families of Awadh in those days,' Abdullah said. 'And Wilayat fell in love with Yusuf. She was married already but attracted to him. One day, she invited herself to his house when he was alone. She was so desperate for him that she threw herself off the stairs inside his house, hurting herself in the process.' Afraid of such passions, the man got himself extricated from the liaison soon, Abdullah said.

Interestingly, he says that the house where they used to live still exists. We bid him goodbye, after he tells us how to reach it.

∽

The directions lead to a jumble of newly built concrete houses, with open drains and badly paved roads. We look for the mosque near which the old mansion stands, according to Abdullah. But there is no such mansion near the mosque, and no one seems to have heard of it.

We walk through the colony and enter another, seemingly older part. It is a slum. An old woman in one of the tenements outside a large courtyard owns some of the houses in the slum and complains about tenants illegally occupying the space she had rented out to them.

She says there is indeed an old mansion. 'It is across the other side of the railway track.' The track lies next to the slum. Right across on a small hill, there is a large building, constructed in the colonial style with red bricks and tall columns. One can imagine that in pre-Partition Lucknow it may have been surrounded by greenery rather than a slum. The city, at that time, had less than 4,00,000 inhabitants, compared to about ten times as many now.[18] As registrar of the university, Inayat must have been a man of standing.

The mansion looks rundown. Clothes are hanging in the veranda, with a balustrade to mark its boundary.

A young man comes out and tells us that his family lives there, but his father is not home. He is not initially keen to let us in to see the house but relents after some cajoling.

The rooms inside are sparsely and haphazardly furnished. The walls seem brittle from years of lack of maintenance. Other than the rooms with high ceilings, there is a large hall in the middle of the house that is almost empty. The fireplace has clearly not been used in ages. The hall leads to a big room, which probably once served as the drawing room. It opens out into a large porch where a craftsman is working on making thread used for stitching; the thread is spread out in the air, with ends tied to small poles stuck in the ground. On a second visit we meet the man of the house, the young man's father. He points out that there are multiple residences around his in what once must have been old mansions. He says he works at Jubilee College, and that's how he came to live here. The building was until

City of Nawabs

some decades ago the residence of directors of the college. What it was before that, he does not know.

~

Ammar Rizvi, the politician, is not willing to say that Wilayat's claims were false. 'I have not seen any government judgement,' he says. 'People say that the government had her claim debunked. If so, that would have been done by the home ministry. But I have no information about this.'

At the same time, he does not think the central government did anything explicitly to accept their claim either. Indira Gandhi ultimately giving them Malcha Mahal should, according to Rizvi, not be seen in this light. 'Mrs Gandhi was very considerate towards ladies. She must have asked someone to help.' Apart from Gandhi, Rizvi does not remember Wilayat getting any support in New Delhi. 'They did not have proof for their claim. And also, the government did not want to side with royals.'

In Lucknow, this was a slightly different story. 'The state government was very sympathetic,' Rizvi says. 'Because of her claimed links to Hazrat Mahal.' He explains that Hazrat Mahal and the way she fought for Lucknow in 1857 still strikes a chord with the people here. 'That's why the government and the people here were very sympathetic.'

He, therefore, gave Wilayat quite the VIP treatment during her stay in Lucknow. But she could not get along with those in power. When she asked to meet Ali Zaheer, Rizvi took her. Zaheer came from a prominent Shia family in Lucknow and had been law minister in a provisional government formed in 1946, in preparation for Independence a year later.

Sakina, in her book, describes Zaheer as someone who 'became defendant to guard Princess Wilayat Mahal's privileges'. She writes that it was Zaheer who conveyed to the Uttar Pradesh government that they could not accept the house that was offered to them in Lucknow, as it was 'not worth their status'.

Rizvi has a different memory. He says that while he and Wilayat were having tea in Zaheer's house, she said to him: 'This house is good. I want this house.' The blunt statement angered Zaheer a lot, Rizvi says. And she left a bad impression with others, too. 'Once Chief Minister N.D. Tiwari was at my house, when I came to know that Wilayat was on her way. Tiwari left abruptly, as he wanted to avoid her.'

Earlier, she had been invited to Tiwari's house, Rizvi recalls. 'When he entered his drawing room, he saw that most of the seats had been occupied by her dogs. She was sitting on his chair and the dogs started barking as soon as they saw him. So he refused to see her after that.'

~

Some suspect that there was more to the initial VIP treatment and attention for Wilayat. 'I don't think there was this much interest because of her royal claim,' says Atul Chandra, a senior journalist with the *Times of India* in Lucknow. At the time of Wilayat's stay in 1975 and 1976, he was a trainee with *National Herald*, followed by the *Pioneer*, and tracked Wilayat's case through reports by senior journalists. We meet him at a cafe in a crowded part of town. 'I believe that what played a bigger role was the Shia–Sunni politics.'

The Shia–Sunni tension that occasionally erupted in violence was at its height in the late 1960s and '70s in Lucknow, centred around the annual Muharram processions. While both sects in places such as Hyderabad participate in the processions together, in Lucknow during those decades they grew more and more into a display of tensions between them.

Aseem Hasnain, a political sociologist, argues in his doctorate dissertation for the University of North Carolina that the roots of these tensions lie in the early twentieth century.[19] Elites and sect-based organizations at that time were enabled in their identity politics by the colonial state—something that was not possible in the authoritarian princely state of Hyderabad.

In post-Independence Lucknow, Hasnain argues, political parties exacerbated the dividing lines between the sects. He argues that the absence of an inclusive Muslim party with legitimacy in both sects allowed other parties to align with either sect. In practice this meant that the Congress Party, the Samajwadi Party and the Bahujan Samaj Party have supported the Sunni community because they form the majority of Muslim voters. Their main rival, the BJP (and its predecessor, the Bharatiya Jana Sangh), with not much chance of votes from the Sunnis, has aligned with the Shias. The rivalry between the parties 'has contributed to sectarian frictions that has often transformed into violent rioting', writes Hasnain, adding that the old town centre of Chowk was the epicentre of this violence.

Chowk and Chawal Wali Gali used to be integral parts of the Lucknow of nawabs, as both were inhabited by Lucknow's famous courtesans. 'Most of the … tawaifs lived in Chowk. Some of them, like Allah Bandi and Najju, stayed in Chawal Wali Gali. The famous Mughal Jan lived in Sabji Mandi; Haider Jan had her house in Parcha Wali Gali; and Mushtri, whose poetry and voice were immensely popular, lived in Nakkhas; and Jaddan lived in Taksal,' writes Ravi Bhatt in his book *The Life and Times of the Nawabs of Lucknow*.[20]

At one point of time, walking alone in the Chawal Wali Gali may have attracted the attention of Lucknow's refined courtesans who used to live here, but today, the aroma of a variety of breads being baked in tandoors and large pans—sheermal, roomali roti and others—wafts in the air. These are being prepared as accompaniments to kebabs, which are served in the many eateries here, or to be had solo, such as sheermal. Other than small hole-in-the-wall eateries, there are residences with low, ramshackle doors and faded paint.

A colour-coded police map of the area, printed in Hasnain's dissertation, shows the well-known trouble points along with areas that are majority Shia, majority Sunni or mixed. During Muharram, the assertion of sectarian identities has meant till date processions going in opposite directions, the performance of mutually offensive rituals and instigating speeches.

'In good years, Muharram would include incidents such as stone pelting or minor fisticuffs between sectarian groups during days of a particular procession,' Hasnain, who grew up in Lucknow, remembers. 'In bad years, there would be stabbing sprees, rioting and arson.'

The year before Wilayat's arrival, 1974, had been a 'bad year', and tensions and politics in subsequent years resulted in a two-decade-long ban on Muharram processions from 1977 onwards. Therefore, to point in the direction of Shia–Sunni politics, as journalist Atul Chandra does, makes sense. Bahuguna, the chief minister in early 1975, who first asked Rizvi to invite Wilayat to Lucknow, was known to be pro-Shia, he says.

'He never said this, and he did not ignore the Sunnis, but this is based on the friends he had. He enjoyed the loyalty of both sects, but had more friends amongst the elite Shias.' The arrival of Wilayat provided him with a challenge, he says. 'He could not desert his traditional followers in favour of her. But at the same time, he wanted to make sure not to antagonize the Shias by ignoring her.'

Chandra points out that Bahuguna was not a Muslim and not even from Awadh. He was from a mountain village that would later become part of the hill state of Uttarakhand, carved out from Uttar Pradesh. His son Vijay became Uttarakhand's seventh chief minister in 2012, representing the Congress, though he later joined the BJP. Similarly, Satya Pal Malik, the Uttar Pradesh assembly member who filed a motion in favour of sympathizing with Wilayat in 1975, had personally not much to do with either Awadh or the Shia community.[21] 'So why did he, of all the MLAs, file that motion?' Chandra asks, suggesting there must have been a political motivation to it that had not much to do with whether he believed she descended from Hazrat Mahal or not.

~

Wilayat, perhaps, made use of identity politics by asserting her own Shia identity. In January 1976, she had presided over the bloody ritual of mourning at the Charbagh Railway Station. And in the summer of 1976, when Dara Nawab asked her to vacate his Sheesh Mahal mansion, the first place she took her children, dogs and luggage was the Shia landmark Shah Najaf Imambara. This place of mourning serves as the mausoleum of Awadh's first king, Ghazi-ud-Din Haider, who had constructed it as a copy of the tomb of Ali, the first Shia imam, in Iraq.

More than external assertion, it seems that Wilayat, as well as Sakina and Ali Raza, had deeply internalized and embraced the sense of suffering associated with the Shia faith.

In a 2017 academic article, authors Behram Hasanov and Agil Shirinov argue that in the Shi'ite identity, suffering functions to maintain the cosmic order. 'Suffering is interpreted as the cost of the battle between the ḥaqq (truth) and bāṭil (falsehood) and of preserving the right way; thus, suffering is glorified.'[22] Taking from sociologist Jeffrey Alexander's work on cultural trauma, they find that Shia Muslims attempted to cope with the pain from the Karbala massacre by making it meaningful. Although other religions also find meaning in suffering, they argue that the Shia faith is unique in the way they have made suffering a social activity. 'This state is one of continuous remembering, that is, remembering via suffering.'

In this way, present-day personal suffering is for Shia Muslims quickly linked to Karbala, write Hasanov and Shirinov. 'In funeral ceremonies for their deceased relatives, Shi'ites also shed tears for Karbala martyrs; meaning that they remember al-Ḥusayn, Karbala, and Imams every time they are sad.'

The authors also mention water as an important daily-life symbol of suffering. Sakina, in her book, indeed links their own struggle to get water in Malcha Mahal to Imam Hussain and his supporters being deprived of water for days before they were killed at Karbala.

This notion of glorified suffering suited Wilayat and her children, who continuously linked their own suffering with that of Imam Hussain and that of the begums of Awadh.

∼

In Lucknow, however, it quickly became clear that they could not stay at the Shah Najaf Imambara. While Wilayat and the children had gone inside, her dogs were locked out by the police. 'It was very chaotic,' Abrar Hussain, the dog trainer, remembers. 'Pentra, the labrador, was barking a lot. After two or three days, they all moved from there to the Charbagh Railway Station.'

Soon after, the whole family returned to Delhi.

The Family Retainer

The whole Lucknow experience was disappointing for Wilayat. That summer, she was provided with another chance to move to Lucknow. We discovered this in a set of photos and documents left by Ali Raza, now in the possession of the Alkazi Collection of Photography in Delhi.[1] The Uttar Pradesh government had again offered her a house in Lucknow. With a short letter, dated 9 June 1976, and directed to Wilayat at her New Delhi Railway Station address, the home ministry informed her of the same. The address of the allotted home was mentioned as: MG/47 in Sector 9. 'You are, therefore, advised to move to Lucknow', the letter concluded.

Wilayat, however, decided otherwise. In the same set of papers, there is a copy of a bitter letter she wrote to Chief Minister Tiwari a month later, in July 1976, the letterhead mentioning her address as the New Delhi Railway Station. It castigates him for 'ruining' and 'destroying' the lives of the 'descendants of Begum Hazrat Mahal and Wajid Ali Shah', through 'continued injustice'.

Around this time, Mohammad Kasim first met Ali Raza at Connaught Place, in the heart of colonial and commercial New Delhi.

As mentioned earlier, Kasim's name was scribbled on a piece of paper we found among Ali Raza's possessions in Malcha Mahal. Though he picked up the phone immediately, it took months for Kasim to agree to meet us. Even then, he initially refused to go on the record, saying that he had promised the family that he would never speak about them. This changed after the publication of the 2019 *New York Times* article and the subsequent media storm. He was shocked by the suggestion that his former employers were frauds and agreed to speak in their defence.

We first meet Kasim in a locale far removed from his days with the royals—near a waterpark in Kapashera, an industrial outpost on the border of Delhi and Gurgaon where middle-sized firms make clothes for international brands; he lives nearby with his family. After leaving Malcha Mahal, Kasim took up a job in one of the many factories in the area under pressure from his family, who wanted him to settle down. It was only after leaving the employment of the family that Kasim finally got married. He now has three children, one of whom is an adult and the others are enrolled in school.

His loyalty, even after all these years, is remarkable. 'They treated me like a son,' he remembers fondly. Asked whether he was paid on time—the financial status of the family never seemed to be stable, and in their final days they were reduced to utter penury and even starvation—he says: 'They had some gold and silver with them. They used to pay me by selling that. They were quite well-connected.'

During an early afternoon stroll in September 2020, in between Covid-19 lockdowns, Kasim opens up about his connection to the family. We are walking down the State Entry Road section near New Delhi Railway Station. State Entry Road is located away from the main station with its two well-known entry points, Ajmeri Gate and Paharganj. Government dignitaries board trains from this point.

The road leads to platform 1, where Wilayat Mahal stayed with her children and dogs. It is early noon on a Sunday, and in the quiet environment we can hear the birds chirping loudly. Kasim recalls the buildings on both sides of the road that existed back then. 'I used to come here to stroll with the dogs,' he says. 'It used to be quiet in the mornings, like it is today on a Sunday.'

Kasim is from Bihar and came to Delhi as a teenager, after finding it tough to do well at school. It was during his very first week in Delhi that he met Ali Raza by chance. 'I came to Delhi with people from my village, who said they will get me some work in Delhi. I got separated from them after arrival, but at the station, I met some people from a shop who had come to collect their cargo. They needed someone to help, so they asked me if I wanted to work. I accepted, but soon, I realized I did not like working there; they used to smoke a lot of pot. So, I left the work. They gave me Rs 40 when I left.' He worked for only four days, he says.

Ready to take the first train home, Kasim made his way to the station, not suspecting the U-turn his life was about to take. 'Then I saw the prince [Ali Raza], who had fallen on the ground after a car hit his bicycle. Everyone passed him by, but I helped him.' He points at the place where the incident took place, right outside the station, in H block, where Plaza Cinema once stood. Now it has been renamed as PVR Plaza. 'On occasion, I would get some money to go and watch a film. I saw films like *Maati Maangey Khoon* and *Ram Teri Ganga Maili* here.'

Ali Raza asked Kasim to accompany him to the platform, and that is how he began to live with the family as a servant at the VIP waiting room at the station.

It is a small space, with iron grills barring the entrance. It is mostly empty and littered with waste. Kasim shows where they cooked in the one-room space, and where they bathed. The station has undergone a drastic shift since they lived here; a new lift has come up beside what used to be the VIP waiting room. The swanky first-class waiting room is next to the ticket counter.

He first met them when they had just returned from Lucknow, he says. They had a lot of stuff in Lucknow, which was brought back to Delhi. It is then that he first mentions Asad.

～

Among the many things that Kasim remembers, his memory of Asad is the most remarkable.

Asad was Ali Raza and Sakina's brother. He lived with them in Kashmir, but did not join them when they moved to Delhi—Wilayat told *Hindustan Times* in 1975 that he was 'holding the fort' in Srinagar. After that article, Asad is never mentioned in any reports or articles from those days.

Nobody else we spoke to recalls Asad ever being at the New Delhi Railway Station or in Lucknow. The *New York Times*, in the 2020 follow-up to the 2019 article, reported him as having been abandoned by his family in Srinagar, where he, according to a rumour shared by a former neighbour, died of starvation.[2] We learnt in Kashmir that the circumstances of Asad's death were more complicated—and will share our findings later in the book.

In Kasim's memory, Asad was not only far from isolated in Kashmir, but regularly travelled back and forth from there. The family even travelled together.

'The first time I went to Lucknow with Asad Sahab, we got two dogs back to Delhi, and some carpets. The dogs were with a relative. We also brought back a trunk.' He says the N.D. Tiwari government had offered Asad a job, but it did not materialize. 'Then Rani Sahiba called me back to Delhi, over the telephone. She was unable to cook on her own.'

Looking around the VIP waiting room, Kasim tells us they had improvised a kitchen and a bathroom in that same single-room space at the railway station.

'Rani Sahiba had these iron grills placed here. There also used to be a park here. Asad Ali Sahab used to stroll there with Rani Sahiba at around 2 a.m. at night, when it used to be quiet.' He casually mentions a visit from Indira Gandhi, who he says came to meet them. Then he continues his description: 'They had a lot of stuff with them: carpets, beds, old antiques … All around this room, Sakina had planted flowers.'

A train whistles loudly as he shows us around. We offer to go to the platform with him. He is a little wary now, although initially, when we had just entered, he had blustered that now that we were there at the station, he did not fear anything. We take his pictures inside. He asks if he should remove the medical mask, which we are all wearing due to the Covid-19 pandemic, and then does so.

While Kasim discusses Wilayat's stay at the station, trains come and go; there is the usual flurry of passengers whenever they hear the whistle of an incoming train.

'Our duty hours were in shifts of three to four hours, after which we would eat and rest. We would climb the wall to go outside to buy provisions, such as milk or meat for the dogs, which we would bring from shops near Delite Cinema.' Kasim tells us that sometimes people would accost him when he went out on errands, asking him questions regarding the family. But since they had forbidden him to talk to anyone, he says he always kept quiet.

'One of the dogs, Himalaya, a doberman, used to stay in front. He was a heavyset dog who would rarely sleep. He had a 40-foot-long chain that weighed almost 60 kilograms.'

Himalaya would lead all the fights, Kasim says, at the railway station. There were many quarrels, he says. 'Sometimes, taxi drivers would come here, looking for a spot to drink. We would first warn them. Or sometimes, some local boys from the area would come. Even government officials would come sometimes, or policemen, or railway officials and their children. This had become a usual occurrence. Railway officials came so many times, with force, to try to get us to vacate this place.'

Kasim claims Asad got a black cobra for Wilayat Mahal to keep. 'It was only then that the quarrels ceased.'

∽

The American writer Ann Morrow visited the family when they were living at the station and wrote about it in her book *Highness: The Maharajahs of India*.[3] Sakina did not like what she wrote and says so in her own book.[4] But it does give a peek into their stay at the railway station. Morrow's book came after the Privy Purse had been abolished and she met many members of India's former royalty, which makes her work a comprehensive account.

She started by observing that a 'Dobermann Pinscher' was 'savaging' a servant's hand when she visited them at the station, amidst the flurry of trains going and coming to various destinations. She contrasted their living conditions with those of others she had met, by mentioning ironically that instead of 'swinging palace gates' to welcome her, she only found a bumpy dirt road that took her to the abode of the royal family on the platform.

Initially difficult to find, she was guided by a ticket collector to the family, which was staying in the VIP waiting room once used by the viceroy, writes Morrow.

She was greeted first by Ali Raza, who was dressed in 'trendy' clothes and shoes.

After shooing her driver away, he told her they once had twenty-seven dogs, but many had been poisoned. Then, he said dramatically: 'I have a hatred of the outside world, it is mean and cruel.' Morrow said that when she visited, the family had twelve dobermans. One of them 'growled viciously' at the prince, who 'moves swiftly like an athlete on springy heels'.

She was reminded of Lewis Carroll's *Alice in Wonderland*, a comparison that must have angered Sakina.

She followed it up with describing another 'outburst' from Ali Raza, which gives an insight into how it must have affected a young man to have spent half his life at a station platform. As another train left, he grabbed his head in his hands and wailed that he had 'grown up' amidst the constant sound of trains and announcements and music that followed every departure and arrival.

Morrow noted their 'five ragged servants'; one of them accidently hit Wilayat on the nose while fanning her, she observed. She mentioned that the family had refused the Uttar Pradesh government's offer of a house in Lucknow, as it was in a 'suburban' area. She described Wilayat as someone with whom she was not allowed to hold a direct conversation—her children acted as intermediaries—and who wore an 'air of pained dignity and melancholy'.

Ali Raza's utterances added to the absurdity of the situation, according to Morrow. He said that he 'hates daylight' and loved sleeping. His visit to England was noted—the family would tell reporters that Ali Raza travelled to London to hand over a petition with their demands to the British royal family. Between their possessions, we did find photos of a young Ali Raza posing in front of buildings of an architectural style typical of English residential townhouses. Unfortunately, the writing on the back gave us no information about whom the houses belonged to. He never told Leonie Broekstra either, when trusting her with the family photos to create a digital archive. Perhaps he visited his brother, Shahid, whom the *New York Times* found to be living in England. Whether it was during this trip that he delivered a petition to Buckingham Palace, we don't know.

The rest of Morrow's piece covered familiar ground, speaking of their grouse against the British for ill-treating the House of Oudh, their Shia sense of suffering, while mentioning that their fate, according to Ali Raza, was due to their being Muslims. 'He has a Moslem intensity and complains that no Hindu prince has ever been treated in the same way,' wrote Morrow, then quoted Ali Raza: 'We are Shiites, used to suffering and mortification, the ladies of Oudh have always stood strong.'⁵

∼

Kasim describes Asad as having a different temperament than his siblings and Wilayat, who were often short-tempered and mercurial. Asad was of a more temperate nature, Kasim says, emphasizing that he never ordered him around. 'He talked nicely to everyone. He was a bit different.' Once, Asad took a child to the hospital in Lucknow after an accident on the street, Kasim tells us. 'He took him to the army hospital and bore the expenses. He was very socially conscious and liked helping others.'

Interestingly, in her book, Sakina writes that Asad had good taste in shoes and clothes, including those for women, and he was the one who shopped for Wilayat. Sakina describes him as extra-sensitive and a bit 'different'.⁶

Unlike Abrar Hussain, the dog trainer in Lucknow, Kasim knew about the family's connection to Pakistan. He tells us that it was from the time of 'Raja Sahab', Wilayat's husband. He remembers that the children would sometimes speak about Pakistan, and their wish to return. 'But Rani Sahiba would get upset and say—don't ever speak of it. She used to say that they had nothing to do with it anymore. Asad Sahab expressed his desire to return several times.'

Kasim believes the family experienced severe trauma. 'They underwent tremendous suffering.'

He links Asad's death to their lack of success in negotiating the return of properties. According to him, Asad took the lead in these negotiations and kept going back and forth between Delhi, Lucknow and Kashmir—which might explain why no journalist ever saw him in the company of his mother and siblings.

'In Lucknow, Asad used to stay in Aminabad,' he says, referring to an area south of the Gomti river, not far from Wajid Ali Shah's old palace of Qaisar Bagh. According to him, it was at the house of a nawab called Bashir Nawab that Asad used to stay at. He says Asad had diarrhoea during a trip to Lucknow but refused medical help; his tendency to refuse medical help recurred later too.

In Lucknow, though the goodwill of the administration seems to have faded, the family still had some support. In 1978, the All India Shia Conference wrote a letter to the then home minister, Charan Singh, expressing its anguish at Wilayat Mahal spending her days in poverty and misery at the railway stations of Lucknow and Delhi.

We find the letter in the trove of papers left behind by Ali Raza, and kept at the Alkazi Collection of Photography in Delhi. It says:

> I may be excused to encroach upon your most precious time, but the gravity of the situation and the significance of the issue compels me to bring to your notice the sad and miserable plight of Begum Wilayat Mahal, the grand-daughter of the great Indian patriot, Begum Hazrat Mahal. This granddaughter of that great Indian lady, Begum Hazrat Mahal, who did not yield to the Britishers despite heavy odds and whose valour and patriotism are too well-known, is now compelled to pass her days, along with her two children in the waiting rooms of Delhi and Lucknow stations, more as a destitute than as the heir of one of the foremost freedom fighters and more in ignominy than in honour.

Signed by Dr B.H. Rizvi, the joint secretary of the All India Shia Conference in Lucknow at that time, it went on to exhort the government to consider her situation favourably and sought a 'better' and 'fair' deal for her. Our attempts to trace the writer of the letter did not bear fruit although the organization still exists in Lucknow, and the current office bearers were able to confirm that B.H. Rizvi had indeed been the joint secretary at the time.

Kasim claims that Asad was in favour of compromising with the government, but Wilayat refused.

From the conversations he overheard, Kasim gathered that they tried to take it to the courts. 'They wanted the government to return their properties. They would have willingly given some of it back to the government, had they been returned. But they did not want to bow down to the government. Neither Wilayat, nor Ali Raza and Sakina.' He claims Asad had approached the Patiala House Court in Delhi for resolving the dispute with the government over their properties in Lucknow. 'But the court asked him to talk to the government about it,' he tells us.

He recalls that the family was in touch with a high-ranking bureaucrat called L.K. Jha, though he calls him N.K. Jha. He remembers going to his residence in Delhi with Asad one time.

Lakshmi Kant Jha was a top bureaucrat who had been Secretary to Indira Gandhi in the 1960s, before spending the '70s as governor of the Reserve Bank of India, and later, as an ambassador to the US and governor of Jammu and Kashmir. In the 1980s, he served as economic advisor to first, Indira Gandhi, and, after her death in 1984, to her son, Prime Minister Rajiv Gandhi. Through other sources, we were able to ascertain that his stint in Kashmir was coterminous with the time Wilayat and her children spent there.

L.K. Jha is also mentioned in Sakina's book. She mentions that Wilayat went to meet him on 4 October 1985, and that this was the only time she ever left Malcha Mahal after moving there.[7] About herself, Sakina writes that she left the monument for the last time on 2 February 1990, to hand over some documents to 'Bhure Lal SECRETARY' in North Block, Central Secretariat, on behalf of Wilayat.[8] Bhure Lal, a well-known bureaucrat who later became known as an anti-pollution crusader, has a long CV, which indeed includes the position of Secretary to the Government of India around this time.

They also tried to make their case through foreign diplomats. Kasim remembers a high-ranked official from the Australian embassy came to visit them once. 'Rani Sahiba gave him an appointment after two years. He said he would forward their papers. He came once more, but nothing came off it. They used to get letters from America as well.'

Press reporters came to meet them at the station, too. 'Someone from the *Statesman* used to come often.' In her book, Sakina mentions the *Statesman* as the newspaper Wilayat Mahal used to read.

In the meantime, Asad's health took a downturn. He would often fall sick with a fever. Kasim used to bring him medicines, away from the eyes of Wilayat, since Asad did not want her to know. 'He used to barely eat, especially anything from outside. Talks of his marriage were going on, when all the trouble started.'

Kasim seems to believe that all the travelling took a toll on Asad. 'When he came to Delhi, Rani Sahiba asked him to return to Kashmir. After he returned on the Jhelum Express, he fell ill. Then she asked him to go to Lucknow. His health worsened further.'

Mostly, he believes that Asad's worsening mental health played a role. 'The government had taken over their property in Lucknow,' Kasim says. 'They tried everything to get it back, including going to the courts. Asad died from the sadness of losing it all.' This is what an earlier story by Elisabeth Bumiller in the *Washington Post*, published in 1986, says too. Bumiller visited the family in Malcha Mahal, soon after they moved there, and saw a photo of Asad on the wall. She was told that Asad died 'of sadness'.[9]

Kasim tells us that his funeral took place at the Alambagh cemetery in Lucknow, and both Wilayat and Sakina attended. We now know this to be untrue, and one can only wonder why Wilayat told him this; perhaps not to let him know about the tragic circumstances in which Asad actually died.

'When Malcha Mahal was offered to them, Ali Raza first went to check it out,' says Kasim. The prince was not pleased. 'It was all broken down. There was no electricity or water.' The divisional railway manager, in a letter to the chief secretary of the Delhi administration, had mentioned that 'the Begum's representative visited Malcha Mahal' and complained about the same. The railway manager requested the administration to 'immediately' provide the facilities that were 'agreed on earlier'.[10]

None of these facilities materialized, however, and ultimately, they moved anyway. According to Kasim, it was on Wilayat's insistence, even though no one else in the family was keen to do so. 'We were also helped by a reporter from the *Indian Express*, who on the family's behalf spoke to authorities, who cleared up the forest around the monument a bit, so the family could live here.'

Initially, it was not even clear that they could stay. As the *Washington Post* reported in December 1986, the ASI was trying to take control over the monument and get the family evicted, since it turned out to be the only well-preserved hunting lodge built by Firoz Shah Tughlaq. A deputy superintendent was sent to investigate and recalled to the newspaper: 'She is living in hell. So many lizards, so many snakes. The bat smell was terrible. Inside the darkness, I had a feeling of horror.' According to the article, the ASI argued that Wilayat was never given the monument: 'The former home minister said nothing was ever decided, and his successors don't know where to find the file.'[11]

It was Indira Gandhi who, after visiting the railway station in 1984, instructed the home ministry to find a suitable accommodation for Wilayat. A letter by the home ministry dated 6 December 1984, a copy of which is included in Sakina's book,[12] says that the 'Home Minister feels that we may agree to the building known as Malcha Mahal being given to her after repairs'. This indeed does not sound like a definite decision. But nevertheless, the ASI gave up the fight and Wilayat and her children stayed on.

~

It is December when Kasim agrees to revisit Malcha Mahal with us. He is dressed in blue trousers, a blue sweatshirt with a narrow strip of red in the middle, a skullcap, and sandals on his feet. First, he trails behind as we make our way towards the monument, but then overtakes us and moves with ease, walking with a measured pace, betraying no particular emotion. The path is overrun with wild and thorny vegetation and tall aloe vera plants, which reach up to our faces.

'They were very determined to make Malcha Mahal inhabitable when they first moved there,' says Kasim. 'We even dug up a well on that rocky ground.' However, in keeping with their history of failed efforts, no water was ever found. 'We used to get water from the market down below, loading it on the cycle. They suffered many adversities. It was only after they had lived there for eight years that they received a water connection from the ISRO Earth Station.'

As we reach the stairs in front of the structure, Kasim pauses and gazes upwards at the mahal, which seems both inviting and forbidding. Then, the stories begin. Kasim tells us how the family liked their breakfast: toast, tea and coffee, always before 9 a.m. They were very particular about that. He walks up the stairs. At the threshold, he touches his head with his right hand, uttering sotto voce the greeting 'aadab arz', paying polite obeisance to his deceased employers.

'It was not so dilapidated when we lived here,' he notes, looking at the pitiful condition of the mahal, with big holes in the wall, and broken columns. He adds that there were gates to keep intruders out. 'Dogs used to lounge about here. We had four Great Danes, ten dobermans and four labradors,' he says with evident pride. 'The dogs liked to hang around Rani Sahiba. As the sound of any car would reach the dogs, the labradors would be the first to run towards it.'

He says once there was a story in the media about a servant who allowed one of the dogs to bite someone, when they were living in Malcha Mahal. He says he had the dog in question with him, but the story was false. Then some other publication or channel reported that they had illegally occupied Malcha Mahal. 'That is why they did not like press reporters. They published stories different to what they had been told.'[13]

As we enter the structure, we first come into the arched hallway, surrounded by the other smaller rooms. 'This used to be the darbar [royal court],' Kasim says. 'This is where they received guests.' The room is littered with dust and all kinds of waste paper, telephone bills, bank slips, newspaper cuttings and ash from a bonfire someone must have built using the wood from the bed that used to be there. 'In this corner was the bookshelf,' he points.

Next to the hallway is the dining space. Here, Kasim says, they also did yoga to keep fit. Shortly after Ali Raza's death, the dining table with some remaining utensils was still standing but now there is nothing left. 'It was almost impossible to live here in the early days. We used to feel as if any kind of accident could take place with anyone, anytime.'

Kasim was one of the few servants to accompany the family when they moved to Malcha Mahal. None of the others stayed for long, he says. 'They were not trustworthy enough,' he says of the other servants.

∽

Among the photos kept by Ali Raza, that are now with the Alkazi Collection of Photography in Delhi, there are a few of the family's servants. Some have words like 'traitor' inscribed on the back—including one that appears to be a young Kasim. Perhaps, in the end, they trusted nobody.

Wilayat Mahal died, allegedly by suicide, in 1993. The means was as dramatic as her life, according to Sakina's account: by swallowing crushed diamonds.[14]

Kasim had left their service shortly before, leaving them in the care of a servant from Nepal. When he came to visit them after that, Ali Raza acted 'strange'. Later, it occurred to Kasim that Wilayat had possibly died by then and, hence, the change in Ali Raza's behaviour.

'I went to meet them, but the prince said Rani Sahiba had gone out. I had a doubt about it. Perhaps he did not wish to tell me about it. He was speaking a bit differently to me than how he did before.' He remembers asking about the dogs and Ali Raza's gaunt face, perhaps due to not eating. 'I had brought along some bananas. He did not let me go towards her bedroom. I felt heartbroken.'

He did visit again, though the last time he had met Ali Raza was almost a decade earlier. 'He asked me to go back and take care of my children and family.' Kasim would still call him sometimes on the landline, and the prince invited him, but, busy with his own family, he never visited again. After Ali Raza died, alone in Malcha Mahal, Kasim got a phone call from the Chanakyapuri police station.

Kasim seemed desolate that he was unable to meet the prince in his last days. 'I feel like all is over,' he says. 'It is such a feeling I cannot put it in words. He never treated me like a servant. He took care of me as a brother as far as it was possible for him. I also think that the kind of statements being made about him, about being a liar, are extremely unfair.'

~

Back at the residence for the last time, Kasim stands in a room adjacent to the entry to the monument, where there is a tank to store water. He says this is where they cooked; it also served as a washroom. The floor is strewn with old clothes, shoes, bedsheets and cushion covers. 'We used to go down from here to get water.' He points in front. 'You can also see a small mosque there.' He used to sleep in this room at night, he says, on a cot.

He starts to identify the clothes, mostly of Western fashion: jeans, jackets, shirts, etc. 'Looking at his clothes lying around like that, I get goosebumps. I know what belonged to whom.'

He finds a pair of dark blue trousers, scouring in the pile. 'This used to belong to me.' Wilayat Mahal stitched her own clothes, he says. He finds a yellow-green pillow cover with designs on the edges. 'This was embroidered by Rani Sahiba. She used to do this in her free time.'

We ask him if it makes him sad to see their belongings lying in such a state. 'I feel remorse,' he says. 'A tremendous remorse.'

We pass by another room, where the floor is covered with bat faeces, and then we move to the dining room where Kasim picks up a broken chair that belonged to the family. Its top and bottom parts come off in his hands. Then we are outside, having exited from the rear door, opening into the forest.

'Many peacocks used to come here. Rani Sahiba liked to feed them,' he says, walking briskly around the building. 'They used to come in droves.' We spot the grave of a dog. There are some bones lying around, and several stones over a hole in the ground that has been filled back in.

Kasim used to bring meat for the dogs from Nizamuddin, he says, a neighbourhood some 7 kilometres southwards. 'Himalaya was there,' he says, mentioning the doberman that had been with the family since their Lucknow days. 'Another was called Brahmaputra. The dogs were very loyal.'

Back in the building's circumference, Kasim picks up a tattered carpet lying in the darbar. 'This is a very old carpet that they brought. It is from Iran. It used to cover the entire hall but it looks like people have cut it up and taken away the parts.'

Our tour of Malcha Mahal is done. Finally, we take the narrow stairs going to the roof, and are outside in the sun, facing the wide expanse of forest around the decrepit palace. Kasim looks around for a neem tree. Wilayat Mahal had planted it, he says.

The tree is very much there, in full bloom. He breaks into a smile, as if he has met an old friend.

The Princess's Diary

'As for a common language, there is no such thing; or rather, there is no such thing any longer; the constitution of madness as a mental illness, at the end of the eighteenth century, affords the evidence of a broken dialogue, posits the separation as already effected, and thrusts into oblivion all those stammered, imperfect words without fixed syntax in which the exchange between madness and reason was made.'
—Michel Foucault, *Madness and Civilization*[1]

'It was a sign. The cruel, nasty nature was demanding the return of princess royal Wilayat Mahal.'

In her book, Sakina starts by addressing her mother's death. Her beloved dogs had a premonition, writes Sakina, which they communicated in a rather dark way: by dying one by one. 'The messengers of the custodian of the dead,' she calls them, and describes how 'the unseen forced them to lay sacrifice their unselfish lives willingly one by one for and on behalf of their fortress; princess Wilayat Mahal.'[2]

It started with the death of two dobermans on 31 December 1992, and two more the following day. February took two Great Danes, Brahmaputra and Kaiser; followed by Himalaya on 14 March.[3] Sakina notes that the dogs were treated with both affection as well as strictness by Wilayat, and in return they only listened to her. 'Princess kept them in discipline; yet had tender attachments for them.'[4]

Five more dogs died in the months leading up to 10 September 1993, a day Sakina keeps referring to in her book as Black Friday. Friday, a day Wilayat had never liked, according to Sakina. No dog died in the month of August; Sakina writes that it was probably because Wilayat was born in that month.

On the afternoon of 10 September, Wilayat had been writing about the history of Awadh, with her 'favourite' newspaper, the Kolkata-based *Statesman*, open before her, and a cigarette packet next to it. At 2.40 p.m., she summoned her children: 'Rajkumarji' and 'Rajkumariji'—Respected Prince and Princess—is what she always called them. When they approached her, Wilayat did not say a single word. Instead, she just placed her head on the stone writing table, never to lift it again.[5]

Eight hours passed, until around 10 p.m., Sakina and her brother decided to move Wilayat's body to her bed. 'We could not have the audacity to touch [her corpse],' she writes. Both she and the prince then sought 'forgiveness' and 'consent' by asking her aloud. The remaining dogs began a 'heart-rending' wailing and the prince and princess wept along, while the retainer—Kasim's successor—stood there in shock; some of the remaining dogs 'placed their heads on the Princess'. They asked the retainer not to disturb them for the next three days as they slept with their mother's corpse without eating or drinking anything.

Sakina writes that this was the first time they slept with their mother without first seeking her permission.

Three days turned into a week, then ten days. They embalmed her with 'ancient ingredients' and the 'diamonds, pearls and rubies', which she wore when alive, were also crushed and used by them for the purpose. Afterwards, they wrapped her corpse in her 7-yard-long cream-coloured silk sari. They slept with her at night, while with great difficulty digging her grave in the day, near the graves of all the dogs that had died before her; it took them a week to dig up a grave for her and 'adjust a stone vault for the Princess'. Inside the vault, they placed marble slabs, then put her body on top of them.

> We never never desired to part move away from Princess. The Grief the deafening silence created Princess's dogs the silent spectators throughout and the fragrance of aromatics forever fresh this was and is the first time our heads of wills was and is shattered beyond measure—disaster reverse fallen on us...[6]

Sakina describes in detail the process of burying their mother.

> Over a week days and nights we broke the rocks removing huge rock layers and stones the soil does not exist in our Malcha Mahal. Our hands elbows feet bleeding yet no intervention of outsiders—
> Only silent observers. The Princess's dogs the sun of the day and moon of the night—
> The vault the mother earth granted a chamber of marble slabs on which princess reposed. It was mid-night the embalmed Alexandrine features countenance un-wavering living-only apparently silent princess on the same marble so not to disturb Princess's style, the etiquette never never thinking H.H. to be subject to this state but princess yet remains our supreme being of stakes and strongly desire the un-seen force for

the incantations to the silent princess to return to us. First Rajkumar stepped inside the vault prostrated himself then I Rajkumari laid myself on the slabs? Why?
So the soul which has a protector over it the existence of Princess should realise that we had not the indecency to rest Princess first no but it is we who had entered before. Equally our conscience desired to raise the spirit of Princess back to existence. H.H. was and is everything ... We sat the whole night alone with Princess's dogs watching silently next to H.H.[7]

Finally, they again asked their dead mother for consent, this time to bury her and close the grave. 'But the chamber of our minds will never close,' Sakina writes.

This is followed by a poignant meditation on the nature of time itself, and what Wilayat meant to them.

By the sickle of time, time is a created thing. It has its mysteries but it is no more eternal than matter. Time has no value for us how it passes grief in sorrow is a life itself. For us Princess's constant countenance constancy in the Malcha Mahal never made us feel that we are in unmeasured adversities created provided by the selfish insensitive governments devoid of petty necessities electricity water or our abode is a ruin.[8]

She reminds the reader that to her and Ali Raza, Wilayat was everything:

Nothing on Earth and never on Earth can anyone replace a Mother not even the Supreme Being.[9]

She goes on to mention that Wilayat had refused all marriage proposals for her because it would cause 'separation, distance, apartness'.[10] After Wilayat's death, she writes that she refused to take care of her hair, allowing it to become 'matted', while hoping Wilayat would return.

> I live life less without Princess full of thought in anxiety agony with thought of separation ... I Rajkumari very much want to give up my life.[11]

She adds that she was closer to Wilayat than her three brothers.

> Princess always had attachments with me more than for them.[12]

~

We had known about Sakina's book for a while. Many of the foreign journalists visiting Wilayat, Sakina and Ali Raza in the decades they spent at Malcha Mahal were shown or given a copy. Some mentioned its existence. But none of them ever found it worth reading in full or quoting in their articles.

It was only after Ali Raza's death that we managed to get a PDF via the Dutch photographer Leonie Broekstra. Ali Raza had asked her to digitally archive the family photos and had given her a copy of his sister's book as well. After that, she had lent it to Ellen Barry, the *New York Times* journalist, who on Broekstra's reference was kind enough to have a PDF copy made and send it to us. Broekstra is one of the few people who have seriously read it; she was moved and quoted from it in a self-published book, combining the family photos and the photos she took of Malcha Mahal. Her book is at the Alkazi Collection of Photography. What interested Broekstra was how the family chose to archive and portray themselves.

Theirs was not a story that could be captured by relying solely on what is termed 'objective' truth or facts. This is why we made the effort of reading and rereading the text, for large parts are written in capital letters and without much punctuation, besides poetic handwritten notes that are quite difficult to make sense of. Nevertheless, it contains a wealth of information, including mostly accurate historical accounts and notes on the importance they attached to them, besides details of the family's daily life in Malcha Mahal, their religious practices and their claimed family tree.

Central to it all is—how could it be otherwise—Wilayat. The cover page reads: *The Un-Seen Presence Princess Wilayat Mahal Oudh*, along with a painted portrait. She is here seated on a couch, dressed in a black sari, hair open and flowing, with a solemn and sad expression in her eyes. This painting was made by a professional painter when they lived at the station; according to Sakina's text, the painter also gave Ali Raza some art lessons.

Inside the cover follows another full-page photograph of Wilayat Mahal, seated, dressed in a black, kaftan-like dress, her right hand holding the paw of a huge dog that Sakina identifies as Castle. In the background, Kasim stands at attention, turbaned, wearing white trousers and a dark-coloured, buttoned shirt. The dog's head reaches the middle of his torso. Wilayat Mahal looks haughty: her intellectual wide forehead and aristocratic hooked nose dominating the rest of her features. Her lips are thin and pursed and her expression is pleasant enough, although she is not smiling.

Sakina calls the dog by the name Egyptians referred to the deity they associated with death, with a man's body and dog's head: the Anubis. 'The Knower's of Premonitions,' she terms them. 'The Princess Anubis do not possess deceitful human calculations.'

She then proceeds to name all the members of the family: the mother, Princess Wilayat Mahal; two deceased princes, Asad and Mehdi, who died at the age of twenty-four and fourteen respectively; and the two remaining members, Prince Ali Raza, for whom she uses the name 'Cyrus Riza', and then acknowledging herself as the author, Sakina.[13] The names of the two deceased princes are also prefixed with the name 'Cyrus', after the Persian king, Cyrus, who founded the first Achaemenid empire. Later in the book, she briefly mentions a half-brother 'who later went his way'.

So, how many children did Wilayat have? How old were they and what happened to them? When was she herself born? In the chapters to come, we will trace Wilayat's history via documents at the National Archives of India and living sources that can shed some light on the lives she led in Karachi, Kashmir and Lahore. For now, let's focus on Sakina's version of the family history. Though some details are missing, vague or unlikely, this is what she presented as her family's oral history, her memory, her truth.

～

Wilayat Mahal, Sakina writes, was born on 13 August 1931.[14] Her mother was Taj Bakht Nasr, an equally proud and stubborn woman who was said to have rejected an offer of a government pension of Rs 13,000 in 1948.[15] Though a significant amount at the time, Taj Bakht found it insufficient. Wilayat's grandmother was called Zamend Tamkeen Mahal,[16] and her great-grandmother was Almas Mahal.[17] We will discuss her possible existence in Chapter 6, as it is this Almas who would be the link connecting Wilayat directly to Hazrat Mahal.

In an interview with the *Chicago Tribune* in 1985, Wilayat had given another name for her grandmother: Zamrud Mahal. She, according to Wilayat, had attended the Delhi Durbar of 1911 and 'appeared before the British party in a conspicuously torn gown to declare that she would never accept a stipend from the British'.[18] Whether it was Tamkeen or Zamrud, none of these ladies seem to be mentioned in history books, as far as we can tell. When we look up the Delhi Durbar of 1911, reportedly only one Indian female royal attended: the Begum of Bhopal who was famously photographed in full purdah.[19]

Despite the great detail in which Sakina narrates her lineage, never does she mention any fathers or grandfathers.

Perhaps this is a result of the Shia tradition of mut'ah marriages, a kind of temporary marriage that would expire after some time and was generally not accepted as legal by Sunni Muslims—some likening it to prostitution. Wajid Ali Shah had hundreds of mut'ah marriages, including his marriage to Hazrat Mahal, a former concubine. Perhaps all of Wilayat's foremothers were born out of such mut'ah marriages that were later dissolved, accounting for the absence of forefathers.

Or perhaps the fathers were just not considered important or relevant. This fits into Sakina's discourse of female strength. Even Wajid Ali Shah is hardly mentioned by her. From the eighteenth-century begums of Awadh to Hazrat Mahal and Wilayat and Sakina themselves, it is the women who take centre stage in her book. They are hailed for their heroism and their strong characters.

For example, Sakina does not name her mother's place of birth, but describes its historical significance by highlighting what she felt was an example of female heroism in the House of Awadh:

> In the fort which had witnessed the events the treacheries of the British walls were silent true observers. It saw 1836 battle between Badshah Begum consort of king of Oudh Ghaziudin Hyder, and the British.[20]

Ghazi-ud-Din Haider[21] was the first nawab to be crowned king of Awadh, in 1819, and Badshah Begum was the title of his main wife. The *Statesman* wrote an article on her in 1986, describing the battle Sakina referred to—although they noted the year as 1837.[22] In a feud over succession, Badshah Begum had her step-grandson Munna Jan coronated, aided by her own army, against the choice of successor that the British had put on the throne. The begum got a lot of support from the people of Lucknow and they held the fort for one night, until the British surrounded them completely and shot most of her men. The begum and Munna Jan were arrested and spent the rest of their days in Chunar Fort, near the city of Varanasi in present-day Uttar Pradesh.

The coronation and subsequent siege took place in a building called Lal Baradari, also known as Badshah Bagh, that is now part of the Lucknow University campus, which celebrated its centenary year in 2020. After the annexation of Awadh, it was auctioned off and bought by the maharaja of Kapurthala, who leased it to Canning College—which was elevated to Lucknow University in early twentieth century. After Independence, it was used as a club for the university staff. It also accommodated a bank for students on campus.[23] More recently, it was evacuated due to its dilapidated state. In the absence of any renovation, one of its walls collapsed in 2021.[24]

~

It is hard to imagine how and why Wilayat Mahal was born in a building that, regardless of the historical significance in the history of Awadh and its fierce begums, already housed a university staff club at the time of her birth. Since this chapter's focus is Sakina's truth, we'll leave it at that.

Wilayat got married at the young age of twelve, which Sakina writes was a 'royal compulsion'.[25] She was the third wife of a man from 'the race of Oudh' three decades older to her—which would make it probable that there were half-siblings. In fact, Sakina mentions stepchildren. Sakina repeatedly emphasizes that the marriage was unhappy and this caused Wilayat a great amount of distress. 'There existed a great distance of disturbance Princess lived separately from her consort not on speaking terms.' She writes that when the husband died, Wilayat was not even thirty years old. He was conscious of the age difference and Wilayat's unhappiness due to it, writes Sakina, showing some understanding for her father:

> Though Princess consort was truthful in his relations with himself incapable of deceiving himself persuading that he never repented in his binding relations with Princess though much elderly All that Princess consort repeated of was that he did not never never succeed in retaining princess happiness inspite of worldly possessions of the nobility grandeurs He might have felt difficulty of his position and perhaps felt sorry for princess and latter for his or rather princess children that is us.[26]

She writes that Wilayat's forced marriage and royal upbringing forced her to become 'reticent' and 'self-possessed'. 'There was neither complete division nor agreement between the Princess and the consort the memories of which had so tortured Princess'.

She mentions that Wilayat liked flying planes and driving; owning a Mercedes, a Ford and a Willys Jeep, which were later sold for a pittance. According to her, Wilayat even owned a pet leopard that would lie in the back seat of her car while she drove.[27]

There is no other information about Wilayat's childhood, her life before Partition, or her life in Pakistan. Sakina also never mentions where the children, including her, were born. She does mention that as children they were cared for by nannies, one of whom was English, Ms Merchant, and another, a courtesan from Awadh, whom she praises highly for her refined etiquette; apparently, Wilayat trusted this courtesan a lot. Other than this, the story of her own life begins when the family was given a residence in Srinagar's Nishat Bagh by India's first Prime Minister, Jawaharlal Nehru—though Sakina writes that Wilayat 'never wanted to acclimatise' in Kashmir and had 'no likeness for' the state. She did love swimming, and they undertook special outings to Ganderbal, 'where cold river water flows'.[28] It was

Nehru who, Sakina says, 'compelled' them to stay in Kashmir, till 1974, even after fire was set to their residence, burning some of their antiques, carpets and other possessions.

From Kashmir, the family moved to the New Delhi Railway Station, which Sakina calls the 'formal declaration of dissent'.[29] Sakina displays some bitterness when she writes of their decade-long stay there, accusing both the general public and the railway authorities of hostility towards her family, and especially the latter for inciting violence towards them. 'Each day and each night had its own untold and open miseries,'[30] she writes about the experience at the station, where, according to Sakina, they faced goons who wanted to oust them.[31]

This is plausible. Kasim also remembers harassment by 'local boys'. It is not known who sent them, but it is possible they came at the behest of some higher authority, according to S.G. Mishra. He is the president of the All India Railwaymen's Federation, an organization that champions the rights of railway workers, and he was a regular visitor to the station when the family lived there. Mishra confirms the harassment they faced and says there was opposition against them by the Railways authorities. Since Mishra also belongs to Lucknow, he says, he took a sympathetic interest in their affairs. He narrates an incident when, in protest against the railway authorities, they occupied the entry to the platform with their dogs for several days.

Sakina writes that many of their possessions, including clothes and antiques, were stolen while they were at the station.

> Memories of the stay at New Delhi Railway Station the station meant for public what surpassed each day each night we had never slept in peace the meannesses of authorities and public the Emergency experiences what bitter sick time jerking Princess us our dogs not spared the railway authorities often let loose the water pipes on the suitcases. Carpets tapestries

portraits which were ruined and much stolen from steel boxes which they broke open the middle brow people enjoyed the sight.[32]

At another place, she writes that Wilayat stayed at the railway station to protest the amount she was getting as an allowance. 'Princess was receiving against her will "Pride of Purse" a small amount as a token of Rs 500'—Sakina calls it an 'intentional humiliation for Princess and us', which 'H.H. resented and objected. Sternly declared formal declaration of opposition for ten years at the railroad station.'[33] According to Sakina, many members of royal houses of the world, such as Russian and Austrian royalty, expressed solidarity with them while they were at the station and even came to meet them.

She mentions Maharani Gayatri Devi and Maharani Vijaya Raje Scindia in this context, the former as someone who expressed 'admiration and esteem' for Wilayat; both of them spent time in Delhi's Tihar jail during the Emergency, Sakina writes, for being opponents of Indira Gandhi. Gayatri Devi, queen consort of Jaipur, was an MP from the Swatantra Party and was arrested during the Emergency. Vijaya Raje Scindia, of the Gwalior royal house, was also initially with the Swatantra Party and later with the Jana Sangh. She, too, was arrested during the Emergency. According to Kasim, Karan Singh, scion of the Kashmir royal house and a Congress politician, had also expressed support for Wilayat, but later withdrew it. V.P. Singh, who later became Prime Minister, and who was a royal from Manda, near Allahabad in Uttar Pradesh, was also supportive of Wilayat, according to Kasim. We reached out to Karan Singh, who is still alive, but he did not wish to comment, citing health reasons. All the others are now no more.

After Asad died—according to Sakina's book on 23 July 1980[34]— Lucknow became more and more a distant dream for the family. They opened up to the next best alternative, Malcha Mahal, without completely giving up on their more ambitious demand. 'The Princess's persistent constant demand repeated for the return of at least two palaces from Lucknow,' Sakina writes in her book. 'This Malcha Mahal in lieu of one of the palaces, as Chatar Manzil Palace is converted into a drug institute.'[35]

As per government documents, it indeed seems that railway officials took the lead in trying to find alternative accommodation for Wilayat and her family. 'In pursuance of cleaning drive being maintained we found that Begum Wilayat Mahal has not yet shifted,' one desperate letter said, written by the divisional railway manager to the chief secretary of the Delhi administration about two months before their move to Malcha Mahal in 1985.[36]

A year earlier, in May 1984, Wilayat had threatened suicide if she were evicted. It was reported by the *Times of India*: 'In a four-page hand-written statement delivered to UNI headquarters by her son and daughter, the begum referred to reports that the railway authorities are planning to evict her ...' In the statement, Wilayat had referred to her claimed family history: 'If the government officers had planned to evict ... then the tragedy of Nawab of Oudh, Sadat Khan, and Begum Sadat Khan, shall definitely be repeated,'[37] referring to the 'historical event in 1739 in which the Nawab drank the cup of poison rather than face dishonour'.[38] Wilayat also made use of the occasion to repeat her demand for property in Lucknow. 'The British empire had no moral authority to transfer our ancestral properties to the other government.'

Finally, the home ministry and the PMO got involved.

Government order to the Princess by the then Home Minister Mr P.V. Narasimha Rao—1984 while Princess was still at the New Delhi Railway station. By the orders of the then Prime Minister, Mrs Gandhi. That Malcha Mahal shall be provided repairs, water, electricity etc.[39]

The railway station took a toll on Sakina's health—she writes in her book that she suffered from pneumonia while staying there, which lasted a long while; she writes that this made Wilayat accept Malcha Mahal, along with Indira Gandhi's death.[40]

Life in the mahal was a challenge, too.

> We stepped here on 28th May 1985—much hue and cry in the Parliament for New Delhi Railway Station, The Princess's abode.[41]

Sakina laments their 'wretched abode', speaking of darkness, snakes, scorpions and the building's bad state. 'Whenever it rains its roofs which are now very weak become a sieve—pouring rainwater flooding everything,' she writes. It had ruined their Persian carpets and Chinese tapestries.[42]

Sakina mentions issues with the water supply, noting that the family paid the municipal corporation for water, but the tankers sent would often not be able to climb up the ascending road that led to the mahal. Sometimes, water from the tankers would fall out in such a struggle and be wasted. This made them dependent on the whims of the authorities of the Earth Station next door. The electricity department, she mentions, had installed a power grid next to the monument much before they moved there, but Wilayat Mahal had it removed due to her fear that the dogs would get electrocuted. Sakina calls the experience of seeking both water and electricity from the Earth Station as 'great humiliation'. She notes that sometimes their retainer would get into altercations with the employees of the station and use 'harsh words' for receiving the supply of water.[43]

She compares their need for water and the humiliation they used to suffer for it with the story of Imam Hussain in Karbala, a foundational story for the Shia community. For Shia Muslims, the Battle of Karbala holds as much significance as the crucifixion of Jesus does for Christians. In the legend of the Battle of Karbala, the denial of drinking water to Hussain and his companions by Yazid's army—which cut their access to the river and forced them to go without water—is a defining motif, which for Ali's followers shows the utter lack of humanity of the opposing side.

∼

Slowly, they learnt to live with the hardships and developed their daily routines in and around Malcha Mahal. Wilayat had an interest in gardening and used to place stones outside to make beds for cacti. She also fed peacocks, which visited them daily. Jackals also came by to have their share of food.

Initially, she describes their troubles with the Bawariya tribe, a nomadic hunting tribe that was stigmatized as criminals by the colonial Criminal Tribes Act of 1871. Sakina calls them 'deadly' and 'notorious' and mentions that she had slapped one of them when they came to visit them at the station. She says they were informed that the tribe admired the House of Awadh. And that when they arrived at Malcha Mahal, some members of this tribe came to know of it. Then, she suspects, with the collusion of their servants, they managed to poison seven Great Danes in the month of May and steal silver crockery including plates and glasses, among other precious things. Wilayat made every effort to get the dogs treated—the President's vet was consulted; attempts were made to fly in medication from Germany. Finally, two of the Great Danes survived.[44]

The siblings maintained a formal distance from their mother, even asking permission to interact with her. Wilayat bathed herself every morning and evening, never eating before she washed herself up. 'Princess has breakfast under different arches, lunch under east arch, dinner west arch, never in the same place and always separately from us,' Sakina describes.[45]

The only day in the year they ate together was on 21st March, Navroz, the Persian New Year. They would have tea and lunch and Wilayat would arrange for narcissus flowers.

Navroz is indeed celebrated by Shia Muslims in Lucknow and other parts of India. Sakina also mentions other customs and traditions they followed. At one place, Sakina writes that Wilayat Mahal did not care for Fridays so much, the holy day for Muslims, but preferred Saturday as the day for repose and contemplation.

Elsewhere, she mentions that both her mother and grandmother worshipped celestial bodies, especially the sun. For them, fire was the emblem of the deity. Wilayat, she writes, 'revered and preferred' Ra, the sun god of ancient Egypt.[46] Again, elsewhere—the mentions of religion are scattered—Sakina writes that they followed the beliefs of Sabaism,[47] a term we had never come across before. An initial online search seems to suggest some connections with both ancient Egypt and the ancient Persian religion of Zoroastrianism, as well as with a group of people mentioned in the Quran as Sabians who worshipped the sun and the moon.

Coincidentally, we later find more clues in the writings of Russian philosopher Helena Blavatsky, the co-founder of the Theosophical Society, the headquarters of which are in Chennai. She is a fascinating figure, with her interest in Indology and her reputation as a psychic; she had a connection with the Indian struggle for freedom as well through her friendships with Mahatma Gandhi and Annie Besant.

Blavatsky, in her works on the history of the world's religions, describes Sabaism as an ancient religion in which the sun, moon and stars are worshipped.[48] In Persia, Sabaism gradually gave way to Zoroastrianism, which also features the worship of heavenly bodies and reverence for fire, and was later replaced by Shia Islam.[49] However, Zoroastrian practices survived, in Iran and among some Shia communities elsewhere. The celebration of Navroz is one example.

The poetic, opaque sections of Sakina's book begin to make more sense with all this in mind. Sakina, for example, invokes multiple times Ahura Mazda, the God of the Zoroastrians, and calls him Yazd, which is the Persian name for God. Considering their dogs as Egyptian gods also fits this picture.

Though people like Kasim and Abrar only remember them following Shia rituals, Sakina, with these references in her book, gives an insight into how deeply connected they were and wanted to be to the Persian roots of the House of Awadh, going back centuries to not merely the first nawab,[50] but keeping alive ancient Persian religious traditions as well. Traditions from Sabaism, Sakina writes, were passed on to them by Wilayat's mother.

∽

After Wilayat died, Sakina and Ali Raza mourned and struggled to move on with their lives. 'Princess has left apparent void leaving us lonely. We now consider ourselves the dynasty of the living dead.'[51]

Ali Raza broke the mirror in which Wilayat glanced at herself, Sakina writes.

> The mirror which glanced on Princess hence it had to be cleft asunder so even we had not the audacity to see our reflection that in which Princess's image was reflected.[52]

All her things—apparel, shoes, riding boots, saddle—were preserved by Sakina and Ali Raza after her death.

Sakina kept a comb of her mother's but never combed her hair again.

> The comb for us carries no meaning now also shun even glancing in the mirror.[53]

According to Sakina's book, even Ali Raza did the same.

After six months, the body was brought back inside and kept for seven days during which period meals were served with formal etiquette, she writes.[54]

A decade after they first moved there, she writes, Ali Raza decided to take an electrical connection from one of the streetlights outside, but it was met with opposition by the staff of ISRO. While she was alive, Wilayat had always counselled against it. Sakina complains of the 'communal attitude' of the ISRO staff. 'Her highness would and could have set these bunch of staff straight,' she rues.[55]

Later in the book, her thoughts turn to her brother:

> The stoic son of Princess Wilayat Mahal the only brother of mine Princess Sakina Mahal must face the world with great courage for the greater sake of the dynasty.[56]

Ali Raza was thinking about Sakina, too. Towards the end of the book, he takes over the writing and describes an event that must have had a devastating impact on Sakina.

He begins quite abruptly but we know it is him, since the language becomes sparer suddenly, even a bit more coherent, and he acknowledges that it is he who is now writing.

> This continued reference towards the Princess's stead = In context = Between the Princess in Rest = And Princess Sakina's regular lighting of the candle = Though in no way had I or Would I like to contest – Between Princess Wilayat Mahal and Princess Sakina … I have no audacity to intervene
> Yet I Prince Cyrus A. R. Had built up a retentive decision for the greater security of the two princesses which I desired not to leave to anyone.
> I have burnt my nights without sleep = I have burnt my days = each day to contest with the following day. Every cruel evening Candle by candle =
> The silent glow =
> I could no longer bear Princess Sakina's state of mind.

Here Ali Raza is referring to the practice Sakina had of burning a candle every evening in the place where Wilayat had died, under one of the arches in the mahal.

He writes that Sakina's melancholy was 'not easy' to observe and that it was 'crushing' him inside. He then made a drastic decision.

On the eve of Wilayat Mahal's next death anniversary, Ali Raza made sure that Sakina was busy having her breakfast, which he says she always had late like her mother.

> I held the crowbar = and silently stepped out = and gave a final glance to her = I solemnly stepped towards the resting stead of princess Wilayat Mahal. Indescribable concealed sorrow in my heart.

He then smashed the other grave that Sakina had made for herself next to where Wilayat lay buried.

> Two strokes of the heavy crowbar—I smashed and struck that future stead of Princess Sakina's reticence which she had counselled—determined for her burial.

He went on to open the vault using the crowbar in which Wilayat was buried and accessed her corpse.

> Same content posture as before 10th September 1993 Before 2:40 PM No difference only extreme silence = This silence was unbearable for me Prince Cyrus. I broke down alone besides immortal princess ... I placed my forehead on the forehead of the Princess. Embraced Princess == I felt warmth in my self.

He took out the corpse and laid it outside, careful enough to put a pillow under the head. Then, he set the corpse to fire.

> I do not need verses and scriptures Then solemnly == with a single match stick of the same match box left over with the

cigarettes on that table 2:40 p.m. That time chosen by the Princess == conferred to the pious flames Now Princess was in the safest guardian of the flames == to remain unseen and untouched by any human.

Later, the siblings would tell reporters that the cremation was a mutual decision, taken because they noticed their mother's body was not preserved as well as they had envisioned with their embalming.[57] But after Sakina's death, Ali Raza reveals what really happened. It had been his plan and executed without Sakina's knowledge or consent.

As the body burnt and fire cracked open the bones and singed the flesh, the sounds it made alarmed the dogs, who began running and 'growling with heavy voices'.

This alerted Sakina, who stepped outside.

Princess came out as Princess saw me = and this foundation and Princess Wilayat Mahal conferred to the flames The flames were at their commanding heights = whilst stepping out = Princess missed the step of the high stone stairs = and stumbled on the rocky ground yet she stood and rushed towards the flames of the fire.
Completely unaware. How severely she was hurt. But I noticed how the blood was flowing all through the neck = Princess stood in pain holding her hurt back but yet rushed towards the fire.
Ali Raza writes that he came in between the fire and Sakina.
Sakina screamed I held her firmly.
Leave Me Alone
Leave Me Alone
Leave Me Alone
I Want To See Princess
I Want To See Princess
I Want To Meet Princess

I Want To Meet Princess
Leave Me Alone
Leave Me Alone.

Afterwards, Ali Raza writes that he remained standing near the flames all day. In the evening, Sakina came out of the monument, followed by the dogs 'because they always walk beside her'. Her eyes were 'completely swollen', he observed, due to the fall earlier, seeing which he 'broke down inwardly'.

She had some difficulty in sitting down opposite him, on the other side of the grave, which no more existed. They did not speak to each other and sat like that all through the night, accompanied by the dogs.

They waited for the hour to become 2.40 p.m. in the afternoon the next day; the date was exactly one year after the death of Wilayat. Collecting her ashes in a glass bowl, they went to the roof of the mahal and allowed the wind to carry them away.[58]

After this, Sakina wrote a few more entries herself, in which she expressed severe depression. 'I am distinctly conscious to experience time further for me is unbearable', she writes,[59] and: 'All that is left is cruelty and darkness- ...Why am I living? What for? The dynasty of the dead must include me whether it is possible or impossible.'[60]

∼

Ali Raza described his sister as melancholic, which is indeed the state of mind that her book seems to reflect. Sigmund Freud described it in his 1917 paper 'Mourning and Melancholia', as summarized by psychotherapist Danielle Trudeau:

> Freud believed that in melancholia, a loss is so unbearable that it gets relegated to the unconscious, where the grief exists but can't get processed by the conscious mind. And so, the person

gets a little bit stuck: the pain is felt *internally*, and without the specificity that the conscious mind could give it, the pain very often becomes directed towards the *self*.[61]

Sakina's book, on the cover of which she refers to herself as *The Self*, is a narration of their internal world. The world inside the railway station and inside Malcha Mahal. The world in which only their claimed family history matters. The outside world hardly plays a part. Government officials and politicians are mentioned in the context of their struggle, but the immense economic and political changes that India underwent in the years Sakina was writing—from economic liberalization to wars with Pakistan and major communal riots—are not mentioned or commented on.

Certainly, there is order to be found in what may seem like a chaotic and incoherent rant with random references and a lack of punctuation. Historical sagas are largely correct, other references all serve a purpose and personal observations are genuine. Sakina continuously tries to make sense of her own life, by connecting her family's story, as she knows it, to history. The injustices done to the begums of Awadh and to Awadh itself tie up directly to the injustices she felt were done to them by the Indian government.

She speaks of 'intended humiliation' and accuses the Indian government of following in the colonialists' footsteps by favouring those royal families that sided with the British.

In 1993—the year of her death—Wilayat Mahal sent letters on two occasions to then President, Shankar Dayal Sharma, about the 'severe distress' the family was in. Sharma did not reply. Calling him 'insensitive' like all government functionaries, Sakina writes that she knew well that the Government of India was used to making false assurances.

Praising the fighting spirit of the begums of earlier centuries, Sakina goes on to state that their 'endurance descended' and was 'inherited by the strong-minded princess Wilayat Mahal of Oudh'. A 'deafening silence' from the side of the government caused the despairing state her mother was in, she argues. Sakina must have known what others thought about them. Avoiding words used by journalists before and after their death, such as 'obsessed', 'mad' and 'eccentric', Sakina addresses this when she writes: 'Nothing was wrong with Princess, only acute anxiety may be the cause.'[62]

By speaking of her mother's mental state in the context of present as well as similar historical injustices done to an entire kingdom, Sakina essentially describes a trans-generational trauma.

The concept of madness, the French philosopher Michel Foucault argued in his work *Madness and Civilization*, is subjective and serves to 'other' and silence those who don't fit into our idea of normal. Sakina was aware of her family being different. 'Our profound conservative ordinate, strange for others,' she remarked, for example. But she also reminds the reader that her mother was a human being. A woman who loved horses, elephants and swimming, who had a great interest in chemistry and physics, and a mother who 'inwardly grieved' for her deceased sons. A woman who deserved to be heard.

In the next section, we will dive into the history that came to define the family's identity and was so important to Wilayat and Sakina that they narrated it to all the journalists who wanted to hear it: the injustices inflicted by Warren Hastings on the begums of Awadh of the past, and the heroism of Hazrat Mahal. These are also recurring themes in Sakina's book, where they are mentioned as evidence of British perfidy towards the House of Awadh as well as testimony to the spirit of the strong women of the royal family, who remained defiant in the face of governmental persecution. We will further explore the claimed family tree and whether it can be proved that they were descendants of Hazrat Mahal.

In addition, we visit Wajid Ali Shah's descendants in Kolkata, the ones who tried to expose Wilayat's story as a hoax, saying that they are the real inheritors of the House of Awadh.

Following these three next chapters, we will explore how their identity was connected to the history of the subcontinent—including the history Wilayat preferred to forget: the years around Partition in Kashmir and Pakistan, and, to come back to Freud's description of melancholy, what unbearable losses they may have relegated to the unconscious.

Part II
History

'Hegel remarks somewhere that all great world-historic facts and personages appear, so to speak, twice. He forgot to add: the first time as tragedy, the second time as farce.'

—Karl Marx[1]

The Looted Begums

On one of our trips to Malcha Mahal, we recover two handwritten pages. The top left corner of these pages—made from handmade paper and foolscap in size—reads:

> H.R.H. (Her Royal Highness), The Begum of Oudh, Shehzadi Wilayat Mahal, Heir to the Last King of Oudh Begum Hazrat Mahal and Wajid Ali Shah.

Written in perfectly intelligible English (with occasional grammatical errors), it is mentioned that the British, and afterwards the Indian authorities, were 'in possession of considerable portions of treasures of Nawab Sadat Khan, Burhan-ul-Mulk and Safdarjung'.

Sadat Khan (also called Burhan-ul-Mulk) and Safdarjung were the first two nawabs of Awadh. The note, which we believe was written by Wilayat,[1] continues:

> It was Warren Hastings who kept behind irons the then Begums of Oudh for many months starved, beaten and

deprived of food. And the treasure of the Begums of Oudh was seized and estates and properties wrested.

The narratorial voice turns prophetic and laments, under a section titled 'Why Knowingly Hiding the Real Realities...':

> Nor his heirs ever in vain thought of fleecing the subjects ... Historians were are and shall be in future always swayed by favouritism and mislead intentionally. It is this Royal House of Oudh in the open portico who shall never waver for our justified return of our ancestral palaces and properties by the Government of India and not the meaningless decision taken by the Government of India the offers of government properties which was refused and rejected by we, the Begum of Oudh, Shehzadi Wilayat Mahal.

The 'open portico' refers to the space they inhabited at the New Delhi Railway Station. While the rhetoric might be lofty, it is correct that Warren Hastings, then governor of Bengal, was accused in the British Parliament of corruption and ill-treating the begums of Oudh, and his reputation suffered a serious blow from these proceedings. The money that Hastings looted from the begums was used to finance the battles that Britain fought with France in the south of India, as part of the Anglo–French War between 1778 and 1783, in order to consolidate its hold over the Indian subcontinent.[2]

While asking for the return of Awadh's palaces, Wilayat and her children also spoke of bigger reparations, though in less direct terms: the injustice done by Warren Hastings in Awadh was so great that it should have been made right in some way; if not by the British empire of the time, then by the independent Indian government, which, in the eyes of Wilayat, had failed Awadh utterly.

Interestingly, Hastings is remembered rather fondly by many in India due to his love for Indian culture. He is known as the patron of the Asiatic Society of Bengal, and his properties in Calcutta, including one named Hastings House, are well-maintained and used for other purposes.

In Britain, too, though Hastings' image was severely blemished during his trial, it was given a purely heroic spin posthumously to support the empire's imperial project.[3]

Only recently has his legacy again been discussed in more critical terms, with the loot of Awadh's begums in the forefront. Most prominently, Indian author and politician Shashi Tharoor used Hastings's looting of Awadh's begums as one of the prime examples of British misconduct in his book *An Era of Darkness*, 2016—the book followed Tharoor's viral 2015 speech at Oxford University where he argued for reparations from the United Kingdom to India for centuries of misuse of colonial power. He called Hastings 'arguably one of the most rapacious of the Company's many venal Governors General'.

> Hastings accepted substantial personal bribes and then went on to wage war against the bribe-giver (one wonders whether to deplore his avarice or admire him for the fact that despite being 'paid for', he refused to be 'bought'). His brazenness in such matters compels admiration: when he tortured and exacted every last ounce of treasure from the assets of the widowed Begums of Oude, Hastings duly informed the Council that he had received a 'gift' of 10 lakh rupees...[4]

(The gift of Rs 10 lakh [1 million] was made out to him by the then nawab and the begums' son and grandson, Asaf-ud-Daula, and Hastings went on to keep it.)

～

For someone who rose to dizzying heights of fame or notoriety later in his life, Warren Hastings, the first Governor-General of British India, came from rather humble origins.

Although connected to minor royalty, his family was not well-off. His mother died while giving birth to him, according to a biography written by Michael Edwardes in 1976.[5] His father abandoned him soon after, and he was brought up by his grandfather.

Hastings's uncle funded his initial education, first at a boarding school, and then at Westminster School, which was one of the best schools of its time. After the death of his uncle, Hastings had to abandon his education and look for a job. It was with the East India Company that he received employment, as a lowly clerk, and was sent to India in 1750. He was only seventeen years old.[6]

India, at this time, was marked by political instability. The Mughal authority was in free fall and influential regional power centres, such as Awadh, Bengal and Hyderabad, were already well-established.

Awadh was ruled by Safdarjung (also spelled as Safdar Jang) when Hastings arrived, having taken over after the death of the first nawab, Sadat Khan, in 1739. Khan had no sons, so his son-in-law Safdarjung became the next nawab of Lucknow. The trend of powerful begums exerting influence on the functioning of the kingdom started during his reign.

In this fluid political atmosphere, the British and the French were involved in a conflict to secure their position as the main trading power. The French, with their headquarters in Pondicherry, were strong in the southern region of India. The British enjoyed a similar position in Bengal.

Warren Hastings, first sent to Madras in the south, and soon after to Calcutta in Bengal, thrived in this political scenario. Within three years of his arrival, he was sent to Kasimbazar as a representative of the Company. Kasimbazar was an important trading town in Bengal, close to the capital at Murshidabad, a city as large as London, according to Edwardes. During his period there, a major clash erupted between the British and the ruler of Bengal.

In 1756, the nawab of Bengal, Ali Vardi Khan, died and was succeeded by Siraj-ud-Daula; not the man the British had expected would succeed Khan. In his book *Sirajuddaullah and the East India Company*, Brijen K. Gupta provides a detailed overview of the economic situation then prevailing in Bengal and how it caused a confrontation between the new Nawab Siraj-ud-Daula and the East India Company:

> Due to the growth of the oceanic trade the Indian economy, which had hitherto been largely agricultural, was gradually taking on a commercial character. The exports were not agricultural products; they were manufactured goods like silk fabrics, calicoes and muslins. It was, therefore, not unnatural that the landed military aristocracy of the Muslims should have lost in importance...[7]

The nawabs of Bengal, dependent on land revenue, were further disadvantaged as the employees of the East India Company used to trade on their own, without paying any taxes to the local government.

The immediate catalyst for the confrontation between Siraj-ud-Daula and the British was the latter's decision to fortify the precincts of Fort William in Calcutta without taking the nawab's permission. The hostilities started with Siraj-ud-Daula taking over the British factory at Kasimbazar on 1 June 1756. Within weeks, Calcutta was also captured by the nawab's army. Hastings, who was taken prisoner, was lucky to be released soon through the good offices of his Indian friends.

For six months, the nawab's writ ran over Bengal and Calcutta, till military help arrived from Madras, with Robert Clive at its helm. Clive, who had arrived to India like Hastings as a clerk, but had risen quickly through military hierarchy, was ferocious in defending British interests in Bengal. He managed to recapture Calcutta, thus setting up the Battle of Plassey in 1757, which the British won. Siraj-ud-Daula was defeated and killed, and succeeded by Mir Jafar as the new nawab.

With the victory in Plassey, the British were now a bona fide power in Bengal. Hastings received a promotion and became the resident at the court of the new nawab. He continued in his position till 1764, the year in which the Battle of Buxar took place; which established the supremacy of the British quite comprehensively as they managed to defeat the combined armies of Bengal, Awadh and the Mughals. The defeat would prove especially costly for the Awadh rulers, and would set the template for their relations with the British in the future, allowing the British to dominate state affairs.

~

In 1764, Hastings sailed to England where he was to spend the next five years. In 1769, he returned to India, serving the first two years in Madras Presidency, before being made the governor of Bengal in 1771; the first-ever to occupy this position.

He was now a rich man with expensive habits, funded at times through personal trade as well as bribes. For example, Edwardes, in his biography, narrates:

> He ... accepted from the Munny Begum some £15,000 as 'entertainment money', on a precedent established by Clive and followed by other governors.[8,9]

Awadh, in these years, became increasingly entangled in a relationship of dependency with the East India Company, which saw it as an important buffer state between Bengal and the Marathas.[10] In 1765, a year after Buxar, Clive had already signed a defensive alliance with Nawab Shuja-ud-Daula, who had succeeded Safdarjung after his death in 1754. In 1773 followed the first Treaty of Banaras, through which Hastings arranged that a brigade of the Company's troops were to be stationed permanently in Awadh—supposedly for Awadh's defence—for which the nawabs had to pay a fixed amount of money.[11]

A second Treaty of Banaras was signed in 1775, the year Shuja-ud-Daula died and was succeeded by his then twenty-six-year-old son Asaf-ud-Daula. An increased number of Company troops took over the command of a part of his army, which was incorporated as a 'temporary' brigade into the Company's forces. With the growth in numbers of the troops stationed in Awadh, the British began to squeeze Lucknow harder monetarily.

The 1775 treaty also brought Banaras, which had been close to Awadh, under the Company's suzerainty. As part of this arrangement, the king of Banaras, Chait Singh, had to pay a fixed annual tribute to the British but other than that, he was free to act as he pleased. The amount was fixed at Rs 23,40,249.[12]

In 1778, Hastings asked Chait Singh to pay additional monies, other than the tribute levied annually, to the tune of Rs 5,00,000; this money was to be used by the Company to shore up its defences against the French and the Marathas. Singh refused and took recourse to open rebellion in 1781, which was subsequently suppressed by Hastings.

Chait Singh's rebellion is where the begums of Awadh come in—the begums whom Wilayat and Sakina regularly referred to in their narrations of historical injustice, and 'the loot' that was central in the trial of Hastings.

The two begums in question were the nawab's mother and grandmother. Bahu Begum, the widow of Shuja-ud-Daula, and Sadr-un-Nisa, the widow of Safdarjung, were no ordinary begums. Both were rich and powerful in their own right, with their own jagirs, or estates, collecting handsome revenues. Bahu Begum's jagir was managed by two eunuchs, Bihar Ali Khan and Jowar Ali Khan. In addition to her jagir, Bahu Begum, who had helped Shuja-ud-Daula buy back his kingdom after the defeat at Buxar, possessed large amounts of jewellery.

What happened between the begums and Hastings is described by Peter James Marshall, in his account of Hastings's trial:

The prosecution's case was that the East India Company had given their guarantee to the lands held as jagirs by the mother and grandmother of the Nawab Wazir[13] of Oudh, and to the treasure belonging to his mother; and that in 1781, on a contrived pretext, Hastings had violated this guarantee by compelling the Wazir to resume the Begams' lands, to seize most of the treasure and to pay the proceeds to the Company. Hastings admitted the existence of a guarantee of the Wazir's mother but not of his grandmother, and also admitted that he had used some influence, though less than compulsion, in bringing about the confiscations. But he asserted that the Begams had forfeited all guarantees by acts of hostility to the Wazir and to the Company.[14]

The 'acts of hostility' mentioned by Hastings referred to allegations that the begums had sided with Chait Singh in his rebellion. It was alleged that they had provided military help to Chait Singh by sending a thousand-strong force.[15]

The second allegation was that they had incited revolt in Bahraich and Gorakhpur, two districts in Awadh. None of these allegations were ever conclusively proved but it was speculated that the begums disliked the British and their patronage of Asaf-ud-Daula.

Following the revolt at Banaras, a new treaty, called the Treaty of Chunar, was signed between Asaf-ud-Daula and the British, allowing the former to take back any jagirs that he saw fit, while paying the due amount for them to the British.

However, the begums were not at all prepared to part with their jagirs and they made it known to the British. As punishment for their defiance, it was decided to seize their treasures as well, writes Marshall:

> On 8 January (1782) Middleton [Nathaniel Middleton, the Resident] decided to take 55 lakhs, or £550,000, out of

the treasure. The process of extracting them was to be lengthy, and the methods squalid. Bahu Begam's chief servants, the eunuchs Bihar Ali Khan and Jowar Ali Khan, were seized, put in irons, and, after 'some few severities', 43 lakhs were taken from 'the most secret recesses' of their houses.[16]

In 1785, Hastings's term as the Governor-General finally came to an end. His reputation was already damaged due to allegations of personal corruption, high-handedness and his treatment of Chait Singh and the begums in particular. Barely a year after his return, Hastings was impeached and charged with over twenty-two charges of corruption and misdemeanour. Seven of these charges were eventually considered, out of which six were then redrafted as 'Articles of Impeachment'. On 10 May 1787, the House of Commons voted that Hastings was to be prosecuted before the Lords, paving the way for a trial, which opened a year later, attracting much attention from the press and the public.

Such was the appeal of the trial for the British public that it was a ticketed affair.

> It was to be excellent entertainment for the fashionable audience, and the black-market price of tickets always went up when it was known that Sheridan would speak.[17]

Three of the best orators of England participated in the prosecution of Hastings—among them the playwright Richard Brinsley Sheridan; the politician Charles James Fox; and Edmund Burke, a philosopher. In his opening speech, Burke spoke for four days.

> There was a display of India's history, so that the paradise that country had once been could be glaringly contrasted with

the hell of the 'avarice, rapacity, pride, cruelty, malignity of temper' the accused had made of it. Hastings was the 'captain-general of iniquity' who never dined 'without creating a famine'. Even after attaching most known crimes and original sin to the accused, Burke could regret that 'the English language does not afford terms adequate to the enormity of his offences'. It was an immensely impressive performance. The fashionable audience greeted it with tears and moans and at least one lady had to be taken out in a fit.[18]

The trial went into the history books as a landmark political trial, the significance of which extended far beyond the accusations against one individual—rather it was about the idea of empire itself.

After six long years of proceedings in the House of Commons, Hastings was acquitted. Opinions remain divided over the damage to his reputation, with some even feeling he was unjustly treated. Marshall, in an entry in Encyclopaedia Britannica, for example, states:

> It is difficult not to regard this long-drawn-out ordeal as a serious injustice. At the most it made some contribution to the process by which standards were being laid down for the future conduct of British rule in India.[19]

In 1818, Hastings passed away. Edwardes writes:

> The death of Warren Hastings, first Governor-General and to many the saviour of British India, was greeted with private sorrow but little display of public regret. There seems to have been no suggestion of a state funeral, the obituaries were curiously guarded, and neither Parliament nor the Company erected a monument to him in either of those reliquaries of accepted greatness, Westminster Abbey and St Paul's Cathedral.[20]

Hastings was buried in his hometown, Daylesford. His widow, Marian, later had a memorial plaque with a bust erected in Westminster Abbey, which speaks of his 'talents and integrity', 'Christian virtue' and the 'affection and gratitude' he received from the inhabitants of Bengal. The church notes on its website:

> Two versions of an inscription were put forward mentioning his impeachment and acquittal but neither was used.[21]

~

Till date, Hastings remains a controversial figure; but unlike some imperial characters, such as General Henry Havelock and Robert Clive, whose statues and street names have been targeted by activists in the UK alongside slave owners and other historical villains in recent years, Hastings seems to have been spared similar opprobrium.

Perhaps because he was a controversial figure when he died, only one statue of his exists in London and it's not for the general public to see. It was commissioned in 1820, two years after his death, by the East India Company for their own headquarters. These days, it stands in the Foreign and Commonwealth Office in Whitehall, which only opens for the public once a year. When the statue was being discussed, not everyone in the Company agreed that Hastings should be honoured. Historian Alfie Banks, in his award-winning undergraduate dissertation, suggests that the debate was actually about the legacy of the East India Company itself. 'Hastings was symbolic of the Company, and his commemoration represented an attempt to defend its legacy amidst parliamentary incursion.'[22] Once commissioned, opponents included prominent philosopher Jeremy Bentham, who suggested that the statue should get a critical inscription: 'Let it but put money into our pockets, no tyranny too flagitious to be worshipped by us.'[23] Needless to say, his advice was not followed—but it shows how divided opinions were on Hastings.

Meanwhile, the British community in Calcutta collected money to honour Hastings with a statue as well. Here, much less discussion took place, notes Banks: it was unanimously approved and they got 342 individuals, out of which 30 per cent were Indian, to donate generously. It took almost ten years for the statue to be unveiled in the Calcutta Town Hall in 1830; Banks notes that it could have been related to Hastings having strong and popular opponents in Britain, notably Burke. These days, the statue stands at the Victoria Memorial in central Kolkata—the present-day name for the capital of West Bengal. It depicts Hastings as a scholar, wearing a classical robe, and accompanied by a Hindu Brahmin on one side and a Muslim scholar on the other.

As critical and divided as public opinion towards Hastings used to be—reflected in history books, newspapers and public magazines— it became eulogistic towards the end of the nineteenth century. Banks links this shift to the imperial fervour after the 1857 Revolt. Historians and journalists alike worked in sync to vindicate Hastings from all his alleged crimes. 'Vindicating Hastings was, like the Empire, a divine mission, taken up with zealous enthusiasm by his biographers.'[24]

In the twentieth century, in the context of increasing insecurity over the future of the empire, this trend continued and amplified into Hastings being portrayed as an 'untouchable imperial hero', along with his predecessor Robert Clive. In 1932, the bicentenary of Hastings's birth was commemorated as a grand affair in London, describes Banks. There was a procession, memorial ceremony and speeches speaking about him as the 'founder of the Empire', as 'the greatest Englishman in the eighteenth century', and as an administrator 'full of kindness'. As self-rule had already been promised at that stage, Hastings was celebrated as the hero who 'built the foundation' of the empire. An exhibition at the British Museum with his papers and portraits was extended due to its popularity.

After India's independence in 1947, a lot of this hero-worship has stuck—Hastings being mostly remembered in the UK as the 'saviour of India' who undertook extensive and efficient reforms. And even today, argues Banks, contemporary concerns influence how Hastings is being remembered:

> Multiculturalism provides the tendency to treat Hastings with a sympathetic eye; his patronage of Indian art, languages and culture sitting more comfortably with present concerns than the policies of his anglicising successors.[25]

Banks, in a footnote, points to William Dalrymple's widely praised book on the East India Company, *The Anarchy*, 2019, as a 'recent example of the sympathetic interpretation of Hastings'.

In India, too, such a 'sympathetic interpretation' is not uncommon. 'Let's redeem Warren Hastings,' wrote historian Zareer Masani in 2017 in an opinion piece for *Open* magazine. Masani is part of a group of scholars that form a non-profit, History Reclaimed, whose stated mission is to challenge 'the abuse of history for political purposes'. In his article, Masani lists the many things that proved Hastings's love for India, calling the charges against him ironical. 'He was fluent in Bengali, had good working knowledge of Urdu and Persian, and pioneered the revival of Sanskrit, rescuing it from the narrow confines of a corrupt Brahmin priesthood.'[26]

In Kolkata, architecture associated with Hastings is cherished and an entire neighbourhood remains named after him, without any protests—just next to Fort William, besides the Hooghly river bridge. 'Kolkata romanced the Raj,' wrote senior journalist Shikha Mukerjee in an article arguing why the 2020 worldwide fury against statues honouring past oppressors—following the Black Lives Matter movement in the US—did not reach Kolkata. She describes how a few dozen statues of colonial heroes survived until the late 1960s, when they were quietly removed by the leftist government of the time and placed in a suburban garden. Many streets were renamed, but the old street names—including Curzon Park, and Clive Row in the above-mentioned Hastings neighbourhood—remain more popular in usage. Mukerjee quotes a former curator of the Victoria Memorial, Chitta Panda, who responded to the idea of removing signs of the imperial past with the argument that Indian society has more pressing issues and injustices than the colonial past, saying: 'There is no tiger; what are we fighting against?'[27]

The anti-statue movement did reach the UK, but Hastings's statue in Whitehall has gotten away with it, for now. A statue of slave owner Edward Colston was toppled; a statue of Henry Havelock—a general during the 1857 Revolt—was vandalized; and a public petition asked for the removal of the statue of Robert Clive in the foreign office. Clive, rather than Hastings, currently seems to embody the evil of the empire in the public mind. Dalrymple, in *The Anarchy*, described him as an unstable sociopath—a widely used quote in the British press. Shashi Tharoor, in a public message on social media to London's mayor, Sadiq Khan, who made it his personal mission to review all statues, street names and plaques in the city for public commemorations to become more diverse, pointed to Clive's statue, calling him 'a ruthless, dishonest, unprincipled leader of an unregulated corrupt corporation that oversaw India's plunder and loot'.[28]

One of the first physical results of Khan's policy was the changing of a street name in south London. Havelock Road in the Southall area, where three-quarters of residents are of South Asian descent, is now called Guru Nanak Road, after the founder of the Sikh faith. For the initiator of the process of changing the name, local MP Virendra Sharma, it was a victory after decades of discomfort with London's street names.

'I started raising this twenty-five years ago,' Sharma, who was born in undivided India in 1947 and migrated to the UK in the 1960s, says over a video call.[29] 'This idea of equality, where it means that the master and servant days are gone, and that we need to bring the history up to date, highlighting what went wrong and why there is resentment—earlier it was seen as an individual's view. Now it is clear: there was a silent majority who wanted to make a change, but were not aware of the ways to do it, by democratic ways.'

For Sharma, the end of Havelock Road is only the beginning. Asked how he feels about the Hastings statue, he says that he has been focused on his own constituency, but he does not agree with Masani and others who emphasize Hastings's love for India. 'Different Governor-Generals had different ideas. But the principal was that they went to India as rulers. These officers who were sympathetic to Indian culture and people—nobody raised their voice, saying that what we are doing is wrong. Nobody resigned out of protest.'

Quoting Tharoor's book, Sharma says he does not believe in financial reparations. 'You can't put right what has happened in the past. But at least acknowledge that it was wrong, for the future generations to understand that.'

∼

Wilayat, of course, demanded financial reparations for herself, in the form of grand palaces, and she expected them to be given to her personally by the Government of India. She was not humble or democratic in her demands, therefore not generating much sympathy. She did not wish for the days of master and servant to be over—rather, she longed for them to return, with her as the queen of a lost kingdom. But that is just one layer of it—the outer, most superficial layer. In her and Sakina's writings, we also detect another longing: for being heard. In one passage, Sakina writes about the two begums:

Put behind bars, starved, their treasure confiscated which was in millions of pounds by Warren Hastings, for the princess did not co-operate with the British rule.[30]

The impeachment trial of Hastings, Sakina writes, has put the injustice on the pages of history in such a way that 'the British can never deny nor erase'.

The passage is immediately followed by one making a connection to the present day, with Wilayat who inherited the begums' 'endurance' opposed to the 'selfish government'. 'The government is weary of our existence. The deafening silence for us.'

Wilayat tried to tell a story of centuries of injustice by embodying it and claiming to be part of the same line of suffering; but it got clouded and overlooked. Her audience was only interested in exoticizing her behaviour, at first, and later in one single question: Was she really a descendant of the House of Awadh? Before we address this question, let us dive into the history of the last begum of Awadh, with whom Wilayat claimed a shared ancestry: Hazrat Mahal, the rebel queen of 1857.

Rebel Queen

'Wajid Ali was weak and contemptible, the wedge of British treachery. But our ladies were always strong and perfect. Nobody could defy Oudh.'[1]

Wilayat made this statement in an interview with the *Chicago Tribune* in 1985. It provides a telling insight into her thoughts on the 1857 Revolt, and why she mostly referred to Hazrat Mahal, rather than Wajid Ali Shah, as her ancestor. She admired her greatly and wished to see herself in the same line of strong women fighting for their kingdom, and for their rights.

The life of Hazrat Mahal, the warrior queen who gave the British a stiff fight during the 1857 Revolt, remains an enigma that has not yet been fully explored.

The initial part of her life, especially her origins, has never been conclusively established; the latter part of her life spent in Nepal has also not been examined sufficiently. Only her role during the 1857 Revolt has received the attention of historians, due to the availability of records from that period.

Perhaps this is why it was possible for Wilayat to claim ancestry from Hazrat Mahal. Her life story was simply not known enough. Even though Wilayat did not provide documented proof, the ancestry was ultimately stated as a fact in most articles, without questions regarding the exact family line, suggesting that they never told reporters either. But, as mentioned in Chapter 4, Sakina does discuss the family line in her book. It is here that we discover how exactly they explained their link to Hazrat Mahal. Wilayat's ancestor, Sakina writes, was Almas Mahal. And Almas Mahal, she claims, was a daughter of Hazrat Mahal.

No other record of this daughter exists. But when records are scarce and history obscure, anyway, unproven theories go around—and in the case of Hazrat Mahal, her having a daughter is hardly the only unproven story. As the saying goes, absence of evidence is not evidence of absence.[2]

~

One of the few books describing Hazrat Mahal's life is *Jaan-e-Alam Aur Mehak Pari*, written by Lucknow-based historian Nusrat Naheed. About Hazrat Mahal, she writes that 'she was born in a poor family in Faizabad'. Her father Umber was the slave to a nawab, called Gulam Husain, from Farrukhabad. Her mother, Meher Afza, was the nawab's 'Khawas', which means something akin to the head of his household staff.

Due to her beauty, Hazrat Mahal, then called Umrao, attracted the attention of two female brokers who worked for Wajid Ali Shah, and they presented her to the king on one of his birthdays. She was admitted into the Parikhana for training in music and dance and given the title Mehak Pari.

Subsequently, Shah married her and she became pregnant, due to which her training could not be completed, writes Naheed. She gave birth to a son called Mirza Ramzan Ali, who was given the title of Birjis Qadr Bahadur. When Shah ascended the throne, he gave Mehak Pari the title of Nawab Begum Hazrat Mahal Sahiba.[3]

Historian Roshan Taqui presents a similar account, but with several different nuances. Citing the research done by Dr A.K. Srivastava, former director of the Uttar Pradesh State Archives at the India Office Library in London, he writes that her father's name was Miya Amber[4] and her mother was called Meher Afza. According to Taqui, Miya Amber was from Farrukhabad and came to Lucknow during the reign of Wajid Ali Shah's father, Amjad Ali Shah.

When Wajid Ali Shah ascended the throne, he placed all his former associates and employees in various positions in the new regime. Miya Amber knew someone who knew Wajid Ali Shah's sitar teacher, and through this connection, he managed to secure the position of daroga (caretaker) at a mausoleum in Lucknow. He died within a year of his new posting. Following his death, Hazrat Mahal, then called Muhammadi, went to live with her relatives who were experts in making caps for the elites of Lucknow. Owing to an incident, which is not historically established but hearsay, on one occasion, a cap that had been commissioned for Wajid Ali Shah was found with a strand of hair in it; when an investigation was carried out, it led to the discovery of Muhammadi—who had apparently worn it before it was delivered to the king; her beauty charmed the king and she became a member of his Parikhana.[5]

Sakina's account differs from all others. She claims that Hazrat Mahal was of Nepali origin and was a princess from the Malla dynasty in Nepal.[6] The Malla dynasty ruled Nepal from the thirteenth to the eighteenth century. The same theory is mentioned in a lengthy article published in the *Kathmandu Post* on 24 September 2019. The article cites a couple of books in this regard: a novel by famous Hindi writer Amritlal Nagar called *Gadar Ke Phool,* and another called *Doon-Ghati Nalapani* by Kumar Ghising, where this speculation finds a place. However, this theory has no historical basis and the article goes on to mention that.

Sakina further writes that Hazrat Mahal's father was the cousin of an aristocratic woman, Lady Sughra, who owned an estate called Munnepore, which lies between Faizabad and Ayodhya. She was already 'impoverished' and was under the control of a local chieftain called Maun Singh; she calls him her 'oppressor'. She gives the name of the father as Syed Mansur Ali and the mother's name as Gayatri Devi. The family had four children, according to Sakina. She writes that although the family was not keen, they ended up presenting Hazrat Mahal to Wajid Ali Shah, perhaps under pressure from the aunt or her 'oppressor'.[7]

∼

Rosie Llewellyn-Jones, in her book *The Last King in India* as well as in several interviews since, gives a new interpretation to Hazrat Mahal's origins. According to her, Hazrat Mahal's father was an African slave. She draws on the research of Nusrat Naheed, but concludes that her father's name was a complimentary name for dark-skinned people, in particular African male slaves.[8]

Taqui, when we meet him at his Lucknow residence, says he disagrees with this interpretation. 'This is not true,' he says. 'As far as Hazrat Mahal is concerned, everybody knows her parents were not [black].'

He goes into the various theories that are there around her origins. 'Some say her father came from Faizabad. There is one reference that her father was the caretaker of a monument. Another story says that her father was in attendance of a nawab of Farrukhabad. There is no third story, as far as I know.'

Taqui reminds us that there are not many objective sources that have recorded Hazrat Mahal's life story. 'She was never in the limelight until the rebellion started. So, when she led the war against the East India Company, both sides started writing things. That's the only period you will find things about Hazrat Mahal from.'

Because of the context of the revolt, we must remember that these sources had an agenda—and not all historians agree on which is more reliable. Taqui, narrating a meeting with Llewellyn-Jones, adds: 'A couple of years back, Rosie told me: don't rely on Urdu references of that period. I asked her, why? I consider the Urdu references of that period more relevant and reliable. The English media was bent upon maligning characters of that period.'

We decide to ask Nusrat Naheed herself, as it is her research that Llewellyn-Jones based her conclusion on. It's not easy to find her, with no contact details or place of work mentioned anywhere online. We decide to ask around at the Amir-ud-Daula Library in Kaiserbagh, a well-known public library in Lucknow, which published her book. The library is housed in a beautiful building, built for the purpose in the 1920s. When we visit, there is a big project of digitizing all their books ongoing and many books are lying in a big pile. But Naheed's book is special and the staff should know where to locate it, a manager tells us. 'She used to be the chief librarian here, a very educated lady. When she worked here, the library was doing very well.' We are given English and Hindi versions of her book to read. When we ask where we can find her, we are told she is retired now, but lives nearby.

In a small living room in an apartment complex above a shopping centre, Naheed offers us tea and shows us her books. Apart from the one on Hazrat Mahal, there is one on several begums of India, and another one on the culture of Awadh. Some of her books are written in Hindi, and some in Urdu. We converse in a mix of these languages and English.

'No,' she insists without hesitation when we ask her about Hazrat Mahal's possible African descent. 'Umber means "sky". It does not mean he was from Africa or dark-skinned. A slave could have come from this region too.' We ask her if she ever spoke to Llewellyn-Jones to discuss her conclusions, and she says no. 'She never visited me.'

She shows us the document where she found the details on Hazrat Mahal's parents. It is in an archive of rent-free landholdings, a one-page document printed in her book in the original English. It mentions that the land was 750 acres in size, contained fifty-five wells, and was in the village of Mahudinaggar. Wajid Ali Shah gave this land to Hazrat Mahal in the year 1840, it says, and in a separate column, it mentions the then occupants' parents: 'the begum is the daughter of "Umber" a slave of Gulam Hossain Ali Khan, and her mother was Maher Afza, Khawas of the same person.' The use of past tense here suggests her mother had passed away at the time this document was written, which was in 1860, three years after the Revolt of 1857. It goes on to describe her: 'This is the notorious rebel begum who has persisted in remaining absent. She has one son, Birjis Kud (sic) 13 years old, who is with her.' The document was the conclusion of an investigation into such landholdings, after the annexation of Awadh. The chief commissioner ordered: 'Sanction of Government to the confiscation of this tenancy solicited.'

~

Another important source that mentions Hazrat Mahal is Wajid Ali Shah's autobiographical book, *Parikhana*. His describes the time when Hazrat Mahal first came to his notice.

Wajid Ali Shah, connoisseur of music and the arts, established an institute called Parikhana—House of Fairies—where training in music and dance was imparted to women, mostly those belonging to the lower strata of society. The prospective candidates were brought to his notice by agents—or pimps, in modern terminology—such as the two names he mentions in his brief description that is reproduced here in full:

> Through Amman and Imaman one *khangi* whom I found worthy of my admiration, was admitted into the group of

'Paris' and rewarded her with the title of Mehak Pari. She then started her training of dance and Sarod.⁹

The meaning of the word 'khangi' is disputed. In the translation of Shah's *Parikhana*, it is translated as a woman involved in sex work. But Taqi, in his book, insists that it means 'a domesticated woman'.

According to the online Rekhta dictionary, the word, as an adjective, means 'domesticated', but as a noun, it means a 'kept woman, clandestine prostitute'.¹⁰ Shah has used it as a noun.

Subsequently, Hazrat Mahal managed to impress him sufficiently and became his wife and then the mother of a male heir, following which she became known as Hazrat Mahal. (Mahal was a title awarded to those women who had produced male children.) This episode, too, is described in *Parikhana* under the heading 'The Birth of Mirza Birjis Qadr'. Shah writes that upon hearing the news of her pregnancy, he 'thanked God' after which he awarded her with the grand title of Iftikhar-un-Nissa, which translates to 'the jewel among women'.

When Birjis Qadr was born, his grandfather and then king Amjad Ali Shah was very happy, writes Shah. Eleven cannons were fired in honour of the new male scion of the House of Awadh.

Towards the end of the book, Shah's father dies and he becomes the king. Post this event, his run-ins with his wives become more frequent. Perhaps his increased authority made him autocratic and this was one way in which it manifested itself.

The first instance of his suspicious attitude towards Hazrat Mahal and other wives surfaces towards the middle of the book when he describes how one of his concubines became pregnant and was evasive about the paternity of the child. Shah writes of his 'utter surprise' at her pregnancy and mentions that he threatened her with a whip over her refusal to name the father.

This suspicion becomes a theme in the rest of the book. After another such incident, he summoned all his wives and confronted them about their lack of loyalty, but they protested and denied it. Although the matter was ultimately resolved, he writes that his suspicions were not allayed.

After he ascended the throne, Wajid Ali Shah gave new titles to all his wives. He writes that although he was well aware of their 'infidelities', he tried to keep them loyal by awarding them new titles and giving them money. As part of this initiative, Mehak Pari, who was earlier awarded the title of Iftikhar-un-Nissa, was now given the appellation Nawab Hazrat Mahal Sahiba.

In a subsequent chapter, he explicitly names the wives whom he found to be loyal and Hazrat Mahal's name is absent from this list of around a dozen women—a rather short list considering he married around 365 women.

He remained besotted with Hazrat Mahal, however, to the extent of breaking his ties with some other wives who tried to win back his affections through unconventional measures, such as barging into the house where he was staying with Hazrat Mahal.

Towards the end of the narrative, he writes:

> One day, after I could not bear it anymore, I sent them all out of the house and sent them to the palace. However, Hazrat Mahal stayed with me in the house of Razee-ud-Daula. When they had all been turned out, they started to writhe in envy like black snakes. Meanwhile, Hazrat Mahal told me—'If you stop meeting me then I swear on God I will kill myself.' Finally, we came to an agreement that she will act in the manner she wished and I would do the same.[11]

In her historical novel *In the City of Gold and Silver*, based on the life and times of Hazrat Mahal, Kenizé Murad also goes into their increasingly strained relationship post the birth of Birjis Qadr. She writes: 'When Allah finally blessed her with a son, she thought she had found a certain security. Quite the reverse, it was the beginning of a war, the covert war of harems, where accidents and poisons are the weapons that mothers must ceaselessly protect their offspring from.'[12]

At this point, Murad introduces an intriguing and mysterious character called Mammoo Khan, who did exist in history. At times described as a eunuch, though not by all, Mammoo Khan was a confidant of Hazrat Mahal. Eunuchs were often preferred by kings, including those from the House of Awadh, to guard their queens, for obvious reasons. Some of them, like Mammoo Khan, came to enjoy great prestige and power over time. But Mammoo Khan and Hazrat Mahal have also become connected in public memory in yet another way. There were rumours, which Murad has woven into her novel. After Birjis Qadr had been crowned the new king and Hazrat Mahal his regent, since he was barely a teenager, a British officer tells his superior that Mammoo Khan was rumoured to be Qadr's father. When the superior objects, saying that Khan was a eunuch, the officer claimed that at times eunuchs who were partially castrated could 'procreate'.

These rumours are alluded to by Sakina in her memoir, in which she also hints at the many other affairs that Wajid Ali Shah himself suspected in his harem, as he wrote in his book. Though he never writes this, Sakina in her book concluded that Shah himself had doubts about Birjis Qadr's paternity:

> The offspring of concubines issued pamphlets to declare claimants the flaws of deceptions carefully hidden the strange stories of courts and harem there was no dearth of rumours and

hissings of poison's intensity above all, the Last King himself knowingly did not know the Prince Birgis Qadr's father was and is with quaint intentions.[13]

In this context, she writes that Shah was not interested in bringing Qadr, then twelve years old, to Calcutta after the annexation of Awadh. Unlike—Sakina claims—Almas, his infant daughter with Hazrat Mahal.

> The king desired to keep the princess of 2 years daughter of Hazrat Mahal with him which Hazarat Mahal rejected (and Princess Wilayat Mahal has the honour to be the great grand-daughter of this 2 year princess of that turbulent time).[14]

Sakina's contention that Hazrat Mahal and Mammoo Khan were lovers and Birjis Qadr was their offspring was indeed commonly speculated during the 1957 Revolt, especially by the British. Sakina perhaps mentions it to discredit the claims of the descendants of Birjis Qadr living in Kolkata, who in 1975 were writing letters to the Lucknow state assembly calling Wilayat's claims a hoax, but there is simply no way to prove it. Many historians dismiss the possibility entirely for various reasons.

In the book *Begums of Awadh*, its author K.S. Santha introduces Mammoo Khan as the 'superintendent of her household'. Later, he writes: 'Firstly, the English records and writers at first stated that Birjis Qadr was forcibly taken away by the army, and later that he was a son of Mummu Khan.'[15]

Santha, a well-regarded authority on Awadh's history, gives no credence to speculations about Qadr's paternity. He writes: 'To question the legitimacy of Birjis Qadr and to cast aspersions upon his mother appeared to be politically motivated in order to ridicule the purpose of the movement and to wean the loyalties of and sentiments of all such citizens, nobles and *Taluqdars* of Awadh who upheld her cause.'

At the same time, there were no rumours about Hazrat Mahal having a daughter or any other children from Mammoo Khan or any other possible lover. Taqui takes this as a sign that it is a very unlikely theory. Asked about Wilayat's claim that she descended from an unknown daughter of Hazrat Mahal, he says: 'The British officers, as a matter of policy, tried to malign her character. Even they did not write anything like this. They could not find anything. So, to me it is very obvious that this claim cannot be justified. That she had a daughter ... there is no reference or book about this anywhere.'

Taqui refers to Shah's autobiography, *Huzn-e-Akhtar*, as further proof. 'In this book he has written about all his wives, sons and daughters. There is no mention of any daughter of Hazrat Mahal.'

Taqui, in his book, also dismisses the speculation about Qadr's paternity. He mentions the British historian P.J.O. Taylor who wrote in his book *A Star Shall Fall* that Qadr's father was Mammoo Khan. But he says this is either an attempt to present a falsehood or mere ignorance. He states that Qadr was born in 1843, whereas Mammoo Khan entered royal service in 1851, although he does not give a source for the second assertion. He also cites from the writings of Wajid Ali Shah, who had accepted Qadr as his son in the book, which he wrote after he had been exiled to Calcutta.

However, it gets more complicated. Historians such as Ravi Bhatt have written that Wajid Ali Shah had divorced Hazrat Mahal, along with eight other wives, 'when he found snake-like marks on their backs'. But, he adds, 'they were later taken back into the harem.'[16]

It is known that when Wajid Ali Shah left for Calcutta, he left Hazrat Mahal behind, along with Birjis Qadr. In her book, Rosie Llewellyn-Jones writes that it was Wajid Ali Shah's mother, Mallika Kishwar, who 'tricked' him into divorcing eight of his wives.

> She also interfered outrageously in her elder son's matrimonial affairs and had already tricked him into divorcing eight of his wives of whom she did not approve, including Begum Hazrat Mahal, the mother of a young son.[17]

This story appears in one of the most important books written in that period, one that most likely led to Wajid Ali Shah's deposition. It was written by William Sleeman, who was the resident of Awadh before James Outram took over; it was the latter who carried out the task of deposing Shah, but Sleeman had already prepared the ground for it. Sleeman had previously acquired considerable fame as someone who had 'eradicated' thuggee during his earlier posting, a subject on which he wrote three books.

A Journey Through the Kingdom of Oude was written by Sleeman after undertaking a tour of the Awadh countryside, in order to report on the situation existing thereof. It is a long and rambling treatise, which contains a lot of gossip and innuendos along with his dispatches from the region.

The story about Shah divorcing Hazrat Mahal appears early in the text. Sleeman writes that Shah had become infatuated with a maid who worked for his mother, Mallika Kishwar, who refused to part with her. According to Sleeman, she made the excuse that the maid had a snake-like shape on her nape, which made her inauspicious. The king believed her and ordered an inspection of all his wives, except his main wife, the mother of the heir-apparent. This led to the discovery of such marks on eight of his wives, including Hazrat Mahal, all of whom he subsequently divorced.[18]

~

When the revolt broke out, the British imprisoned Wajid Ali Shah in Fort William as they suspected him of having secretly instigated the revolt despite professing allegiance to British rule. After the revolt had been subdued, they informed him that Hazrat Mahal had fought in his name, which is why they had detained him. When he came to know this, Shah, according to Llewellyn-Jones, responded that he was 'unaware' of the use of his name in the revolt and proceeded to disown both Hazrat Mahal and Birjis Qadr.

However, as shown above, Taqi cites from his autobiographical work, *Huzn-e-Akhtar*, which he wrote during his imprisonment in Fort William. It shows that he was aware that Hazrat Mahal was leading the revolt against the British and that Birjis Qadr had been anointed king. He expressed admiration for both, while acknowledging Qadr as his son. Hence, the stance he took before the British contradicts his earlier attitude towards Hazrat Mahal and Birjis Qadr. Most likely, he had to disown them in front of the British to save himself from further punishment at the hands of the British.

Sakina gives a detailed account of Hazrat Mahal's role during the revolt of 1857. She writes:

> The then Begum of Oudh Hazrat Mahal was in war with the British. They wanted to capture Hazrat Mahal to avenge they could not. Those who were caught were either hanged or slaughtered who sided with the Begum of Oudh. She was the noblest bravest and ablest of that time. Even the best of her enemies admired the ivory Hazrat Mahal ... Princess Hazrat Mahal had shown more sense nerve than all her generals. She had dignified face of character. She stood firm against the British the illegal annexation 25 February 1857. She fought at four forts with them.[19]

When Hazrat Mahal lost Lucknow and fled, Sakina writes:

> ... [she] then mounted on an elephant went to meet her mother and infant daughter then proceeded to Nepal to

become the homeless the Begum of Oudh those who deserted though many of them courtiers in the court of the last king of Oudh … Begum Hazrat Mahal the prince and princess heir to her were lawful sovereigns but became wanderers in Tarai Nepal.[20]

Sakina goes on to describe what happened to those who had sided with Hazrat Mahal. She mentions Tatya Tope,[21] who had also sought refuge in the Tarai region of Nepal, but was captured and hung in 1859. She notes the fates of other chieftains from Awadh who were either killed or exiled. She refers to the role played by the king of Nepal who allied with the British against the revolutionaries but allowed Hazrat Mahal to take refuge in Nepal. She compares Hazrat Mahal with the Rani of Jhansi and writes: 'Rani of Jhansi's valour known to all She had received exaltation in eulogy and glorification.'

When writing about Hazrat Mahal's fight against the British and subsequent events, Sakina's account matches what other historians have written, including the names of local chieftains who allied with her—such as Rana Beni Madho—and who betrayed her—Raja Man Singh. The comparison with the Rani of Jhansi is quite relevant and, in fact, forms the subject of a recent book by historian Rudrangshu Mukherjee, *A Begum and a Rani*.[22]

In his book, for descriptions of her early life, Mukherjee relies on Llewellyn-Jones's account, which has already been summarized: daughter of a slave who ended up in Wajid Ali Shah's harem through the Parikhana, bore him a son, and was later divorced and left to fend for herself.

Mukherjee starts by recounting the books written to eulogize Lakshmibai and notes that Hazrat Mahal did not receive the same treatment, although she was also written about. One of the first books to be written on the 1857 Revolt by an Indian was by Vinayak Damodar Savarkar, revolutionary-turned-Hindutva-ideologue.

In it, Savarkar praised Lakshmibai to the moon but was reserved in his appraisal of Hazrat Mahal. Others—historians and politicians—took a similar approach but we will come to the possible reasons behind this later.

Mukherjee writes:

> The making of Lakshmibai into an iconic figure relegated, without anyone quite intending it, another woman rebel leader into relative oblivion. Hazrat Mahal, unlike Lakshmibai, was not a late entrant into the rebellion but had been a leader of the rebels in Awadh from the very beginning of the uprising.[23]

He adds:

> For the 150th anniversary of the uprising, Hazrat Mahal was scarcely commemorated.[24]

The revolt of 1857 started in Meerut on 10 May; it took twenty days before Lucknow revolted. Awadh was already seething due to the unfair annexation of the province by the British, and the revolt could not have found more fertile ground. Soon, almost the whole of Awadh raised the banner of revolt, following the example of Lucknow. The native forces drew first blood by defeating the British comprehensively in the first battle at Chinhat. Meanwhile, the British population of Lucknow took shelter in the Residency compound, a small city within a city, with many other buildings inside it. The rebel forces began to shell the Residency daily but the British stayed put, hoping for a rescue.

Looking for a leader from the royalty, the rebel commanders agreed upon Birjis Qadr, the twelve-year-old son of Wajid Ali Shah and Hazrat Mahal. But since he was a minor, Hazrat Mahal was appointed his regent and, in effect, the supreme commander of the rebel forces. 'It was during the preparations for the coronation that

Hazrat Mahal made her entry into the annals of the uprising and thus on the stage of history.'

Around seven years earlier, in 1850, Hazrat Mahal along with five other wives had been divorced by Wajid Ali Shah, Mukherjee writes, and adds that at the time this was rumoured to be due to their 'lowly origin'.[25] He argues that the story about the snake-like marks, as mentioned above, was probably a rumour spread by the royal family to cover this up. So this was a huge change in fortune for Hazrat Mahal.

Jhansi, unlike Awadh, had never been an 'independent sovereign state', writes Mukherjee. Starting out as a province under the control of the Peshwas, it had been taken over by the British. Lakshmibai was married to its nominal king, Gangadhar Rao, who died in 1853. (Little is known about her childhood, like Hazrat Mahal's.) He had adopted a son before dying and in the subsequent years after his death, Lakshmibai pleaded with the British to acknowledge him. When the British finally decided to annex Jhansi, Lakshmibai protested.

When the revolt broke out in Jhansi in 1857, the rebels slaughtered the British population, and, taking the opportunity, Lakshmibai declared herself the queen. She tried to make sure she was not blamed for the massacre and informed the higher British officials of what had transpired, but they believed her to be behind it and considered her an enemy from thereon. This was why she had to ultimately face the British on a battlefield, where she fought with great bravery before being killed, and is rightly celebrated for her valour.

In Lucknow, the resistance to the British was well-organized. Mukherjee credits it to Hazrat Mahal. '[T]here was a concerted attempt made to defeat the British. Such an attempt could not have been possible without a decision-making body that was overseeing and guiding operations. That body existed in the court of Hazrat

Mahal. It was from this court that orders emanated and plans of attack and resistance were formulated.'

The resistance was divided into two parts: taking care of the administration and directing military operations, which included issuing orders to local chieftains to fight the British. After the British re-established control over Delhi, 'Lucknow became the focus of both the resistance and the British counter-insurgency measures,' writes Mukherjee. By January 1858, the rebel army in Lucknow consisted of 1,00,000 soldiers.

However, the British managed to mount a serious counter-offensive, which included rescuing the British population under siege in the residency and taking back Kanpur.

Repeated setbacks led to Hazrat Mahal issuing an ultimatum to the rebel commanders who reassured her that they would continue to fight the British.

By February 1858, the tide had turned in favour of the British forces. 'Within one month—towards the end of March—the city, the British claimed, was free of rebels,' writes Mukherjee.

Before leaving Lucknow, Hazrat Mahal's rebel army gave the British a stiff fight. But having lost, she moved to another district in Awadh, Bahraich, with 5,000 soldiers; from here she continued to issue orders to local chieftains, urging them to fight and act against those who had betrayed the cause.

By the end of 1858, the revolt finally petered out. Mukherjee writes:

> Hazrat Mahal, whose former husband had agreed to surrender his kingdom but had refused to give up his dignity, fled to Nepal with 1500 followers. That was the swan song of the revolt in Awadh.[26]

In his article in the *Kathmandu Post*, journalist Prawash Gautam has described Hazrat Mahal's stay in Kathmandu and traced those who came with her, some of whom remain attached to her memory. But, unfortunately, no one has any real information or insights into her stay there for twenty years. What is conclusively known is that she settled in a residence given to her by the king, and either renovated or constructed a new mosque, with those who came with her settling around it. This is where her grave lies and is also where the descendants of those who came with her still live. Her son Birjis Qadr married a Mughal princess called Mahtab Ara, the granddaughter of Bahadur Shah Zafar, in 1869; the princess was also granted asylum by the king of Nepal. Gautam mentions that Birjis Qadr was a poet who read in local mushairas. Some of his poetry has survived.

> Indeed, all that the members of Kathmandu's small Muslim community—the community closest to Begum Mahal and Birjis Qadr—can say about the lives of these historical figures in the Capital are variants of the same story.[27]

The article goes on to mention that when the 100th anniversary of the 1857 Revolt was celebrated, the government did not honour Hazrat Mahal. Her descendants based in Kolkata protested and met Prime Minister Nehru to complain about this negligence in honouring her. Subsequently, a search was mounted to locate her grave. 'Under Nehru's direction, the Indian embassy in Kathmandu promptly located the grave.'

Wilayat and her children were also concerned about the grave and the state it was kept in. In the papers we accessed at the Alkazi Collection of Photography, there is a short letter by a Nepali acquaintance of Wilayat, someone called Rhodos Mahan. The letter, dated 2 July 1987, written from Kathmandu, addressed to Wilayat, says:

> Enclosed are some photographs of the grave of Begum Hazrat Mahal, which Prince Ali Reza requested I send to your Highness. I am sorry that I have not a better camera, but these should give your Highness an idea of the present condition of the site. I myself, was pleased to see that it has been enclosed by a fence in the past year which gives it a little more of the sanctity it deserves.

We don't know in what year Wilayat's contact in Kathmandu took the photo. But after this, the grave was again neglected, until an Indian ambassador made the upkeep his mission. Ranjit Rae, who was posted in Kathmandu from 2013 to 2017, recalls in his book, *Kathmandu Dilemma*, a visit by Akhilesh Yadav, then chief minister of Uttar Pradesh, for a family wedding in 2014.

> He asked me about the location of Hazrat Mahal's *mazhar* in Kathmandu. Much to my embarrassment, I was unaware of this history. Immediately after the visit, I made enquiries with the Muslim community and found that the grave was lying in a derelict state in a small corner of the Jame Masjid in central Kathmandu.[28]

This is when he decided to organize the annual commemoration on 7 April by laying a wreath of flowers at the grave. The Jama Masjid, according to him, agreed reluctantly, which he says was because Hazrat Mahal was a Shia and those in charge of the mosque are Sunni.

In the years after Rae left, the annual commemoration was continued, but lately, it has been stopped. When we checked with the mosque authorities in April 2023, they told us nothing was planned in terms of a commemoration.

∾

In Lucknow, Hazrat Mahal was honoured with a park in 1962—the old Victoria Park was renamed on Independence Day that year. Nationally, a postage stamp in Hazrat Mahal's honour was issued in 1984. The Indian Ministry of Culture mentions the stamp on a special website. A detailed account of Hazrat Mahal's life and her role in the 1857 Revolt can be found here. It does not go deep into her origins, only mentioning that she was from Faizabad and her name was Muhammadi Khanum. But it calls her 'one of the primary figures' behind the uprising of 1857. It names Nana Sahab and Maulvi Ahmad Ullah Shah as her 'closest allies'.[29] The latter was more a rival than an ally, according to Rudrangshu Mukherjee. As he writes:

> The leadership and authority of Hazrat Mahal and her court did not go opposed in Lucknow. The main challenge came from Maulvi Ahmadullah Shah, about whose antecedents not much is known.[30]

The website further praises Hazrat Mahal's leadership and bravery in battle:

> Begum Hazrat Mahal often called meetings to encourage soldiers, asking them to be brave and fight for the cause. She wrote letters of instruction for the movement and is reported to have appeared on the battlefield on February 25, 1858, mounted on an elephant.[31]

The account provides some details about her escape to Nepal and her stay there, till her death. It claims that she did try to come back to India in 1877, two years before her death. 'Begum Hazrat Mahal could not come to India and had to reside in Nepal permanently. She died for the great cause in 1879, in a land foreign to her. The grave of Begum Hazrat Mahal is in Kathmandu.' Praising her, in conclusion, it says: 'The indomitable Begum became one of the few women to fight against the British in the first war of Independence.' A picture of her grave in Kathmandu, along with other photographs and illustrations concerning her life, accompany the write-up.

However, these words of praise have not been followed up with much action in terms of memorials in Hazrat Mahal's name. In 2002, a government scholarship for girls from minority communities was started in her name—but in 2023 the government decided to scrap it for classes one to eight, retaining it only for classes nine to twelve. Critics say this is a result of the Hindu nationalist Modi government's attempts to exclude Muslims from education benefits.[32]

In 2011, the government sponsored a half-hour documentary film on her life, called *Begum Hazrat Mahal: The Last Queen of Awadh*, produced by the Films Division under the Ministry of Information. There was no promotion for the film, which can be watched online on the Internet Archive.[33] The film is informative and covers her entire life, but it is mainly her role in the 1857 Revolt that is in focus. Most of the information conveyed in the film—her early life, her role in the war, and the end in Nepal—has already been summarized, and does not necessitate a repetition. Two members of the Kolkata descendants of Birjis Qadr, Dr Kaukab Quder and Nayyar Quder, are interviewed about her legacy; the rest consists of a voice-over narration in chaste Urdu, over images from Lucknow and Calcutta.

The filmmaker, Mohi-ud-Din Mirza, told *Hindustan Times* in 2016 that he came upon the idea of making a film on Hazrat Mahal while researching another unsung freedom fighter in the India House library in London, Madame Bhikaji Cama.[34] He told the newspaper that he wished to make a full-length feature film on Hazrat Mahal, but this does not seem to have come to pass.

According to Mukherjee, the two main reasons behind the Rani of Jhansi's posthumous fame are her 'high descent', her caste—Brahmin—and the fact that she was the de facto queen of Jhansi, whether or not the British accepted it, unlike Hazrat Mahal, who was from an impoverished background and trained as a tawaif, and who became queen or technically regent to the young king through accident. According to Mukherjee:

> Lakshmibai was a Brahmin; her father was in the service of the Peshwa. She was not born into wealth, but her father had the resources to educate her and to train her in horse riding and the use of arms. She was married into minor royalty, and following the death of her husband, she was forced to take over the administration of Jhansi ... Lakshmibai's lineage, both in terms of caste and royalty, was important. Hazrat Mahal's origins were altogether different. Her beginnings were humble and somewhat unclear ... If the rebellion of 1857 had not happened, Hazrat Mahal would have been a nobody.[35]

The other factor which distinguished the Rani of Jhansi was that she was a martyr who died on the battlefield, unlike Hazrat Mahal, who went into exile. Mukherjee writes:

> But in the end she became a fugitive—she fled, leaving her people with no choice other than to renounce the resistance. Lakshmibai, on the other hand, had been initially reluctant to join the rebellion but when she had joined the revolt, she did not flee; she died in battle like her people.[36]

Mukherjee raises the question: 'Who were the people that nominated Lakshmibai to her unique place in the pantheon of Indian nationalism?' He answers the question himself:

The nominators were a varied group—from Savarkar to Subhas Bose to Jawaharlal Nehru to novelists and poets and historians … What influenced the choice was the ideology of nationalism that privileged the explicit and outward show of valour.[37]

Wilayat, with her protest and her writing, tried to restore Hazrat Mahal's honour. She was not the only one—the descendants of Birjis Qadr in Kolkata had the same goal. But with her demands for palaces in Lucknow, Wilayat became a rival rather than an ally to them.

Seeing Wilayat receive attention from the media, local politicians and even the fact that other royals addressed her as the begum of Awadh and great-granddaughter of Hazrat Mahal caused one person in particular a great amount of frustration. Anjum Quder, a grandson of Birjis Qadr and one of the few officially recognized descendants of Wajid Ali Shah and Hazrat Mahal, could not stand the 'hoax', as he called it. From his base in Kolkata, he met officials and wrote letters to convey this message. To the MLA who spoke in Wilayat's favour in the Uttar Pradesh assembly, Quder wrote in April 1975:

> We, the members of the House of Awadh, were surprised to read in a Calcutta newspaper today of your adjournment motion in the Vidhan Sabha to sympathize with a lady you named Begum Wilayat Mahal, who seems to claim that she was the great-granddaughter of queen Hazrat Mahal. I am constrained to inform you that the claim is a hoax, and the lady is unfortunately impersonating.[38]

It is to Kolkata, Wajid Ali Shah's 'little Lucknow', where he was exiled in splendour, that we travel to meet the real heirs of the House of Awadh.

The Real House of Awadh

Metiaburj is only half an hour away from where we are staying in Esplanade; it is the neighbourhood just south from the Hooghly river, where Wajid Ali Shah stayed after the British took away his crown.

The driver says he does not know the exact place we want to go to first—the Imambara or the mausoleum that Wajid Ali Shah built there—but is willing to look for it.

We go through a series of short, winding streets alongside the Khidderpore docks. Boats are anchored on both sides in the river, with shipyards and factories lining the streets. The influence of Awadh in the area is visible. One shop is called Sheesh Mahal; another has Lucknow in its name. We cross a street called Karl Marx Sarani as we get closer to Metiaburj, according to the GPS.

Metiaburj is a jumble of small, one- or two-storey concrete houses and shops. There are even mosques and a tall clocktower, built recently. The local MLA is Farhad Hakim, a cabinet minister in

Mamata Banerjee's Trinamool Congress government, and his smiling face with folded hands is on several posters.

After going through the narrow streets of the locality for a while, the mausoleum appears. It is painted blue, and a plaque on the arched gateway says it is the mausoleum of Nawab Wajid Ali Shah and his son, Birjis Qadr.

Inside, there is a large courtyard, raised on a plinth, with stairs to reach it, placed right after the entry. On both sides of the courtyard are small rooms, all of which are locked; their doors are painted blue, as are the pillars and beams supporting the deck covering the large porch that is made of marble. In the front is the main part of the mausoleum, with three doors to go in, one of which is open. Closer to the second door is a large, rectangular inscription, bordered with thick, black stripes on the marble floor. Underneath is the grave of one of the three grandsons of Birjis Qadr, Prince Nayyar Quder. A narrow, rectangular, golden plaque on the wall reads: 'Prince Anjum Qadr President All India Shia Conference (82–97) addressing World Shia Conference London 12th August 1984).' But there is no accompanying picture with it, only an oval-shaped wooden clock adorned with engravings.

Four men wearing lungis and shirts are sitting on chairs and on the floor. They are employed here as helpers in various capacities. One of them says the manager will arrive soon.

Behind the chairs, on the wall, there are two framed articles about Hazrat Mahal's time in Nepal, where she spent almost two decades. The first is the earlier cited article from *Kathmandu Post* by journalist Prawash Gautam. Another article has more details on Birjis Qadr and his poetry, as well as on his participation in mushairas or poetry readings in Kathmandu. There is a portrait of Qadr in one of the articles. It shows him wearing an achkan and a waistcoat buttoned up till the neck. His sideburns are long and cover almost half his face. His sharp nose and dark eyes give him an intriguing look.

A plaque next to the framed articles says: 'Struggle of the Awadh dynasty started by King Birjis Qadr in 1857 hampered by his assassination in 1893 was refurbished by his grandson Prince Anjum Qadr in 1974.' It goes on to say in smaller letters under the main text that it was placed here in 1982, by the then British High Commissioner to India, who saw this as an example of 'An Historic Reconciliation in a Spirit of Mutual Generosity'.

∼

Wasif Hussain, the manager, is an unassuming man. Even when we mistake him for the caretaker of Wajid Ali Shah's mausoleum, he is too modest to correct us.

'It was built beforehand by Wajid Ali Shah. The masons came from Lucknow. This place is run by a trust. There are three trustees. Irfan Ali Mirza, Moin-ul Ali Mirza and Dr Talat Fatima. Dr Fatima is a lawyer. Every four to six months they hold a meeting; all of them live outside [Kolkata].'

We ask him if all the trustees are from the family. 'Yes, trustees are all from the family. But managers can come from outside, like us.'

He shows us a taziya next to the ornate grave of Shah. A taziya is a miniature replica of the tomb of Imam Hussain, which is taken out in processions during the month of mourning, Muharram. 'This was built in his [Shah's] time,' says Hussain, the manager. 'We refurbish it every year. We have to change its paper. Or the wood, if it goes bad.' It is a rectangular structure, made with coloured paper pasted over a tall column of wood.

Using the Persian word for emperor when speaking about Shah, Hussain says: 'Badshah got it built. It is made of sandalwood.' He shows another taziya, made with black paper, giving it a more sombre look, placed next to the last one. 'They are all 100–150 years old. They are taken out on the tenth day of Muharram. Badshah used to sit

Wilayat, Malcha Mahal, c. 1990.
Photo by Sondeep Shankar
Courtesy: The Alkazi Collection of Photography

Ali Raza in Malcha Mahal, c. 1990. QSS print.
Courtesy: The Alkazi Collection of Photography

Ali Raza outside Malcha Mahal, c. 1990. QSS print.
Courtesy: The Alkazi Collection of Photography

Ali Raza, outside Malcha Mahal, c. 2000. QSS print.
Courtesy: The Alkazi Collection of Photography

Ali Raza with the car of a diplomatic visitor in front of Malcha Mahal, c. 2005–2010.
Courtesy: The Alkazi Collection of Photography

Wilayat and Sakina in front of Asafi Kothi, the mansion where they lived in Sheesh Mahal, Lucknow, c. 1976.
Courtesy: The Alkazi Collection of Photography

Asafi Kothi in February 2022, the mansion in Lucknow where Wilayat, Sakina and Ali Raza briefly lived in 1976.
Photo by Abhimanyu Kumar

The ruined mansion in Lucknow, February 2022, where Wilayat and Inayatullah lived before Partition.
Photo by Abhimanyu Kumar

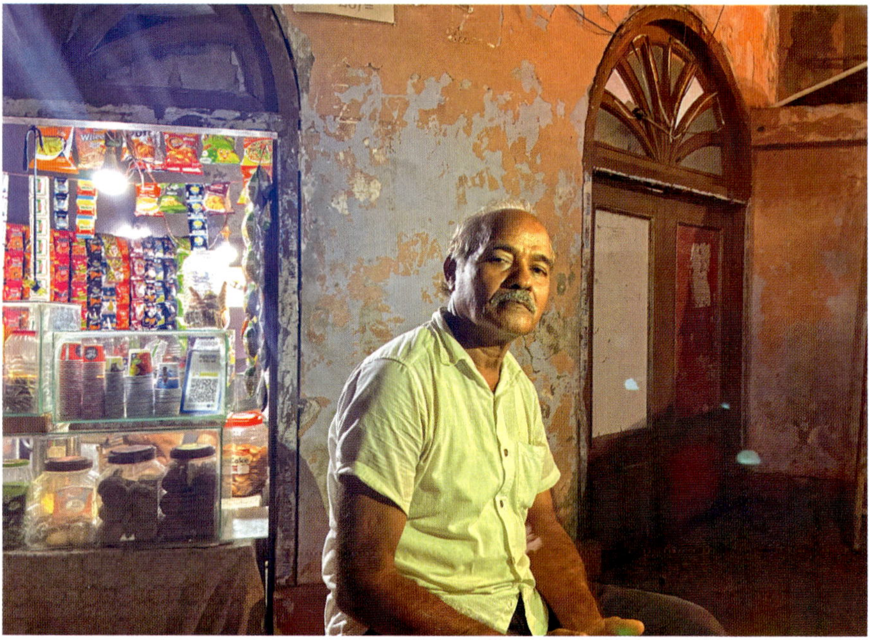

Abrar Hussain next to his shop in Sheesh Mahal, Lucknow, in August 2022.
Photo by Aletta André

H. R. H.
THE BEGAM OF OUDH
SHEHZADI WILAYAT MAHAL
Heir to the LAST King of OUDH
BEGAM HAZRAT MAHAL and
WAJID ALI SHAH

The Rulers of OUDH
in Exile
State Entry Road
New Delhi Railway Station
New Delhi-110055
India

TELEGRAM

5th July 1976

Chief Minister.
N. D. Tewari.
Lucknow.

Explain Clearly – What Decision – And Connivance has taken between You and Home Ministry – in – Ruining Precious Decendants of Begam Hazrat Mahal – Wajid Ali Shah of Oudh – This Continued Un-justice – Shameful indeed – Authorities Desire – How much more to Destroy – Lives – Belongings and time – Concerned Could – understand Verbal and Written truth – My letter of 26th May 1976 had Reached you through your Cabinet Minister Mr: Amar Rizvi – And M. P. Aziz Imam – Who Met You At Delhi and Lucknow – to get your Friend heads for us – And your Continued Promises with him –

The intentional dangerous Polices to Ruin truth – And Lives – this Communal Hatred – Expertness of Bureaucrats indignant Manners – Not Hidden – Reason of Return from Lucknow the Same Day – District Magistrat tuckroo – Should – Explain to you – Whom we Showed

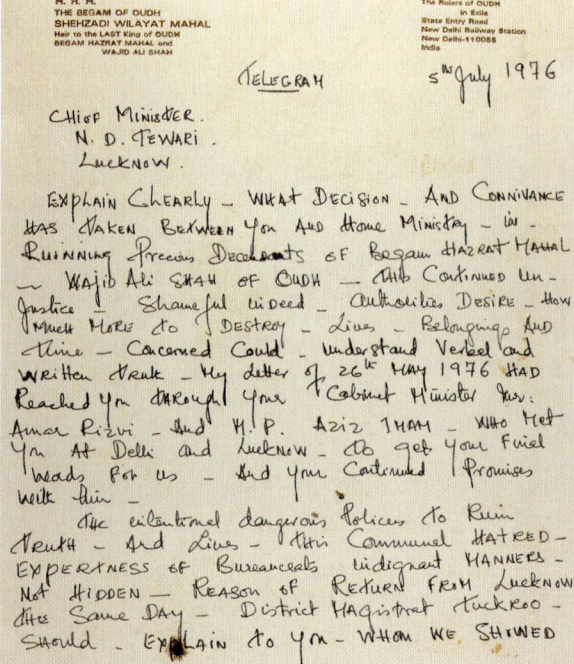

Letter from Wilayat to Chief Minister N.D. Tiwari, 5 July 1976.
Courtesy: The Alkazi Collection of Photography

Wilayat and Sakina in the waiting room at the New Delhi Railway Station, c. 1980. Gelatin silver print.
Courtesy: The Alkazi Collection of Photography

Ali Raza in London, c. 1981. He lost his passport there. The new passport he applied for in London further shows visa and travel stamps for Greece in 1986 and 1987 and Egypt and Syria in 1987. QSS print.
Courtesy: The Alkazi Collection of Photography

Wilayat in Malcha Mahal, c. 1990. Kasim identified himself as the servant in the background.

Courtesy: The Alkazi Collection of Photography

Mohammad Kasim at Malcha Mahal, December 2019.
Photo by Aletta André

Letter from Wilayat to Home Minister P.V. Narsimha Rao, 24 September 1984.
Courtesy: The Alkazi Collection of Photography

Princess Wilayat Mahal's 'vault', c. 1993. QSS print.
Courtesy: The Alkazi Collection of Photography

Sakina, Malcha Mahal, c. 1990. QSS print.
Courtesy: The Alkazi Collection of Photography

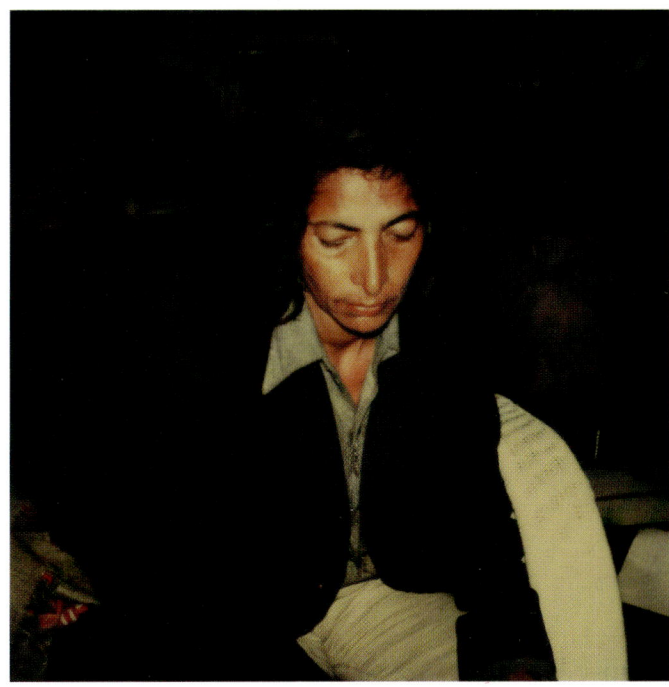

Sakina, c.1980.
Polaroid print.
Courtesy: The Alkazi Collection of Photography

Portrait of Ali Raza, c. 1980. Gelatin silver print.
Photo by Sankarshan Thakur (attributed)
Courtesy: The Alkazi Collection of Photography

KARACHI NEWS IN BRIEF

Begum Inayatullah Butt, in a statement thanks all friends and relations who sent her condolence messages on the sad demise of her husband, Mr Inayatullah Butt. She regrets her inability to acknowledge the messages individually.

* * *

Fun Fair Proceeds: At a meeting held at St Patrick's Library on Sunday presided over by the Archbishop of Karachi. Sister Alma Julia of the Holy Family Hospital was presented with a cheque for Rs 20,667-3-3, being the proceeds of the "Fun Fair" held last December in aid of the New Holy Family Hospital.

* * *

Dramatic Competition: In the Inter-Collegiate Dramatic Competition held under the auspices of the Karachi Students Union on Sunday the Dow Medical College won the Katrak Running Trophy and the NED Government Engineering College and the D J Sind Government Science College stood second and third respectively.

Dawn, 15 January 1952.
Courtesy: Dawn library, Karachi

Begum Butt is declared lunatic

By Dawn Staff Reporter

Forty-five-year-old Begum Wilayat Butt was declared a lunatic by the City Magistrate, Mr S. M. Qureshi, yesterday.

She was ordered to be taken to lunatic asylum in Lahore, immediately.

The magistrate gave the order on receiving a medical report from the doctors who kept Begum Butt under their observation in the Karachi Central Jail and the Civil Hospital for 10 days.

Begum Butt, it may be recalled was arrested in apprehension of breach of peace on her interrupting the Prime Minister's speech on the Independence Day.

Her interrogation by the police gave suspicions of her being a lunatic. A report was made to the City Magistrate who ordered her detention for 10 days for observation under the Lunacy Act.

Begum Butt was alleged to have made statements in which she professed to be under the influence of a "jinnee", who at times made her to do acts beyond the scope of human beings.

Dawn, 18 August 1954.
Courtesy: Dawn library, Karachi

Wilayat and Ali Raza, c. 1975, likely in Kashmir. Gelatin silver print.
Courtesy: The Alkazi Collection of Photography

Sakina as a college student, c.1965. Gelatin silver print.
Courtesy: The Alkazi Collection of Photography

A photo found in Malcha Mahal, shortly after Ali Raza's death, between his other posessions. Multiple former neighbours in Kashmir identified the man on the photo as Asad, some time in the 1970s.

The resthouse in Ganderbal, June 2023, where the family lived for about two years after arriving in Kashmir in 1962.
Photo by Nasir Hassan

Ali Mohammad Dar kisses the phone with Sakina's photo.
Photo by Nasir Hassan

The house on Water Works Road in Srinagar, June 2023, where Wilayat, Sakina, Ali Raza and Asad lived in the 1960s and '70s. It is a school building now.
Photo by Nasir Hassan

Inayatullah Butt, undated.
Courtesy: Mr Butt, our family source in Lahore.

here and listen to the Majlis. Badshah would also attend the Michil, which is the procession taken out during Muharram.'

He shows a few other things: a shield-like plaque made of bronze, depicting motifs from the seal of Wajid Ali Shah—two mermaids and a lion; a painting depicting a scene from the Battle of Karbala, the death of Hussain; there are more taziyas, smaller in size, placed on a low table; along with boxes made of transparent glass, and wooden cabinets. Behind the table, there is another grave, of another son of Wajid Ali Shah.

Towards the end of the hall, there are three posters placed next to the low table. They are about Wajid Ali Shah, Hazrat Mahal and Birjis Qadr. A longish text follows a picture of each, except for Shah, who is described more briefly. He is presented with his full regal title of Abul Mansoor, Sikandar Jah Padsha-e-Adil Qaiser-e-Zaman Sultan-e-Alam Meerza Muhammad Wajid Ali Shah, Shah-e-Avadh. Hazrat Mahal's introduction is an excerpt from the *Who's Who of India Martyrs Vol. III*, published by the Ministry of Education and Social Welfare on 15 August 1973. It describes her role in the 1857 Revolt, her retreat after Lucknow fell, her exile in Nepal, and praises her valour and tenacity.

'Her family members go there sometimes,' the manager says. Wasif Hussain has been working as the manager for the last three years, after retiring from his government job in a defence factory. He has known the family for many years. 'My forefathers came with the Badshah. We have been living here for around 150 years.'

Attached to the main hall is an antechamber with two more graves. One of them is of Anjum Quder. The other is of his father, Mehr Quder, the son of Birjis Qadr.

At one end of the room is an article in Urdu, framed and hung on the wall, about the mausoleum. 'It came out some time ago in a local newspaper. The journalist is now dead.'

We ask him about the changes that have taken place in the last few decades. His words and voice are full of the admiration he clearly feels for Wajid Ali Shah.

'There has been a downfall. When Badshah came, he brought along a few people, among whom were Hindus, Muslims, Shias and others. This whole area used to be a jungle back then. That is why the British brought him here: to harass him by sending him to a jungle. He cleared parts of it and built his residence. He did not distinguish amongst Hindus or Muslims. He brought here the same tehzeeb that Lucknow is known for. If you go a bit further from here, you will come upon a man, a paanwallah—his family also came from Lucknow with the Badshah—where a picture of the Badshah is put up on the wall. He is also very knowledgeable. He does not start his work before he has taken the Badshah's name. Till now, there are Hindus here who do not start working without first uttering his name in the morning in gratitude. First, they go to Bichali Ghat to take a bath, pay homage to his name, and then start their day.'

He tells about the famous menagerie that Shah built for his collection of animals—numbering up to 20,000, according to Sudipta Mitra in his book *Pearl by the River*, which is about Wajid Ali Shah's time in Calcutta.[1] Mitra writes that there were mostly birds, including pigeons that Shah was fond of. There were also reptiles and tigers, one of whom escaped once. Animal trade was flourishing in the colonial era with a huge demand for exotic animals from the tropics and the Orient.

'Badshah had a pond in which he kept fish. All the fishes knew his voice. He had given them golden nose rings. He could even distinguish between individual fishes. He wanted different animals in his menagerie to coexist peacefully. The English wanted to annihilate him and his name, even from the records, so they troubled him a lot. They arrested him when he came here and kept him in Fort William. Even there, he managed to write two or three books. He did not like to be idle. He had a unique temperament.'

Hussain also has a take on the famous story about Wajid Ali Shah introducing the potato in biryani, the way the fragrant rice dish is liked in Kolkata. 'Potato came to India from outside. Only the rich had it. The poor did not even know of it. In those days, Badshah was short of funds. His chef said he wanted to try making biryani with potato (replacing some of the meat). Badshah really liked it. Then it spread all over India.'

In awe of another pastime of Wajid Ali Shah, he says: 'Badshah would throw ink on a white sheet of paper. Then he would crush the paper. I have also tried it, but I get weird shapes! Badshah could make a lake, or a boat, or mountains this way. I read this in a small book.'

The population of the area has increased manifold in recent times. 'Many Biharis came here, Partition onwards, as this was a Muslim area. Whenever there would be a riot there, we would get a new influx of people. The old culture is now lost. Earlier, there used to be mushairas, there was a certain tehzeeb, people went out in sherwanis ... All that is gone. Everything you got in Lucknow, you got it here too. But not anymore. Children have no idea about all this.'

One of the helpers tolls the bell in the courtyard, attached to a wooden structure. It is one o'clock. 'It is from the time of the Badshah. Back in the day, this is how the people learnt the time. It was rung at every hour of the day. The same practice continues till date.'

Suddenly, it starts to rain heavily. We wait for the rain to stop, which happens soon enough.

Hussain has sent the electrician who works at the mausoleum, Shabbir Alam, along with us to explore the Metiaburj of Wajid Ali Shah. He lives in the area, but does not have a connection with Lucknow, other than his work.

Alam takes us to the Bichali Ghat first, where Wajid Ali Shah arrived from Lucknow with his large entourage of wives, princes, household employees and others. We go through a small marketplace to arrive there. It is a busy time as a ferry is about to leave. The river is wide in its expanse. On the other side are the Company Gardens, a botanical garden that Wajid Ali Shah liked to visit in the evenings, Alam says. He takes us inside the enclosure for passengers, at the ghat, with a built-in ticket counter. He is greeted by several people as we walk in and we are allowed passage although we do not have a ticket. He shows the location of the king's residence from there; it does not exist anymore, and other buildings have come up in its place, mainly warehouses.

As we come out, we spot a shop selling kites. Kites were brought to the area by Shah, and kite-flying has continued to be a popular activity in Metiaburj.

~

We walk towards the old mosque where Wajid Ali Shah used to pray, one of the few remaining buildings from those times. The Mausoleum Trust owns properties in the area, but many have been encroached upon. 'The former managers were mostly corrupt and allowed it to happen in cahoots with a local corporator.' The face of the corporator is on many self-promoting posters in the area.

The mosque lies almost hidden from view, tucked in between white-washed boundary walls of small, concrete houses with tiled roofs and shop fronts. A narrow passageway leads to it. 'This is a rare kind of a mosque because you can go all around it to pray,' he tells us.

The mosque has a somewhat desolate air. It is quite small, with an open area around it; a flower-tree is in full blossom. The inner chamber, where a devotee is sitting in prayer, is made of marble. An antechamber is attached to it where two men are sitting and conversing. Alam greets them and they respond warmly. He tells them he is showing us, writers from Delhi, around. They smile approvingly.

Behind the inner chamber is a very small rectangular pond with fishes swimming in it. Around us is a garden. A solemn afternoon light falls all over.

Later, we go to the paan shop whose owner is reputed to be well-versed in Lucknowi lore and known for admiring Shah. It is a small shop, occupying the corner of a row of similar shops, cubicles tucked inside walls. We see a framed photograph and a painting of Shah on the back wall of the shop. The shop front is littered with cigarettes, gutka pouches and other items of daily use.

Someone else is sitting inside the shop today, a young man by the name of Ramesh. The owner, who was also called Ramesh, died a few days ago, we are told. Young Ramesh vouches for the love the older Ramesh had for Shah. 'If you come to the house, you can meet the family members and talk to them. Or you can call me later and I will get you to speak to them.'

We leave, as Alam wishes to show us the area where the residence of the king used to be. A high wall used to belong to the king's palace. The empty land was taken over by jute factories, which closed down two to three decades ago. Now the same land is occupied by warehouses, which are used to store factory products and other goods.

The visit is hardly a success. First, we are stopped as soon as we enter, by a young man in plain clothes acting as a security guard. After some persuasion, he allows us to look around. But as we go further, crossing a pathway, lined with warehouses, we come across a muddy stretch that seems too difficult to cross on foot—so we trace our way back.

~

Soon after Wajid Ali Shah landed in Metiaburj, he was imprisoned, as the British thought he was responsible for instigating the revolt. They put him in Fort William, their original settlement in Calcutta.

A map from British times, preserved in the Asiatic Society of India, shows how Calcutta developed: the British constructed Fort William over the three villages they first received as a grant, occupying one end of the city, near the Hooghly. The Esplanade and Metiaburj were both close by. The Esplanade, which separated the fort from the city, is where the British built several other buildings, many of which can still be seen in the area. Their Grecian-inspired architecture with carved pillars, high ceilings and endlessly long corridors stand in stark contrast to the newer buildings in the rest of the city. All around the Esplanade today is the Maidan, which is a large, open field. Both the Maidan and Fort William are now in the possession of the Indian Army. Civilians are not allowed inside Fort William.

The British continued to expand, with the acquisition of more villages over the years, giving Calcutta its present shape, but fell foul of the nawab of Bengal, Siraj-ud-Daula, over the fortifications they had made, among other issues. This ultimately led to the Battle of Plassey in 1757. Although the British won, they suffered heavy casualties. The famous Black Hole incident of Calcutta a year before Plassey, in which many Britishers perished from suffocation closeted in a small chamber inside Fort William, became part of British myth about the cruelty of the natives, a colonial trope.

The victory in Plassey convinced the British that they were a power to reckon with in India, at par with the others. In the next hundred years, they consolidated their power, through force and subterfuge, becoming a pan-Indian power, which propped up the nominal Mughal authority at the centre.

The deposition of Wajid Ali Shah was a result of the long-running British policy to intervene in the affairs of Awadh and to reduce its nawabs to puppets in their hands. But Shah made them wary from the start with his approach to governance. One of his first decisions after assuming power was to reorganize the army, which did not go down well with the British. From thereon, the relationship continued to deteriorate.

Incidentally, what could have expedited the entire episode of Shah's deposition was a rumour that had started to circulate, predicting the ouster of the British in 1857, exactly a hundred years after the Battle of Plassey, based on a prophecy.

∼

Keen to see something from those times, we get into an autorickshaw already crowded with other passengers. Alam directs the rickshaw driver to take us to the cemetery where some members of the royal family are buried. Though the driver does not know the precise location, he agrees to try and find it.

It takes some asking around as the cemetery is sort of concealed by some buildings and the long grass growing on the land around it. The land is for the purpose of constructing a hospital, which is to be named after Shah. A board next to the plot states: 'Site for 8 Storied Nawab Wajid Ali Shah Memorial Hospital'. It adds that it will also be a 'Nursing and Paramedical College'.

The walls and the gate of the cemetery are painted blue, like the mausoleum. It matches the clear blue of the sky, dotted with fluffy white clouds. A paved path leads inside to an open space, with a boundary wall all around it.

After walking for a couple of minutes, a series of low arches made of red bricks come into view, with a huge blast furnace in the background, behind the boundary wall. Wild grass covers the space beneath the arches where the tombs are. The names and epitaphs for the dead are inscribed in Urdu upon headstones made of white marble. A couple of labourers are sitting next to the tombs, resting and smoking. But they do not know anything about the tombs or the dead interred there.

∼

Later, we come to know from Manzilat Fatima, Hazrat Mahal's great-great-great-granddaughter, that the tombs are of other members from the House of Awadh.

While the current nawabs of Lucknow, such as Jafar Mir Abdullah and Ibrahim Ali Khan, may or may not be able to make a real claim to belong to the House of Awadh, the direct descendants of Hazrat Mahal's son, Birjis Qadr, certainly can. Manzilat is the daughter of Kaukab Quder, who died in 2021, and was one of the three grandsons of Birjis Quder. Anjum Quder, the grandson who was actively penning letters about Wilayat's claims being a hoax in the 1970s, was her uncle.

Before we left the mausoleum, Wasif Hussain, the manager, handed us Manzilat's visiting card. It said 'Great Great Grand Daughter of Wajid Ali Shah King of Oudh & Begum Hazrat Mahal Heroine of 1857', along with her name and contact details. 'Please meet her,' he told us. 'She would be able to tell you more. She is also an expert on Calcutta biriyani,' he said.

Manzilat is a known name due to the fame of her restaurant, the eponymously titled Manzilat, where she serves Awadhi cuisine. When we go to the restaurant to meet her, she is busy, as it is Eid the next day and she has too many orders to deliver. Her restaurant is on the terrace of a building with several floors. The walls next to the staircase, which goes to the top, are filled with newspaper cuttings about the family's lineage, framed family photographs and pictures of celebrities who have visited the restaurant.

We are told to come the day after, and so we do. We are asked to wait in an anteroom adjacent to the restaurant, which has a seating area outside on the terrace, but electricians are working there.

Manzilat Fatima comes in wearing an apron; she is a diminutive woman in her fifties. Her manner is brisk and business-like. She sits down opposite us, with a table in between. We are offered tea. We tell her the purpose of the visit. She does not let any emotions show on her face when she hears we are writing about Wilayat and her family. She mentions the *New York Times* story and says it has already revealed the truth about them. But we tell her that as per our research, the *New York Times* story is not complete.

She starts off by talking of the news reports that appeared after Ali Raza's death in 2017. 'Most of the newspapers …[and] there are press agencies, UNI, PTI, one of them releases a story and everyone starts echoing that … one of them wrote that he was the last prince. I was very troubled by that, and my father was not in a very good mental state to give interviews. We told him what had happened. He shrugged it off and said these are useless discussions and that we should let it go. But we knew Baba is not going to survive for very long and that we will have to take it up. So we told him to make a video recording, stating what he thought about Wilayat Mahal. I don't know how much you will be able to understand, because his speech had become very slurred by then.' She offers to share a link to the video.

'My uncle Anjum Quder had sent my father to meet Wilayat Mahal when she first came to Delhi. But she was not willing to talk to him. When he asked her what proof she had that she was from the royal family of Awadh, she was only showing him newspaper cuttings about her. The newspapers at the time were full of reports about her arrival.'

Manzilat does not remember which year her father met Wilayat. Her father was the second among three brothers: the eldest was Prince Anjum Quder, and the youngest Prince Nayyar Quder. 'My father let go of the title Prince, so he was called Dr Kaukab Quder. He never used the title Prince.'

Referring to the video her father had made before he passed away, she says he never came across her name in all the research he conducted on the history of Awadh and the royal family. 'She has not mentioned any link to her past … I am telling you: I belong to the line of Birjis Qadr, the last king of Awadh, and his son Mehr Quder was my grandfather. She never said she was from so and so line, who were her ancestors.'

We tell her about the claim by Sakina, that Hazrat Mahal had a daughter from whom Wilayat claimed to have descended. She is surprised, but quickly counters by saying Hazrat Mahal never had a daughter.

'There is no such thing. Birjis Qadr was the only son. Two of his children were killed when he was assassinated. He had one daughter, Jamal Ara, who survived, and then my grandfather was born posthumously. This is what our elders have told us. And in all the documents, there is no mention of a daughter.'

She says she did ask her father about the government giving them a property to live in and what it signified. 'Because we still have not got anything, not even a room in this whole country. After Birjis Qadr's assassination, his wife came to live in a house in central Calcutta. Later she bought a smaller house and that is the house my brother lives in.' She mentions an attempt made by the family to seek compensation from the government, as Hazrat Mahal's descendants, when their economic condition was not good. 'That did not come to pass and my father was the last one to receive a government pension.'

She believes the government never took much interest in their branch of the family because they never 'dramatized' their claim like Wilayat did. 'With dogs, and sitting at the station. Creating such a problem for the public. My father repeatedly said that they slammed the [property] on her just to silence her, because she was a public nuisance.'

She says the best way to understand Awadh's history would be to either speak to many researchers or get it straight from the horse's mouth. 'And who is the horse here? It is Wajid Ali Shah himself, since he put down the details of his entire life in his books.'

Shah, however, wrote in Urdu, a language many chroniclers don't know well, says Manzilat. She expresses disappointment that her father did not write in English. 'Now my sister has taken up the task of translating my father's book in English.' Her sister, Talat Fatima, also one of the trustees of the mausoleum, is based in Rajasthan and is now a retired academic.

She mentions Shah's book *Parikhana*, which he wrote when he was imprisoned in Fort William. In that, he wrote about his wives and children. 'Hazrat Mahal is mentioned there and so is Birjis Qadr. In order to understand Shakespeare, you need to read Shakespeare. In order to understand Wajid Ali Shah, you need to read him ... Only then you can understand the true story about him and his wives; how much consideration he had for each of them.'

She says they talk about their family history 'even if my brother and I meet for ten minutes'. 'My brother has been posting about it on social media. I tell you honestly, his language is not very strong. But the facts he mentions are amazing and have drawn so many people to him. That is our success. People understand that here is a genuine descendant who has genuine material. And those who are scattered in Lucknow, and the authors who are writing their book by talking to them, are useless.

'We have faced such things all our lives and it has always been like this. We have never tried to impose ourselves upon others. Till date there are these fake nawabs in Lucknow, but we have never confronted anyone. This is how our father liked it.'

She mentions her elder sister again and says that the students at her college came to know of her royal lineage only after she retired. 'She never made any use of it.'

We ask her how many siblings she has. 'We are six in total: four sisters and two brothers. My eldest sister and I are more active. The other two sisters maintain a low profile. My elder brother [Irfan Ali Mirza] and sister are both trustees of the mausoleum.'

She talks of her uncle, Anjum Quder, who was quite a public figure and known as the president of All India Shia Conference. 'He was active in Calcutta also, but mostly in Lucknow.' According to Manzilat, her uncle knew Mulayam Singh Yadav, a former chief minister of Uttar Pradesh, closely. 'He was also a member of the Babri Masjid Committee.'

Anjum Quder died of a heart attack in Delhi, she says. 'After his death, our family name became obscure. Baba was never in the public eye. Nayyar Quder was based in London; after the death of Bade Abba [Mehr Quder], he came to Metiaburj and died there too; he is buried at the mausoleum. We used to note that unscrupulous people in Lucknow were claiming to be nawabs and showing off things in their house, with supposedly royal legacy. But we never had such things to show. We do have a couple of things that are priceless, not just for us but for the country—such as the seal of Begum Hazrat Mahal.'

She explains that since Hazrat Mahal was on the run, she had to give away her jewellery to pay for her upkeep, including to the king of Nepal who gave her refuge. 'Now see, I have this paandan from my mother. People ask me if it belonged to Begum Hazrat Mahal. I say no! She was not going around with a paandan. When Mahtab Ara Begum escaped after her husband [Birjis Qadr] was assassinated, she did not carry a paandan with her! So we do not have much to show but we do want to tell people: this is Wajid Ali Shah's family; this is Birjis Qadr's family; and we are still around. My grandfather was as yet unborn when Birjis Qadr was assassinated. This is what ailed my father, in fact, that we could not avenge it. My father was deeply pained by the fact that Birjis Qadr was assassinated. This is not widely known and is rarely told to people. The conspirators were in cahoots with the British and were lavishly gifted by the latter for what they did. My father and two uncles believed that the assassination was to snuff out the ruling line. But providence had other plans. Mehtab Ara Begum was unwell that day, so she did not join him, and that is how she and the baby in her womb lived on. That is why even I am sitting in front of you today.'

She says she wanted to let people know about these historical events and took up cooking as a medium to do so.

About her restaurant, she says it was a result of her interest in cooking Awadhi cuisine. 'People told me I could do something with it. I did a one-day event first, then another a few months later.' She says people in the family were initially disapproving of her cooking for others. 'No one had ever done any sort of business in my family. Education was always more important.'

Another reason for starting a restaurant was that her children—a son and a daughter—had left Kolkata for Mumbai and that left her with more time on her hands.

'Even now, some family members do not think well of it. But I think a buzz has been created through this about our family history.'

Manzilat undertook other efforts to enhance Hazrat Mahal's place in collective memory. She arranged, for example, for the documentary mentioned in the previous chapter to be screened publicly for the first time, years after it was released by the government. She got in touch with the director in 2015, after she realized that the film had never been screened formally.

She tells us that she asked Mirza why the film had not been screened. 'He told us that his job was limited to making the film, and that it was up to us to have the film screened.'

After making several efforts to reach the right people who could help her with the screening, she managed to find a sponsor in Lucknow. The film was screened in Paryatan Bhawan in Lucknow. Manzilat's father, Dr Kaukab Quder, was able to attend it, and there was a press conference too. Dimple Yadav, wife of Samajwadi Party leader Akhilesh Yadav, released the film. 'All the history lovers swarmed the venue. When my father gave a speech, I had goosebumps.'

We ask Manzilat if she believes that Hazrat Mahal has got her due. 'Of course not,' she says. She mentions a new BBC report on her, citing historian Rosie Llewellyn-Jones, with whom she expresses displeasure for never bothering to seek out her father's views on Awadh's history and on Hazrat Mahal.

In her biography of Wajid Ali Shah, Llewellyn-Jones does credit Manzilat's father in her acknowledgements, for writing what she describes as the 'most comprehensive catalogue to date of the king's works' and for sharing some images with her of Garden Reach, the king's palace in Calcutta.

Manzilat says Llewellyn-Jones's claims about Hazrat Mahal's African origins and her marital status are not necessarily correct. 'Even if she was divorced, how does it affect the lineage?'

She accuses Llewellyn-Jones of going by hearsay. 'Hearsay is very different from fact. You have a huge readership. One wrong message and it goes to the elite classes, the educated people who are reading your book. We are very, very unhappy with Llewellyn-Jones's work when it comes to Begum Hazrat Mahal. Even when she says Wajid Ali Shah is the last king of Awadh, she says it from the English mindset.' Manzilat makes the case that it was Birjis Qadr who was the last king of Awadh, as he was crowned by the mutineers when they laid siege upon Lucknow in 1857. This argument that Birjis Qadr was the last king is what her branch of the family bases their claim on for the 'title' of descendants of the 'last king'—as opposed to other descendants of Wajid Ali Shah.

Manzilat's dismissal of Hazrat Mahal's so-called African origins is based on her observation that none of the descendants have any African features, skin tone or hair. Even Llewellyn-Jones mentions that Hazrat Mahal has no African features in her portraits, unlike a few other wives of Wajid Ali Shah. 'Perhaps it is racist to talk like that, but biologically speaking, in my entire family, no one has any such trait,' says Manzilat. 'Hazrat Mahal was one of the most beautiful queens of Wajid Ali Shah. Africans are beautiful too, but there is no mention of her skin [being dark].'

We ask her if she has been to Nepal. 'We all have. My eldest sister, my brother ...' Of her first visit in 2006, she does not have many happy memories. She says the family was not treated well by the person in charge of the upkeep of Hazrat Mahal's grave. She also complained that a water tank had been constructed next to the grave of Hazrat Mahal, which gave it an ugly appearance.

In 2017, they went again on the invitation of the then Indian ambassador to Nepal, Ranjit Rae, who had started the annual commemorations.

We ask her if the family had ever demanded or received any material benefits from the government. She says they had some promissory notes from pre-Independence times worth crores of rupees, but they have not received any money from them. 'We have some documents in which the details about the promissory notes are there ... We could make a claim to the British government, but it is not an easy task. If it had been, my uncle would have done so as he was based in London ... There was this Supreme Court lawyer who told us he could help. He made a lot of videos of Baba and got some papers signed [by him] ... He made the point that the British would pay if you showed them the promissory notes, out of a sense of prestige. We told him he could take his fees from the money if he could get it for us. But it never came to pass.'

She says her grandfather had approached the first Prime Minister and President in this regard. 'Nothing came of it too. Only one thing was accepted and that was the demand to acknowledge the grave of Hazrat Mahal.'

∼

In the National Archives of India, a copy of the memorandum submitted by Mehr Quder, Manzilat's grandfather, is preserved along with the response by the government.² It was handled by the political branch of the home ministry. The title page of the memorial, which was submitted on the occasion of the 1857 centenary celebrations, says:

> Memorial to free India's first President from the survivors of a valiant fighter for Indian Independence

The first page of the archived file summarizes the contents of the memorial and the immediate response of the home ministry, putting it up for Nehru to go through it. It says:

> A brief note on the memorial from the Oudh Prince Meher Quder Zahid Ali Mirza is placed below for P.M.'s information. The note is really a brief history of the Oudh family pensions. The request of the Princes however requires further examination in consultation with the Governments of U.P. and West Bengal. The Princes have taken the occasion of 1857 centenary celebrations to make a request for a compassionate grant to relieve them of their debts etc. Such an ex gratia grant is hardly appropriate as an item in the commemoration of the 1857 centenary.

Right away, we can see that the home ministry was not keen to disburse any monies to the family in Calcutta. It did not think the request was necessarily connected to the centenary celebrations, and the tone of its note—hinting at the opportunism of the princes and then calling their action 'hardly appropriate'—reveals its annoyance.

Underneath this note is a comment by Nehru himself. He spoke quite plainly and said 'no elaborate enquiry' was needed in the matter. 'The only point to be considered is whether the pension, or whatever it is called granted to Meher Quder Zahir³ Ali Mirza, should be increased for his life or not.' Nehru appears sympathetic to him and wrote further: 'He is an old man and Rs 500 do not go very far now.'

However, he declined to issue an order to this end, mentioning that he had 'not gone into this matter more carefully'. Finally, he ended his missive by repeating his lack of a deep engagement with the issue at hand: 'I am only suggesting that no elaborate enquiry is needed as to what happened a hundred years ago.'

Soon after the memorandum was sent to the home ministry, an anonymous petition against it was sent by a 'Calcutta Citizen'. While the petition was submitted on 17 August 1957, within a week the petition against it had also reached the home ministry.

Let us look at the memorandum itself before going into the representation against it. It mentioned the occasion that was the centenary year of 'the First War of Indian Independence which commenced on the 10th of May 1857'. It noted 'India's current efforts to extend recognition to those who, a century ago, sacrificed themselves and all they possessed so that Hindustan may be free' and 'the oft declared express policy of the government of India to ensure due restitution as far as practicable to those who lighted the Torch of Freedom a hundred years ago'.

The memorandum listed the three sons of Meher Quder Zahid Ali Mirza, descended from Birjis Qadr and Hazrat Mahal: Sahibzada Anjum Quder Roushan Ali Meerza, Sahibzada Kaukab Quder Sajjad Ali Meerza and Sahibzada Nayyer Quder Wasif Ali Meerza.

In a point-by point style, it went on to list the demands of the 'memorialists':

The first was to construct a memorial to Hazrat Mahal in Lucknow and for the maintenance of her last resting place in Kathmandu, where, it said, she 'died neglected, impoverished and in anguish'; the second demand was for the 'recognition of the just and lawful claims of the direct descendants of Queen Hazrat Mahal in the way of suitable financial provisions'; the third was for the 'restoration of jagirs unlawfully confiscated by the victors of 1857 as a penal measure and/or equivalent compensation on this account'. (Jagirs were feudal landholdings.)

The other demands included a 'refund of Government Promissory Notes confiscated vindictively' and 'revision of political pensions'.

The memorial acknowledged Meher Quder as the 'only son of Prince Birjis Quder ... who was the eldest surviving son of His Majesty Wajid Ali Shah and of Hazrat Mahal'. Calling her the 'Patriot of Avadh', it mentioned that she willingly chose a life 'of misery, poverty and exile' in Kathmandu. About Mahtab Ara Begum, Birjis Qadr's wife, the memorial mentioned that she was a 'near relation' of His Majesty Bahadur Shah, 'a hero of the War of 1857'.

It complained of the British attitude towards the House of Awadh, 'and particularly Queen Hazrat Mahal and Prince Birjis Quder', who, according to the memorialists, 'failed to get recognition of their due political rights and of their claim to emoluments befitting their royal descent'.

Calling it the 'opportune' time for setting right the wrongs of the past, the petitioners sought 'some measure of redress of iniquities of the past', beseeching the President to provide 'some recompense for the historic services of the past'.

The petitioners expressed their satisfaction about what they feel had been 'a gratifyingly true reappraisal of the events of 1857 so long stigmatized as a mere mutiny', calling it the 'seed-bed of Indian struggle for freedom culminating in the Independence of a decade ago'.

Birjis Qadr's coronation by British forces is mentioned, along with the fact that afterwards, the Indian soldiers fought under him as their king and sovereign in Awadh for nine months, till their conclusive defeat in March 1858.

It went on to provide more details of the role played by Hazrat Mahal, including her efforts to provide for the rebels throughout the war, her uncompromising attitude in 'spurning tempting overtures' made by rival British officers, her stay in Nepal, from where she is said to have continued to make attempts to restart the battle against the British, and her end in 1879, when 'the Queen drew her last breath and lies to this day in a common-place grave, unmarked, untended', wrote the petitioners, emphasizing the misery of her final years and her unacknowledged legacy.

They, too, compared Hazrat Mahal to other queens who fought against the British in 1857: 'Permanent monuments and statues to the hallowed memory of the great Rani of Jhansi have been erected all over India.' They noted that 'Permanent monuments to the memory of Tatya Tope, Beni Madho and many heroes of 1857 have been erected in several parts of the country.' Comparing her grave to that of others, they wrote: 'And only the grave of the lamentable Queen Hazrat Mahal on this date remains unhonoured, dilapidated, and crumbling in remote Nepal.'

They did appreciate, they said, that the government of Uttar Pradesh had the 'honours bestowed on the memory of the Queen by the free people of Republican India recently on May 10, 1957, by the dedication of a gate in her hallowed name on the occasion of the current commemorations at Lucknow of the centenary of Remembrance attended by the State Governor among others'.

This gate, it is later mentioned, was temporary and taken down the next day. After continuing in this vein for a few more paragraphs, they sought to establish how Hazrat Mahal suffered personal financial losses due to her opposition to the British. They pointed out that her personal jagirs in Farrukhabad and other places in Uttar Pradesh were confiscated by the British as a 'penal measure'.[4] Then came the mention of the promissory notes. They stated that 'the Queen's and the Prince's personal cash of Rupees Two and a half lakh each in Government Promissory Notes was then also confiscated and still remains unreturned.'

The petition went on to detail the circumstances of the return of Birjis Qadr to Calcutta. According to the petitioners, he returned to continue the fight against the British and was assassinated, leaving his wife, a daughter and a son still to be born. This son, Mehr Quder, was born four months later, it is stated. It then said: 'Among the Memorialists is that son of Prince Birjis Quder who makes this approach for a re-appraisal of loyalties in view of the change of sovereignty.'

They claimed that their branch of the family had been treated with 'vindictiveness' by the British and emphasized their 'present distress'.

After this brief historical background, they contended that 'according to the law and traditions of the dynasty of Avadh, the Memorialist Prince Meher Quder Zahid Ali Mirza is unquestionably the chief inheritor in most interests and the main survivor-in-interest in others of the last of the rulers of Avadh'.

At this point, the petitioners presented some statistics to buttress their claims. They mentioned that Awadh's revenues, at the time of being taken over by the British, amounted to Rs 1,39,00,000 annually. Mehr Quder received a pension of Rs 75 per month initially, awarded to him as an infant, which was later raised to Rs 300 and afterwards to Rs 500 in 1929. They revealed that Quder made many attempts 'for considerations of his lawful claims' in 1945, but that these were ignored by Lord Mountbatten, the last Viceroy.

Upon the death of Mehr Quder, they said, they would be eligible to receive only Rs 75 per month, to be divided among the three sons. They pointed out that the 'younger members of the family of Prince Meher Quder actively participated' in the Quit India movement in 1942. Once again, they pointed out that they were unable to receive higher education due to their poor financial position. 'The family has no savings and has no assets except a small house in Calcutta in which they reside. In fact, the Memorialists are in heavy debts to the extent of Rs 50,000 due to deficit family budgets over last fifteen years on account of the huge and increasing cost of living, and low and fixed income.'

The petitioners reminded the government that others whose families participated in the War of 1857 received educational grants and even jobs. They cited the specific case of Raja Kunwar Singh of Jagdishpur, whose jagirs, they said, were returned to his descendants after Independence by the Indian government. The case of Tipu Sultan is also referred to, whose descendants, according to the petitioners, were being looked after 'generously' by the government.

Then came a reference to a statement by the then deputy home minister, B.N. Datar, on 11 April 1955 that the Indian government was willing to pay allowances to the dependants of those who had fought in the War of 1857, and suffered in it, 'if representations were made in this regard'.

They reminded the government about the promissory notes—'refund of the confiscated Government Promissory Notes is lawfully due, even as a token recompense for the privations and hardships visited on the family directly as penalty for taking part in the 1857 War'.

They reiterated the demand for the return of the jagirs to Mehr Quder but added that if that were to be not possible, being 'opposed to the trend of the times', they should be paid an amount in lieu of that. They complained that the pension—Rs 500—given to Mehr Quder was too low for even his medical expenses and had remained unchanged for thirty years.

They made their demand for a lump sum of money to pay off their debts and requested a pension 'in line with the Privy Purse allowed to the ex-rulers and descendants'.

~

In response, the government took the line that the pension of Mehr Quder could not be increased without doing the same for others from the royal family of Awadh. 'There are 11 grandsons of the late King of Oudh and if the pension of Meher Quder Zahid Ali Mirza is increased, the pension of the other 10 grandsons may also have to be increased.'

At this time, the anonymous petition also met its target.

This petition claimed that facts were being 'suppressed' by the petitioners from the family of Mehr Quder. It also alleged that Anjum Quder had been 'convicted' by the Calcutta High Court and 'sentenced to ten years (sic) rigorous imprisonment for forgery and cheating'.

Providing more details, it said that Anjum Quder 'was convicted in 1950 by Justice P.B. Mukherjee of the Calcutta High Court in a Pensions Trial along with one Agarwalla for offences under S.467/468/420 I.P.C'. This was for allegedly forging signatures of one Bagraia of McLeods and trying to cheat to the extent of Rs 2 lakh.

According to the anonymous Calcutta Citizen, the case was investigated by the detectives of the Calcutta Police. It went on to say that Anjum Quder, also known as Roushan Ali, stayed in jail 'for long' and alleged that he was finally released 'by bribing doctors and others on bogus T.B. plea' after paying a fine of Rs 5,000.

It then upped the ante and made other charges. 'This man is a notorious habitué of police courts. He is a gambler running a gambling den at the Santragachi railway club with one years (sic) licence from the Howrah magistrate even though the police super objected.'

Manzilat, when we ask her about these allegations later, expresses surprise. 'Honestly, I have no clue as the matter was never discussed (if there was any such thing) in front of youngsters as I was born in 1968,' she responds via WhatsApp, and requests for some time to consult with her brother, Kamran Mirza, who at that moment is on pilgrimage to Karbala. A bit over a month later, she shares his written response. Mirza calls the allegations false and alleges that the Calcutta Citizen was, in fact, an 'envious family member'. He says that different branches of the family became jealous of theirs, when Hazrat Mahal was named as a freedom fighter during the 1957 centenary celebrations of the 1857 Revolt. 'This branch had an upper hand before the government because they came from the ruling line when compared to the other branches who were British supporters.' He suspects that the anonymous petitioner wanted to 'delay the decision and place obstacles before the authorities to throw them off track and divert their attention from the main subject i.e., the recognition of the main line of the Wajid Ali Shah.'

If this was indeed the goal of the Calcutta Citizen, he succeeded to some extent. The government at the time felt that if the allegations made in the petition were correct, 'the memorialist does not deserve any sympathy'—though no attempts seem to have been made to investigate whether the said allegations were, in fact, correct.

Meanwhile, the brothers Anjum Quder and Nayyar Quder reached Delhi—their visit even made it to the newspapers—and met government officials in a failed attempt to expedite their case.

The Union government's view was to first consult the West Bengal government, '... before the question of increase in the pension of Meher Quder Zahid Ali Mirza is considered'. It was decided to write to the West Bengal government and to the Ministry of Finance to find out about the promissory notes. It also planned to 'trace' old papers about jagirs that had been confiscated.

The brothers met the Prime Minister too. They wrote a letter about the meeting with Nehru to the deputy home minister, B.N. Datar. The letter stated that the Prime Minister enquired about their family for 'a long time'. They added that after going through the documents they presented to him, he 'expressed profound sympathy with our plight'. This made them hopeful, they said, that his 'sympathies will take practical shape'.

∼

Along with the papers in the dossier, there are notes on the royal family of Awadh before the kingdom was usurped by the British.

They allow us an insight into how the new government of India saw the events that transpired more than a hundred years ago in Awadh.

The government's note on the House of Awadh starts from the time when the nawabs of Awadh became sovereign kings under the patronage of the British, no more under the control of the Mughals in Delhi. From this period onwards, the note says, 'they embarked on a totally dissolute palace life', paying little heed to the advice from the East India Company to introduce reforms in the administration of the state. It mentions the book written by Colonel Sleeman, who toured the entire Awadh. Continuing in this vein, it says that finally, the British lost patience and 'felt compelled' to take over the administration of the state. It notes that Wajid Ali Shah refused to sign a treaty to this effect with the British and was exiled to Calcutta, receiving an annual allowance of Rs 12 lakh.

The government believed that Wajid Ali Shah should have accepted the treaty, as in the cases of the nawabs of Murshidabad and the princes of Arcot. The note states:

> After the grant of the 'diwani' to the Company by the Emperor Shah Alam, Mir Jaffar's descendants still continued to hold the office of the nawab-nazim of Bengal, Bihar and Orissa. This office was taken away from them later, but a nizam-faineant continued to be maintained by British Government and even today the Nawab of Murshidabad gets a political pension of Rs 2.3 lakhs per annum from us. As this pension is in lieu of cessation of territory, the pension has been guaranteed in perpetuity.

The nawab of Arcot received Rs 1.5 lakh, once again, in perpetuity. Like the other two, Wajid Ali Shah also gave away his kingdom, or territory, the document noted, but 'because of his failure to sign the treaty, he was treated differently'.

After Shah's death, the annual allowance of Rs 12 lakh was stopped, but a prince, Kamar Kadr Mirza, was recognized as 'Head of the family' and allotted a pension worth Rs 3,000 for his lifetime. This was stopped after the prince died in 1919, says the document. From then onwards, pensions of Rs 500 per month started to be paid, to all eleven grandsons of Wajid Ali Shah. Great-grandsons were granted Rs 75 per month, and granddaughters and widows of grandsons belonging to the male line received Rs 50 per month. The total amount that was being paid to various descendants came to around Rs 1.3 lakh annually.

The document then looks into the specific case of Hazrat Mahal. Calling her 'one of the numerous wives' of Shah, it acknowledges the role she played in the 1857 Revolt against the British but adds the caveat that she might not have been acting independently and was perhaps forced to do so by Bahadur Shah Zafar, the last titular Mughal emperor in Delhi at that time.

It joins issue with the suggestion made by the petitioners that she had been treated differently, compared to the side of the family that was 'loyal' to the British by not fighting in the 1857 Revolt.

The petitioners had argued that only the jagirs of Hazrat Mahal and Birjis Qadr had been confiscated by the British, while jagirs owned by his other wives and sons of Wajid Ali Shah continued to be in their possession. When land reforms took place in Uttar Pradesh after Independence, they say, the descendants of the other wives and sons were compensated for this land, and the petitioners demanded a similar compensation. 'Only the Memorialists have suffered alone the loss of their Jagirs for their ancestors' part in the 1857 War', they write.

But the government, in its note, avers that this perception was 'not in accordance with the facts'. It cites as proof the pension received by Mehr Quder, which was equal to what the other grandsons received. It rejects outright any demand related to the jagirs that had been confiscated or the promissory notes that were seized, and states that the only question was whether to increase the amount that was being paid to Mehr Quder.

The note then delves into the somewhat curious case of another scion of the Awadh royal clan, Prince Yusuf Mirza. It says:

> Prince Yusuf Mirza who had himself crowned as King of Oudh on August 15, 1947, at Lucknow, has made a representation requesting that he be recognised in place of Prince Mehr Quder as the 'Head of the family' and given the special pension of Rs 3,000/- p.m. It is doubtful if there is any justification at this stage to revive the position of the 'Head of the family.

The incident of Yusuf Mirza, a grandson of Wajid Ali Shah from another wife gives a peek into the dispute between the two branches of the family, and how they adjusted to the new sociopolitical realities post-Independence.

In the same dossier, there is an extract from an article published in the Bengali newspaper *Amrita Bazar Patrika* (Calcutta), on 15 September 1957.

It was written by one K.M. Munshi and is titled: 'An Act of Treason?' Calling it an 'amusing incident', it starts: 'The story of Wajid Ali's dynasty would not be complete without mentioning an amusing incident which took place in 1947.'

It then goes on to mention that Mirza lived in 'pensioned luxury' in Calcutta. Munshi wrote that someone 'advised' him, after India won its freedom from the British, that he could claim his kingdom, Awadh, according to 'the doctrine of legitimacy'. 'Surrounded by a host of flatterers, therefore, he arrived at Lucknow, ready to resume his patrimony. A huge shamiana was constructed to celebrate the event.'

However, things did not pan out as the prince had desired.

> When the aspirant arrived at Lucknow to assert his sovereign rights the police informed him that the passage of ninety years had brought about a change in the situation and that any

attempt at resurrecting a claim to the sovereignty of Avadh might land him in trouble.

Munshi, clearly enjoying writing about such an absurd event, which showed how completely out of touch former royals were with a changing world, then described with sardonic humour what transpired next.

> The claimant took hurried counsel and issued a Proclamation. He announced that, on the British leaving India, he as the rightful sovereign of Avadh had assumed his authority and had appointed Shrimati Sarojini Naidu as Governor and Pandit Govindvallabh Pant as chief minister. Having performed this solemn ritual, he returned to Calcutta, the comedy ended.

The extract from the article is accompanied by a photograph, showing Yusuf Mirza in his regal dress, wearing a long robe that came down to his shoes, over a pair of white trousers and a shirt buttoned up to his neck. His expression is neutral. It is in black-and-white and hazy due to the passage of time. Underneath it, the caption says: '"KING OF OUDH". Prince Yusuf Mirza grandson of the last king of Oudh, in his "coronation robes". He was "crowned" in Lucknow on August 15 last.' Beneath it is a handwritten remark by Anjum Quder, stating that the photograph was published by the *Illustrated Weekly of India* in August–September 1947. The text and photograph were submitted by Anjum Quder to expose Yusuf Mirza as a deluded imposter. In 1947, Meher Quder had himself written to the Congress president of Uttar Pradesh to warn him that some 'eccentric and reactionary elements' had organized themselves into an organization called the Oudh Restoration Mission.

In the end, the government decided against raising the amount that Mehr Quder was receiving, noting: 'If we enhance Mehr Quder's pension and the pensions of his sons, we shall have to lay down new scales and apply the scales uniformly to all the descendants of King Wajid Ali Shah.'

The note from the home minister, meant for the Prime Minister, further stated that no preferential treatment should be expected for their ancestors' role in the 1857 Revolt. 'There are many others whose ancestors sacrificed their all in 1857 but their lot is pitiable now. None of them is getting any pension.' In other words, the home minister felt that the descendants of Hazrat Mahal were already better off than many others and, hence, they should have been satisfied with their present status in life.

Nehru agreed with the home minister. He accepted that he had underestimated how vexing the issue was. 'This question is not quite so easy as I had thought it at first.' However, he did not dismiss the matter entirely and suggested: 'We might agree to give them some educational allowance to those who are studying in school or college.'

The home minister directed his bureaucrats to look into the suggestion made by the Prime Minister.

His senior advisor, H.K. Tandon, asked the officials to 'examine' the issues and then contact the Prime Minister again. He remained circumspect about the viability of the suggestion. 'This allowance will perhaps have to be granted from funds available with the ministry of Education, or failing that from the Home Ministry's grant.'

Meanwhile, another letter from Mehr Quder had reached Nehru, as the memorialists had come to know that a letter against their petition had been sent to the government.

However, the Prime Minister was already becoming suspicious about the authorship of the petitions from Mehr Quder. 'From the account we received about him from the West Bengal Government, he is ill and not in his right mind. Obviously, the letter is written by somebody else.' The doctor treating Quder later clarified in a letter that the mental condition of his patient was 'normal', but till then, it was repeatedly questioned.

The West Bengal government had written that Meher Quder had been 'traced' to an address in Central Calcutta.

> He is an old man aged about 64 years. According to him he was born posthumously in Metiaburz, Calcutta in the year 1893 about 4 months after his father, Prince Birjis Quder was assassinated. Meher Quder had an attack of cerebral haemorrhage in November 1953 and since then he has been very ill and has also lost his memory to some extent.

The reply also gave a detailed report of the 'very poor' financial status of the family. The furniture was said to be 'very old' and the members of the household were observed to be dressed 'very poorly'.

A list of his four children and a brief account of their social status and activities followed. His only daughter, Gulshan Ara Kamini Begum, was mentioned first: forty years old, a widow, who was living with Meher Quder.

Then the three sons were mentioned. Out of them, two—Anjum and Kaukab—were married with children. Anjum Quder was 'unemployed', the note said, while the other two were still studying at Calcutta and Aligarh. Kaukab was studying for his MA and LLB, while Nayyar was preparing for IAS examinations, according to the note.

The first chief minister of the state, B.C. Ray, observes in an attached note that Quder 'is a quiet man and his reputation in the area where he lives is good. Politically, there has been no adverse comments about their doings.'

More opposition to the petition reached the government, however. The general secretary, M.M. Ali, of the Calcutta-based Oudh Royal Family Association, wrote a letter, stating that he had been directed by the members of the royal family descended from Wajid Ali Shah to object to the 'representation' made by Meher Quder and his children. He reiterated the same theme of Meher Quder's illness and deteriorating mental condition to buttress his argument, describing his mental condition as akin to 'insanity'. He ended the letter by raising a controversy that seems to have dogged the descendants of Birjis Qadr, especially Meher Quder and his children. This is what he wrote:

> We also wish to put on record that when Birjis Quder died he left only one issue and that was a girl called Nawab Husan Ara Begum, who died on 15.9.1949.

It is clear from this letter that this other branch of the royal family did not accept the possibility that Birjis Qadr's wife was pregnant with a son when he was assassinated, or even if they did, they did not believe that the son belonged to Birjis Qadr. This was a scurrilous allegation, since the family of Meher Quder maintained that he was born four months after the assassination of his father.

This controversy started to play out in the Calcutta press. While the central government was being petitioned by different branches of the family, it was reported that a defamation case had been filed by the descendants of Birjis Qadr against another rival prince who wrote an article in an Urdu journal regarding the paternity of Meher Quder.[5]

Around this time, yet another petition from some of Shah's other descendants landed on Prime Minister Nehru's desk, making similar allegations as M.M. Ali and the anonymous Calcutta Citizen, regarding Meher Quder's paternity and Anjum Quder's alleged gambling habits and conviction for cheating. They called the family of Kaukab Quder 'pretenders' and their representation 'false … propaganda.' It suggested that the government should consult the Office of the Political Agent in Calcutta 'where all records of the Oudh Family are preserved'.

This petition was bolstered by the signature of at least forty to fifty members of the Oudh dynasty; some members—as they would later contend—had signed not knowing all the details of the matter. Subsequently, some of them sent another petition disassociating themselves from the previous petition against Meher Quder's memorial. They said that their signatures had been obtained fraudulently, keeping them in the dark about the actual motives behind doing so. They claimed that since their English was not up to the mark, they could not make out the actual contents of the letter they had signed. This change in stance on the part of these descendants of Wajid Ali Shah from wives other than Hazrat Mahal was sent to the government in March 1958, perhaps a bit too late.

The government conveyed to the family that their demands had been rejected on 4 January 1958. In the end, it was decided to grant educational scholarships worth Rs 125 to Nayyar Quder and Rs 75 to Kaukab Quder, Manzilat's father. The government reasoned that although Nayyar was younger, he had to pay hostel charges as a student of Aligarh Muslim University, which was not the case for Kaukab Quder, and, hence, it decided to pay more to the former.

Stung, the family sent a revised memorial, expressing their feelings of being 'hurt and insulted' at the government's decision to treat them on par with other princes such as Yusuf Mirza. The second version of the memorial went into further details about the legitimacy or the lack of it, of princes born from mut'ah or temporary wives, such as Yusuf Mirza, as alleged. But no further notice of it was taken by the government.

Looking up the archives, we came across another set of papers that showed that Nayyar Quder was later given a substantial loan by the central government to pursue a law degree in London. But he seemed to have spent the first instalment of the loan fairly quickly, which worried the government. The loan also created a controversy among the family about the house and who owned it, because it was the security on the basis of which the loan was provided.

~

It is interesting that Birjis Qadr's ancestors would argue that children of mut'ah wives were not equally legitimate—considering that Hazrat Mahal herself was a mut'ah wife of Wajid Ali Shah. At the same time, they base their claim to royal lineage and to being the 'real' descendants of the rulers of Awadh on the fact that Birjis Qadr was appointed king in 1857—which would make the question of his legitimacy perhaps irrelevant.

The memorandum and subsequent responses by the government and other petitioners do make a few things clear. One, that Wilayat was by far not the only one at odds with the ancestors of Birjis Qadr, who had been fighting for recognition of being the 'real' House of Awadh since Independence; and, moreover, that the government ultimately did not believe that whoever was related to either Wajid Ali Shah or Hazrat Mahal deserved any extra pension for it, let alone compensation for lost landholdings or palaces.

All of this leaves us with further questions. Who can claim to be the real House of Awadh? Even if Wilayat's ancestor really was an unknown daughter of Hazrat Mahal, for which we have found no proof, certainly this would not make her a more rightful claimant than Manzilat and her grandfather? Does it come down to who, in Manzilat's words, was more 'dramatic' in demanding what they believed was their right?

And moreover, what would be just in terms of reparations and to whom, if the annexation of Awadh were to be formally accepted by the Indian government as unjust? Individual pensions and scholarships for descendants? Better care for monuments, memorials to commemorate ancestors? One thing is for sure: not many people would agree that Wilayat's demand for royal palaces to be given to her personally was just.

~

At this stage, we ask each other why we are pursuing this story. Are we also guilty of looking at them with the Western, Orientalist gaze that likes to imagine an India of palaces and royalty? Is the story worth pursuing only if they were royals and their demands were just in the court of public opinion? Is it only a matter of them not being compensated, as they had demanded, with more money and palaces? Of them not getting their due?

But what would have been their due, if not a palace or two in Lucknow?

Earlier, we wrote that they deserved to be heard, and that's what we did: in the previous sections, we heard their story. But for any attempt to *understand* the story, we need to dive deeper. We must now look behind the outer layer of Awadh royalty, and return to the past that Wilayat herself had hinted at when she spoke to *Hindustan Times* in 1975. The past that she later preferred to forget. The past that involved Partition, Pakistan and Kashmir.

Part III
Identity

*Kitnā hai bad-nasīb 'zafar' dafn ke liye
do gaz zamīn bhī na milī kū-e-yār meñ*[1]

—Bahadur Shah Zafar

Paradise Lost

After her interview with *Hindustan Times* in 1975, Wilayat never spoke about her pre-Partition life in Lucknow and Pakistan again and hardly ever mentioned her time in Kashmir. She chose to fully embrace the identity of Hazrat Mahal's royal and spiritual heir, adopting her title as a second name. A wronged princess, embodying a century-old history of injustice. Sakina and Ali Raza followed this path.

But as we found out through our interviews in Lucknow, before Partition she had been Wilayat Butt, wife of Inayat or I.U. Butt—which is a Kashmiri surname.

In newspaper archives, we found the first clues that Wilayat's initial resettlement in Jammu and Kashmir could not have been a coincidence. Despite what Sakina wrote in her book, Wilayat seemed to have had a deep connection to the region that went beyond her husband's last name.

In August 1954, Wilayat Butt made it to the headlines of several Pakistani dailies. She was present in Karachi's Jahangir Park on

Pakistan Day, celebrating Pakistan's seventh year of Independence amongst Karachi's elite, and reportedly interrupted Prime Minister Mohammad Ali Bogra's speech.

The incident was reported in the Urdu newspaper *Daily Jang* on 16 August, two days after it happened.

> Mrs Butt, who was sitting near the dais on chairs reserved for guests, started yelling, objecting to the Prime Minister for delivering his speech in the English language. 'PM is a liar. He did not do anything for Kashmir.'[1]

The English daily *Dawn*, on the same day, describes quite a scene.

> The rest of what the lady said was drowned in loud shouts from the dais. She was seen making threatening gestures at other women on the dais who tried to stop her; after that she was escorted out.[2]

Both papers kept following up on the case. The next day, *Daily Jang* reports that Mrs Butt was sent to jail for observation for ten days. Though she was arrested under a law for maintaining public order, the police had by then 'observed that she is not mentally well'. It was noted that: 'Butt was a former president of Jammu and Kashmir Muslim Conference and treasurer of the Muslim League Women Wing.'[3]

Keeping track of these ten days, *Dawn* followed up with the conclusion of a medical report:

> Begum Wilayat Butt was declared a lunatic by the City Magistrate, Mr S.M. Qureshi. She was ordered to be taken to lunatic asylum in Lahore, immediately.[4]

The same article also provided details to explain why Wilayat was suspected by the police to be a 'lunatic' in the first place:

Begum Butt was alleged to have made statements in which she professed to be under the influence of a 'jinnee', who at times made her to do acts beyond the scope of human beings.

Two days later, both papers reported, Begum Butt was released into the custody of relatives.

The order to send her to a mental institution in Lahore was reported in Ellen Barry's *New York Times* piece, as Wilayat's England-based son, Shahid, had remembered it.[5] This punishment was the confirmation many contemporary commentators needed to describe her as mentally ill and delusional—even as far back as the 1950s. Saeed Naqvi, for example, wrote that Wilayat 'spent time in a Lahore asylum for her grand delusion'.[6]

However, a closer study of the politics of the time shows us that Wilayat's disruption was, in fact, an act of political protest. This was also the conclusion of one newspaper of that time, the *Times of Karachi*, which questioned the police's alleged observation of mental illness in an editorial called 'Mrs Butt'.

> The lady who interrupted the Prime Minister's speech has been put behind bars, ostensibly for the cure of her alleged mental derangement, actually for having the temerity and daring to heckle Mr Mohammad Ali; for treatment could have been more easily provided outside the four walls of that God-forsaken place, called the Karachi Central Jail.
> We do not approve of Mrs Butt's manners, but we do uphold her right to differ from and voice her opinion against the Government's policy, as indeed is recognized all the civilized world over and conceded even in Pakistan. If it is a sin to criticize the government, then indeed all vocal elements are sinners; we of the Press the worst sinners of all.[7]

The column calls to attention the age-old method to silence people (and perhaps, in particular, women) with an opinion or behaviour that challenges the 'normal', the 'mainstream' or status quo. Because what did Wilayat mean when she claimed Bogra did not do anything for Kashmir? And what was the stance of the organizations that she was a part of, the Jammu and Kashmir Muslim Conference and the Muslim League? They continued to support Wilayat, with the Lahore branch urging the government to release her on 22 August, as reported by *Dawn*.[8] They certainly did not consider her protest the act of a lunatic. In fact, 1954 was a pivotal year for Kashmir.

～

The first organization to espouse the Kashmir cause was the All India Muslim Kashmiri Conference. It was formed in 1896 by Kashmiris settled in what is now the Punjab province of Pakistan, mainly Lahore, and had the great poet Allama Iqbal as its first general secretary. Sheikh Abdullah, the first elected Prime Minister of the Indian state of Jammu and Kashmir after India's independence, writing in his memoir *The Blazing Chinar*, said: 'The basic objective of the Conference was to highlight the deprivation suffered by the Kashmiris who had migrated to Panjab.'[9] By that time, there was a significant Kashmiri Muslim population in Punjab who had fled famines and discrimination by the Hindu Dogra dynasty that ruled over Kashmir.

In 1924, workers at a silk factory in Srinagar revolted against their exploitative working conditions. The same year, an attempt had been made by prominent Muslim citizens of Kashmir to take their grievances to the British Viceroy, Lord Reading, when he was on a tour of Kashmir.

Resentment against Dogra rule continued to mount till the situation got out of control in 1931, following a provocative speech by a Kashmiri Muslim called Abdul Qadir. Protests broke out all over

Kashmir and the Maharaja resorted to a strong show of force to quell the rebellion of his subjects.

The same year, the All India Kashmir Committee was formed at a meeting of Muslim intellectuals and other prominent members of the community, at Shimla. The committee's formation was followed by the establishment of the state's first political party, the All Jammu and Kashmir Muslim Conference—Muslim Conference, in short—with Sheikh Abdullah, then twenty-six years old, as its first president.

'On this occasion, the All India Kashmir Committee [AIKC] dispatched an elected delegation comprising Mir Abdul Rahim Dard, Maulana Ismaeel Ghaznavi, and Sayyid Habib, editor of *Siyasat*. It was proposed that the new organisation would be called the "All Jammu and Kashmir Muslim Conference",' wrote Abdullah in his memoir.[10] Clearly, the AIKC—with poet Allama Iqbal once more a part of it as its general secretary, like with the Muslim Kashmiri Conference—had an influence over the new party based in Kashmir. While the organization continued to expand and hold annual sessions, differences of opinion started to appear between leaders, especially Abdullah and Chaudhry[11] Ghulam Abbas, another important leader and rival of the former. The latter hailed from Jammu and did not speak Kashmiri, so his appeal in the Valley was limited.

In 1935, Mohammad Ali Jinnah visited the state for the first time, writes Abdullah. The idea of Pakistan was by then already in the air.

> The Muslim Conference organised a reception in his honour. Replying to the welcome address, Jinnah said that Muslims were in the majority in the state, and so they and their leaders were duty-bound to ensure not only the peace of mind of non-Muslims but also to consider them equal partners in their political and economic life so as to get their full support.[12]

Two years later, Abdullah met Nehru as well. Nehru gave him the same advice as Jinnah: to broaden the mass base of the party by including non-Muslims.

> He advised me that we should leave open the doors of our organisation for everyone in the state regardless of religion so that those of the non-Muslims who wanted to join the movement could do so without any inhibition.[13]

Abdullah changed the party's name to the National Conference [NC] to give it a more secular character, which ultimately decided in favour of Kashmir's accession to India.

But not everyone in the old Muslim Conference supported this line. 'The conversion of the Muslim Conference to the National Conference was a painful process,' Abdullah states.[14] He faced opposition from many leaders of his party, including Chaudhry Ghulam Abbas, Bakshi Ghulam Mohammad and Mirza Afzal Beg.

> Chaudhri Ghulam Abbas and some of his friends feared that this would undermine the movement as non-Muslims would get in with the design of setting up within the organisation a front to safeguard their own vested interests.[15]

The other fear was that Nehru's Congress Party would run the NC from behind the scenes. Abdullah writes that he managed to win over his opponents for the most part, including Abbas. In 1938, the name was officially changed to National Conference at a session chaired by Ghulam Mohammad Sadiq, who would later become chief minister of the state.

The change in name had serious repercussions and made a section of Muslims insecure, Abdullah writes. They resorted to reviving the original party, the Muslim Conference. 'For two years, Chaudhri was adrift in a state of uncertainty. He finally staged a comeback to politics and actively supported the cause of reviving the Muslim Conference.'[16]

The British historian Victoria Schofield writes about the same sequence of events:

> Those Muslims who were discontented with Abdullah's pro-Congress stance, especially the non-Kashmiri speakers, became staunch supporters of the Muslim League. In 1941, Ghulam Abbas broke away from Abdullah and joined with Mirwaiz Yusuf Shah in reviving the Muslim Conference, which eventually came out in support of the movement for Pakistan.[17]

Subsequently, while the National Conference became more and more aligned with the Indian National Congress, the Muslim Conference took guidance from the Muslim League. In 1946, the leaders of the Muslim League and the Muslim Conference were arrested together after Ghulam Abbas launched an agitation similar to Jinnah's Direct Action Day, which was seen as a call-to-arms by Jinnah. It led to what is now known as the Great Calcutta Killings, setting off an orgy of violence in the Indian subcontinent, culminating in Partition.

Maharaja Hari Singh of Kashmir's Dogra dynasty kept his options open after Independence and did not choose either India or Pakistan. Sheikh Abdullah preferred Nehru and Gandhi over Jinnah and was in favour of merging Kashmir with India.

Schofield further notes that supporters of the Muslim League and, by extension, of the Muslim Conference, were quite certain that Kashmir would accede to Pakistan.

> In the state of Jammu and Kashmir there were staunch Muslim League supporters who believed they would become part of Pakistan at independence and when freedom came at midnight on 14 August, they rejoiced. The Pakistani flag was hoisted on most of the post offices until the government

of the Maharaja ordered that they should be taken down. All pro-Pakistani newspapers were closed ... Those whose hopes were dashed at not becoming part of Pakistan set in train a sequence of events which was rooted in their past disappointment.[18]

The Maharaja's dilemma did not have the luxury of an elongated brooding period. In October 1947, barely a couple of months after both countries became independent, Pakistan launched an invasion of Kashmir, which it did not own at an official level, maintaining that it was a spontaneous uprising led by 'tribals'. Even if there was a spontaneous character to its start, it was certainly backed by the Pakistani State at a later stage.[19]

Sardar Ibrahim Khan, a leader of the Muslim Conference, writes Schofield, was active in leading the rebellion, which started from Poonch and was later assisted by tribals from the North-West Frontier Province, along with the support of the Pakistan Army.

The Maharaja turned to India for help. As is well-known, India wanted him to first sign the Instrument of Accession before sending its troops and starting operations by its air force. This treaty, perhaps because it was allegedly signed under duress by the Maharaja and without really ascertaining the views of his subjects, has long been a subject of dispute, with Pakistan never giving it much credence. Kashmiri politicians and people of the region have also questioned its legitimacy as well as the exact sequence of events in which it is said to have been signed.

India, of course, was aware of what Sheikh Abdullah favoured. And that made India feel it had a moral advantage, regardless of the circumstances in which the treaty was signed. This is why it took the matter of the so-called tribal invasion of Kashmir to the United Nations, seeking a plebiscite. The Indian State, confident of its position, thought the result of the plebiscite would vindicate its actions in Kashmir.

In the meantime, since the Instrument of Accession was signed by the Maharaja, at least 'officially', according to India's stated position, Kashmir became a part of India. But Pakistan disagreed, resulting in the first war between the two newly independent countries, after which the conditions of a ceasefire divided Jammu and Kashmir between them. Almost one-third in territory of the original princedom came under the control of Pakistan.

The Muslim Conference took the lead in establishing a government in this region, which was renamed 'Azad Kashmir' under the Pakistani government and which India refers to as 'Pakistan-occupied Kashmir' (PoK). While the Pakistani government controlled the major issues concerning Azad Kashmir, such as defence and foreign relations, the local government managed the daily administration.[20]

The party started actively expanding all over Pakistan after Partition. In April 1950, *Dawn* reported that over 3,00,000 people were enrolled as members of the All Jammu and Kashmir Muslim Conference. 'This comes to about 25 per cent of the total population of Kashmir nationals in Pakistan and the Azad Kashmir territory. There is still a heavy demand for membership forms.'

It was noted that its branches were functioning in every important city.[21]

This party, the All Jammu and Kashmir Muslim Conference, with Pakistan-administered Kashmir as its main area of operation, was the organization to which Wilayat was connected; in fact, she was an office bearer of the party. Hence, we have good reasons to believe that like any political activist, she must have kept a close track of developments regarding Kashmir. As reported by the *Daily Jang*, she even served as president of its Karachi branch, as well as treasurer of Karachi's Women's Muslim League. It is, therefore, more than likely that she subscribed to those parties' positions on Kashmir.

The Muslim League had been the driving force behind the creation of Pakistan, which from the outset was thought of as including Kashmir. And after the Maharaja signed for accession to India, the All Jammu and Kashmir Muslim Conference continued to push for a plebiscite to be held in Kashmir to decide its future, hoping that it would accede to Pakistan as a result or perhaps become independent. In fact, the Pakistani State continues to make the demand for a plebiscite in Kashmir till today.

But it was only until the year Wilayat got arrested that this plebiscite seemed to be a realistic possibility.

~

Almost seventy years after Wilayat's arrest in 1954, we spend a summer morning searching the digitized archive of the *Dawn* newspaper to find out if more of her political activities were reported on. After some running around, we get access to the cosy, brown woodworked library at its Karachi headquarters, where the librarian settles us down behind an old-fashioned desktop computer. Sure enough, Wilayat's name pops up on a few more occasions, the earliest one being in December 1951. As treasurer of the women's Muslim League, Wilayat commented on a public mourning ceremony for Pakistan's first Prime Minister and Jinnah's right hand, Liaquat Ali Khan. He was assassinated on 16 October 1951. The mourning ceremony, or Chehlum, took place on 25 November and was attended by Liaquat's mother. The meeting was disturbed by 'certain elements', as reported by *Dawn*. 'Efforts were made to disrupt the meeting by cutting off the microphone and the electric wires, raising slogans and even throwing dust on the dais where Quaid-i-Millat's mother was seated'.[22]

Wilayat made the news with a condemnation of this disturbance about ten days later.

She accused them of un-Islamic ways and said they were being used by a certain faction 'in the Muslim League to prop up its waning influence.' Concluding, she warned: 'These women' to behave decently and not to spoil the good name of Muslim women, otherwise, the Almighty God will, sooner or later, chastise them.[23]

This incident and Wilayat's comments made it to a recent book by historians Sarah Ansari and William Gould in a section about how women defined citizenship in post-1947 Pakistan[24]—though Ansari clarified to us that while writing it, she had no idea about Wilayat's later fame in India. The women's movement of the new Islamic republic was debating questions relating to the veil, polygamy and women's rights to work and education—essentially what it meant to be a Muslim woman and good citizen of Pakistan. Wilayat, it appeared, played a very active part in this movement.

What stands out for us is that Wilayat's name comes up in relation to this Chehlum—as she had mentioned Liaquat's assassination in her interview with *Hindustan Times* in 1975: 'After the assassination of Liaquat Ali Khan, Inayat Hussain was in difficulties and later died,' the paper had reported. 'According to Wilayat Mahal, there were allegations that Inayat Hussain had a hand in the murder of Liaquat Ali Khan which, according to her, were baseless.'[25]

If there were indeed any serious allegations against Wilayat's husband, they were not publicly known or at least not reported in *Dawn* at that time. The only time we find his name in the newspapers, in any context, is some weeks after he died. This must have been not long after Wilayat's condemnation of the disturbed Chehlum meeting. On 15 January 1952, she placed a brief personal note in *Dawn*.

Begum Inayatullah Butt, in a statement thanks all friends and relations who sent her condolence messages on the sad demise of her husband, Mr Inayatullah Butt. She regrets her inability to acknowledge the messages individually.[26]

There it was, in writing. Wilayat's husband was, in life and death, called Inayatullah, or as recorded by Lucknow University, I.U. Butt—and not Hussain. She must have added that name after her return to India to make sure that there would be no doubt about her credentials as a Shia royal. The original names of her youngest children, we later found out, were changed to represent a Shia identity as well.

～

But first, back to 1951. The year 1951 was seminal in the history of Pakistan, with both a failed coup attempt and the assassination of Liaquat Ali Khan. Again, Kashmir was the axis on which everything revolved, in Pakistan's early history as well as the lives of the members of Wilayat's family.

In the early years after Partition, the loss of Kashmir rankled Pakistan's political and military elite. The military, in particular, resented the political elite for not backing it enough on Kashmir. The military had a grievance, for example, that even during the ill-fated and unsuccessful 'tribal invasion' it did not receive the required support from political functionaries to carry on with the operation, and to take it to its rightful conclusion.

In his book, *The Time and Trial of the Rawalpindi Conspiracy 1951*, Hasan Zaheer has written: 'Broadly speaking, the Conspiracy was regarded as having its origins in the failure in Kashmir and of the cease-fire there', along with 'the presence of British officers in the armed forces'.[27] The presence of British officers, Ishtiaq Ahmed writes in his book on Jinnah, scuttled the government's plans to 'send regular Pakistani troops', as the commander-in-chief of the Pakistan Army. at that point in history was a British officer, General Gracey, and he refused to comply with the wishes of the Pakistani government.[28]

The other issue was that in its early days, Pakistan had not made up its mind on whether to ally with the US or the USSR, the two big world powers that were bitter rivals. The Cold War had begun and every nation was expected to make its loyalties known.

The Pakistani intelligentsia remained in favour of allying with the Russians, especially the leftist intellectuals who enjoyed popularity among the masses. Sajjad Zaheer and Faiz Ahmad Faiz, some of the biggest literary personalities of Pakistan, were two such intellectuals. Zaheer, coincidentally, had also come from Lucknow—like Wilayat and Inayatullah. Faiz had a relationship with Kashmir and its people, too. He got married there, for example, to the London-born Alys Faiz, and the couple lived in Srinagar before Partition. They were close to Sheikh Abdullah and G.M. Sadiq, who was part of Abdullah's pro-India National Conference and later became the chief minister of Jammu and Kashmir.

However, the political elites of Pakistan were aware of India's association with the USSR, a communist State—although in the initial period, the latter remained somewhat neutral on Kashmir. The personality of Nehru also played a part here because he was perceived to be pro-USSR. Indeed, Nehru admired the USSR and its communist system and would often say so publicly.

In 1950, Pakistan's first Prime Minister, Liaquat Ali Khan, visited the US on a State trip. Although the Pakistani government was already negotiating with Moscow for a State visit by Khan, it did not materialize in time and he chose to go to the US instead. This was widely perceived as him preferring the US over Soviet Russia. Subsequent developments strengthened the view that Pakistan was in the US camp. An anonymous former ambassador of Pakistan wrote in 2010 in *Dawn*:

> This was shown by Pakistan's support for the use of force by the UN in June 1950 against North Korea to secure its

withdrawal from South Korea, as also support for the peace treaty negotiations with Japan in 1951. The Soviet Union opposed both of these developments.[29]

These two factors—the perception that Liaquat Ali Khan had chosen the US over Soviet Russia and the loss of Kashmir—are said to have contributed majorly to the coup attempt and his assassination, both of which took place in 1951. The coup attempt, known as the Rawalpindi Conspiracy Case, was never really put into motion but was discussed among army officers and leftist intellectuals. It was led by Akbar Khan, an army general who was discontented with the government over the Kashmir issue. He had participated in the 'tribal invasion' and rued the lack of support from the political establishment, which he believed led to the failure of the army to liberate Kashmir. Among the intellectuals, Zaheer was very much in favour of the coup and managed to get it cleared by one vote by the central secretariat of the Pakistan Communist Party, of which he was general secretary at the time.[30]

However, someone in the know of the conspiracy leaked it to the government, which moved swiftly to arrest those it saw as the key conspirators—from the intelligentsia as well as the military. Both Zaheer and Faiz, who was editor of the leftist newspaper *Pakistan Times*, were jailed.

Later, in the same year, Liaquat Ali Khan was shot dead by Said Akbar, an Afghan tribesman, while addressing a rally. His assailant was also shot dead by the police present at the spot and his identity and motive have remained a mystery, leaving room for a wild variety of rumours.

Initially, the enquiry commission into Khan's assassination had investigated Akbar's political motives, after apparently his widow stated he had strong views relating to Kashmir. They even had reason to suspect that he had been part of the tribal invasion of 1947. It ruled these out, however, concluding in its report:

There is no evidence whatsoever, apart from what Musammat Malmal Bibi (widow of Said Akbar) has stated, that Said Akbar had any strong political views or political activities, or that he belonged to any political party. Earlier information about him, that he had taken part in the Kashmir Jehad, turned out to be unfounded.[31]

Some believe the assassination was carried out on the USSR's orders, because of Ali Khan's perceived pro-US policies. Others say the US was involved in a conspiracy relating to Iranian oil—which is the more popular theory now. Many believed, and continue to believe, that whoever the conspirators were had hired Akbar and rewarded his family generously. In March 2023, the Urdu newspaper *Daily Jang* reported that Akbar's widow had passed away at the age of 106, claiming that she received a house, security and an allowance until her death.[32]

∼

While it remains unclear how, Wilayat's husband Inayatullah was linked to the rumours surrounding Liaquat Ali Khan's assassination. This is where Wilayat's troubles with the Pakistani government began, culminating in the incident at Jahangir Park three years later.

It could have been because Inayatullah had links to Air Force officers who were said to have been behind the coup attempt—to *Hindustan Times* Wilayat had after all said that he had been defence secretary in Pakistan.[33] Perhaps his Kashmiri roots had made him an easy suspect. Wilayat mentioned the 'difficulties' he faced after the murder, when she spoke to the *HT* reporter in 1975, as well as the allegations of him having had 'a hand in the murder'. Whether his death, not long after Khan's, was in any way related to the allegations, we can only speculate. But it is telling that twenty-four years after the event, Wilayat still felt obliged to deny that the allegations were true. This could only mean that even if it was nothing more than a rumour, it had persisted.

The events of 1951 left Pakistan shattered, and Wilayat a widow with minor children. Despite this, and the allegations towards her husband, Wilayat did not give up on politics. In 1953, she entered the stage as president of the Karachi branch of the All Jammu and Kashmir Muslim Conference.

On 13 July 1953, Begum Wilayat Butt is quoted by *Dawn* as president of the All Jammu and Kashmir Muslim Conference; this day was observed by the Muslim Conference as Kashmir Martyrs' Day, a commemoration of the killing of twenty-one Muslim protesters by the Dogra army of the princely state in 1931. The day was observed in India, too—Sheikh Abdullah had named and announced the annual commemoration that same year.

In 1953, a meeting of Nehru and Bogra was scheduled in Karachi. Wilayat, according to the newspaper report, was pleading for the inclusion of prominent Kashmiri leaders in that meeting.

> She said: 'This day should remind Pakistanis of the great sacrifices the freedom-loving Kashmiris have given to liberate their land.' She referred to the Kashmir Martyrs Day as a day of renewing determination for the final liberation of Kashmir.[34]

Although this has been largely forgotten, till 1954, the possibility did exist that India and Pakistan might be able to resolve their differences on Kashmir on their own. The proposal for the plebiscite, which is today considered Nehru's folly, was seen differently back then. As mentioned earlier, India took the Kashmir case to the UN because it felt, in those days, that it had the moral advantage due to Sheikh Abdullah's support and wanted Pakistan punished over the invasion in 1947. India believed that a plebiscite would actually expose Pakistan's position as a hollow claim over Kashmir and show the world that Kashmiris wanted to be with India.

Bhola Nath Mullik, who served as the chief of the Indian Intelligence Bureau from 1950 to 1964, writes in his memoir, *My Years with Nehru*, that India and Pakistan came quite close to an agreement.

> There were several meetings between the Prime Ministers of India and Pakistan and an understanding was arrived at in London when both the Prime Ministers had met there at the time of the Queen's coronation in June, 1953.[35]

After this, Nehru visited Bogra in Karachi—the meeting Wilayat referred to—followed by a visit to Delhi by Bogra. Mullik writes that Bogra and Nehru decided that they would have an administrator from a small country, rather than from the UK or the US. But, according to Mullik, Bogra was under pressure from the US to have an American as the administrator and he backed out from the agreement.

'This was an unfortunate development since the agreement had brought India and Pakistan very close to each other in settling this outstanding dispute ... The Pakistan–United States Aid Pact of 1954 changed the situation completely.'

India, says Mullik, was wary that Pakistan would use the money from the US to buy arms and use them against India. 'The U.S.–Pak Aid Pact also automatically brought the USA on the side of Pakistan.'[36]

While negotiations did continue between Nehru and Bogra, Pakistan turned to the US for a military alliance. C.P. Srivastava writes about this in his book about India's second Prime Minister, Lal Bahadur Shastri, who was the home minister in the early 1960s. Srivastava, an officer in the Indian Administrative Service, was Shastri's private secretary.

> The United States was looking for allies in Asia who could provide military bases and political support for the USA in its efforts to combat the expansion of Communism. The membership of such an anti-Communist alliance carried with it the benefit of military assistance under the Military Alliance Programme (MAP) approved by the Congress as a part of its Mutual Security Legislation.[37]

The decision to bring Pakistan into the fold of a military alliance created a debate and a controversy within US politics, with the Republicans supporting the military aid to Kashmir and the Democrats expressing their reservations about it. The press in India was also incensed, writes Srivastava. Pandit Nehru told the Parliament that things would change irrevocably if the US went through with the plan.

However, the inevitable happened.

> The views of vice-president Richard Nixon, Senator Knowland and others of the same mind prevailed. And the Mutual Defence Assistance Pact between the US and Pakistan was signed in Karachi on 19 May 1954.[38]

Wilayat, as well as the Government of India and others who followed the Kashmir affair closely, must have known that this indeed changed everything as far as holding a plebiscite was concerned. That ship sailed in 1954, something that Wilayat probably understood very well when she confronted Bogra during his Independence Day speech that year. She did this, reportedly, even before he came to the part about Kashmir.[39] After she was escorted out of the meeting, Bogra spoke the following lines:

> At one time it seemed that the settlement of the Kashmir dispute was within sight. A year ago—in August last—the

Bharati Prime Minister and I came to an agreement that the Plebiscite Administrator would be inducted into office by April of this year in order to clear the deck for the holding of the plebiscite to decide whether Kashmir should accede to Bharat or Pakistan. Unfortunately, I have failed to get the Bharati Prime Minister to agree to the settlement of the preliminary issues, which would pave the way for the implementation of that agreement.[40]

Blaming Nehru for the failure, Bogra ended the part about Kashmir with words that are true till today:

The continuance of this dispute can do no good either to Bharat or to us in Pakistan. It stands as a most serious potential threat to peace in this region. (…) We shall not rest in peace until it is resolved honestly, justly and to the entire satisfaction of our brethren in Kashmir.[41]

For sure, there were other factors that led to Pakistan signing a defence pact with the US. Things in Kashmir were never static after Partition. Although Sheikh Abdullah had initially favoured India, the wrangling over Article 370—which gave special status to Kashmir—and the role of the Maharaja in the new set-up had started to make him suspicious of the Indian regime under Nehru, as lawyer A.G. Noorani has written in his book on the making of Article 370.[42] Abdullah's suspicions grew over the years, resulting in utterances that made the Indian government suspicious of him in turn. In 1953, Nehru dismissed his government and he was jailed over unsubstantiated charges of treasonous activities,[43] and he remained imprisoned for almost a decade. A trial in the so-called Kashmir Conspiracy Case started in 1959, until the charges were dropped and Abdullah was released in 1964. This perhaps eroded Pakistan's faith in India being serious about holding a free and fair plebiscite. Moreover, in 1954, the Jammu and Kashmir assembly ratified the accession of Kashmir to India as valid.

For India, the pact between the US and Pakistan meant the former now backed Pakistan on Kashmir, and a plebiscite on Kashmir under the United Nations would no longer be impartial due to perceived American influence over the organization.

Sheikh Abdullah writes about the episode in his memoir:

> India somehow wanted to get rid of the bone stuck in its throat—the plebiscite and was trying to find a way of doing so. As stated earlier, Jawaharlal had assured the Kashmiri people as well as the world that India had no designs on Kashmir, and that it had sent its armed forces there only to safeguard its right to a plebiscite to decide its future. It was the Baghdad pact and Pakistan's other defence pacts that now provided India with an excuse to go back on its commitment in this regard. In all this, America had left it in the lurch, to India's advantage. Backed by Russia's support, India declared that Pakistan's participation in the defence pacts had changed the whole scenario to the extent that India was no longer bound by the commitment it had internationally made with the people of Kashmir.[44]

Meanwhile, Kashmiris were facing insecurity. For a long time after Partition, those Kashmiris who had moved to Pakistan were not considered citizens and did not get the same rights to refugee property as other refugees from India.

What may also have played a role was that Bogra was from East Pakistan, a former diplomat who had been thrust into his position by circumstances. He was deeply influenced by America and supported it over Russia. His Bengali origin made his loyalties suspect in the eyes of the people of West Pakistan, and his commitment to Kashmir, as a result.

Indeed, as part of the same editorial in which the *Times of Karachi* defended Wilayat's right to voice protest, Bogra was criticized heavily for backing a politician from East Bengal and for claiming that people in East Bengal were protesting 'exploitation and injustices' by West Pakistani authorities due to 'enemy propaganda'.[45]

In other words, Wilayat, in all likelihood, was protesting the fact that Bogra had signed a defence pact with the US in 1954—three months before the alleged heckling. With this pact, the opportunity of a plebiscite vanished.[46] And Bogra was very much blamed for the failure by the West Pakistani intelligentsia, a stance that may have influenced Wilayat.

We called Sarah Ansari, the historian who had mentioned Wilayat in her book's chapter on the early post-Partition women's movement in Karachi, for a second opinion. Ansari suggests that given the era and this context, Wilayat's admission into a mental institution by no means proves that she was mentally ill. It may have provided her relatives a way of saving face and at the same time diverting attention away from the motives behind her protest, she says.

If the matter had gone to court, Ansari suggests, it could have put an uncomfortable spotlight on the government's actions. Therefore, and she emphasizes that this is a 'speculative reading', she says it is possible that Wilayat was released with a deal that saved both the government and her family from embarrassment. If this is the case, this deal had life-changing consequences for Wilayat herself.

After her arrest, Wilayat's name comes up in the newspapers only once more. A month after her arrest, on 15 September 1954, it is reported that her car gets taken from outside Jahangir Park, where it may have been parked the entire time since the Independence Day event that took place there: 'A car belonging to Begum Wilayat Butt has been impounded by the Traffic Police for non-payment of taxes.'[47]

After that, she seemingly disappears from public life.

Is this why Wilayat ultimately decided to relocate to India? Were her social life and standing disturbed, if not ruined, after being publicly shamed as a lunatic? Was her impounded car the tip of the iceberg of the harassment she faced? Or was her move related to the fate of Kashmir, after all? Was she Kashmiri, and did moving to Jammu and Kashmir seem the only way to keep a connection to what she considered her homeland, after Pakistan lost its best chance of getting it back? And why did India allow her, a woman who very prominently fought for Kashmir to get 'liberated' from India, to resettle there? We find some of the answers at the National Archives of India.

Kashmiri Citizens

In July 1962, the office of Prime Minister Jawaharlal Nehru received a typed letter from Wilayat Butt, sounding somewhat desperate. She wrote about her fear of getting attacked, of ruin, torture and murder conspiracies in Pakistan, while requesting Nehru's help to get her application for resettlement in India approved.

This letter was the first in a series of letters and telegrams exchanged between Wilayat and Indian government officials.

In early 2022, we received from the National Archives of India, aided by an application under the Right to Information Act and after paying a requested fee for photocopies, a set of papers from the home ministry. On top of the front page it was marked 'Secret'. It included these letters as well as internal notes between officials discussing Wilayat's appeal.[1]

The subject of the dossier, scribbled in hand, on top, reads: 'Request of Smt. Wilayat Butt, widow of Inayatullah Butt, for permanent settlement in Jammu and Kashmir.'

The very next page contains a typewritten note that suggests that the Intelligence Bureau should be consulted about the matter.

This is a request from one Mrs Wilayat Butt, Pakistani national, for grant of permanent settlement facilities in her favour in Jammu and Kashmir. D.I.B. [Director of Intelligence Bureau] may please see and let us know if there is anything adverse against her which makes it undesirable that she should be allowed to go to the State for permanent resettlement.

An IB official replied that enquiries were being made and the 'result will be communicated in due course'. The official suggested that the Kashmir government should be consulted for their opinion on the matter.

Following a further exchange of notes between multiple officials, there is the remark: 'We may perhaps send a reply after she reminds us.'

~

Was the government hoping Wilayat would forget about her request? Or maybe it was not something very high on the priority list of the government at that moment—in the summer of 1962 tensions between India and China were rising high, ultimately leading to the one-month Indo-China War fought in October and November of that year.

Wilayat, of course, did not forget; it was her last gambit to find a foothold for herself and her children. She was already staying in India: she informed Nehru in her letter to have 'reached Bombay by S.S. *Sabarmati* on 20 June, 1962', and requested permission to proceed to Srinagar. Though she initially mentioned four children in an enclosed letter to the State Bank of Pakistan while requesting Indian currency, she ultimately travelled with three of her children, as is clarified by her inclusion of a total of four visa numbers in her later application.

The SS *Sabarmati* was one of the boats ferrying regularly between the two port cities of Karachi and Bombay, until the Indo-Pakistan War of 1965 ended the sea link. Author Salman Rushdie describes the journey, which he made several times in his childhood with his parents and sisters, in the essay 'Step Across This Line'.

> The steamers plying that route were a pair of old rust-buckets, the Sabarmati and the Sarasvati. The journey was hot and slow, and for mysterious reasons the boats would always stop for hours off the coast of the Rann of Kutch, while unexplained cargoes were ferried on and off: smugglers' goods, I imagined eagerly, gold, or precious stones. (I was too innocent to think of drugs.)[2]

In Wilayat's next letter, addressed to the Government of India and dated 11 August 1962, she applied for Indian citizenship. Apparently, the permission to proceed to Kashmir had been granted, because this letter was written from Ganderbal, a picturesque little town about an hour's drive on a motorbike from Srinagar known for the famous Kheer Bhawani temple.

While looking for Wilayat's file in the National Archives of India, we noticed that her request was part of many such requests made from all over the world by people of Indian origin living in foreign countries such as Pakistan, including the erstwhile East Pakistan. These requests to return and settle in India followed the passing of the Indian Citizenship Act in 1955. Interestingly, many Muslims chose to return from Pakistan to India. One of the more prominent ones was Sajjad Zaheer, writer and first secretary-general of Pakistan's Communist Party. He spent four years in jail after his arrest for the Rawalpindi Conspiracy Case in 1951, and was granted Indian citizenship by Nehru after his release.

The Citizenship Act of 1955 is an important piece of legislation in India's history. In 1947, India won its freedom as an independent nation but retained the status of a British Dominion. It was only in 1950 that India relinquished its Dominion status and became a sovereign Republic, after its Constitution came into effect on 26 January 1950. Pakistan rid itself of the Dominion status in 1956.

Due to the previous status of its citizens as British citizens, a large mass of whom then became Pakistani citizens, it was necessary to define who was an Indian citizen. India had a large diaspora as well, many of whom wished to become Indian citizens, as the applications in the records of the National Archives of India show. The other aspect was of Indian acquisition of territory previously held by colonial powers such as France and Portugal, which happened after Independence. Goa, for example, was taken over in 1961 and for many years after (till 1975), Portugal did not consider Goans as Indian citizens.

The Act allowed people to claim citizenship based on birth, descent, registration and naturalization. It allowed those born in India after 1950 to claim citizenship based on their birth. In the case of those born before 1950 and domiciled in India, they automatically became Indian citizens when the Constitution came into force in 1950.

A distinction was made for those who wished to migrate from Pakistan to India. They were considered to be of Indian origin if their parents or grandparents were born in Indian territory, as defined by the Government of India Act, 1935. They could register themselves as Indian citizens if they had stayed in India for over a year before applying.

The section dealing with migrants from Pakistan, 5(1) (a), is what was referred to in the official remark to Wilayat's appeal to resettle in Pakistan. The section, at that time, read:

Subject to the provisions of this section, and such conditions and restrictions as may be prescribed, the prescribed authority may, on application made in this behalf, register as a citizen of India, any person who is not already such citizen, by virtue of the Constitution or by virtue of any of the other provisions of this Act, and belongs to any of the following categories:-
(a) Persons of Indian origin who are ordinarily resident in India and have been so resident for six months immediately before making an application for registration;

The term 'Persons of Indian origin' is explained in the footnote right after the section which consists of four other categories ends. It reads:

For the purposes of this sub-section, a person shall be deemed to be of Indian origin if he, or either of his parents, or any of his grandparents, was born in undivided India.[3]

Clearly, the ambit is so wide that anyone with roots in any part of India, Pakistan or Bangladesh could claim to be a person of Indian origin and needed to spend only a year in the country before applying for Indian citizenship. Of course, this section has since been amended multiple times to increase the period of residence required, and when the government started to issue Person of Indian Origin status cards in 2002, applicants from Pakistan were declared ineligible. But in the first decades after Partition, it allowed for many people to change their minds, to make their own decision after they followed relatives or to postpone their decision if they found themselves stranded in a third country.

However, a request to resettle in Kashmir was a special case. On the first page of the dossier, a deputy secretary's handwritten remarks say that as per government policy, 'permanent return' to Kashmir for Pakistani nationals, 'even if they are of Kashmiri extraction' is not usually allowed. But it goes on to say that 'it may be permitted to make exceptions in very special circumstances'.

―

Wilayat tried to convince the government of her special circumstances, emphasizing two things: her connection with Kashmir and, because this alone would not be enough, her political persecution in Pakistan.

In her first letter to Nehru, she started by saying that she wished to meet the Prime Minister because only he could understand her circumstances. This was perhaps an attempt to establish an emotional connection with Nehru, who was of Kashmiri origin and hailed from Allahabad in Uttar Pradesh.

The next couple of lines in her letter are intriguingly worded.

> I am submitting before you the following facts, as suffered by a Kashmiri in Pakistan, for the cause of the Nation. This will also clarify my position against any attack on me on political basis, as they have already ruined my property, health, time, children and their future.

She closed the letter by appealing to Indian authorities to consider her case favourably and to let her proceed to Srinagar 'immediately', claiming that she had 'immoveable property at Nanibug, teh: Kulgam'.

The 'cause of the nation' that Wilayat spoke of appears to be the cause of Kashmir. By remaining vague, she made it seem like the persecution must have happened for being in favour of the *Indian* position on Kashmir. But the facts suggest the opposite. As a member and former branch president of the All Jammu and Kashmir Muslim Conference, she would have been in favour of the plebiscite, with accession to Pakistan as a result or perhaps independence.

In the next paragraph, Wilayat emphasized that she had been 'forced' to leave for Pakistan, following an alleged attack on her husband, and that she had not taken a Pakistani passport until it was needed for her recent travels to India, which would show her as loyal to India.

Here, she provided more information about her husband. 'My husband died at Karachi in 1951, by poisoning, while holding the post of Secretary, Pakistan Aviation Ltd., Karachi.'

Pakistan Aviation Ltd was an institution formed by the new government to provide maintenance and repairs to the civil airlines of Pakistan as well as the Air Force.[4] Regarding the alleged poisoning, this remains unverified. We found no such reports in the newspapers of the time. It does play into the hand of the persistent rumour that Inayatullah was involved in Liaquat Ali Khan's murder. He died shortly after the murder, which could be taken as a suspicious coincidence.

The 'poisoning' is a brief, almost casual remark in Wilayat's letter, after which she went on to state that she was entitled to concession under the Transfer of Residence Rules. This was a facility that allowed those who returned to India—after having stayed abroad for a minimum of three years, although this is now reduced to two years—to bring their things back with less import duty imposed on these goods. Clearly, she had a good amount of valuable household goods to import, to request for such concessions.

Wilayat went on to describe the events of 1954, saying that she 'voiced for the Kashmiri nation in a public meeting on the 14th August 1954 at Jahangir Park' after which she suffered 'inhuman tortures' at the hands of authorities in Pakistan in various 'custodies'. It is also in this letter that she mentioned the death of a son in an Air Force crash and claimed it was a conspiracy. She said she was president of Karachi's branch of the All Jammu and Kashmir Muslim Conference at that time, which means it must have been around

1953. By giving this information, she was not entirely concealing her political allegiance, though not explaining it in detail either.

In her subsequent application to the government, Wilayat repeated some of these points. She also stated that she met the Prime Minister of Jammu and Kashmir, Bakshi Ghulam Mohammad, to discuss her case on 6 August 1962. He 'expressed his understanding and sympathies in my unique case', she wrote.

Later that month, Wilayat sent two telegrams reminding the government of her request. In late October, she wrote another letter, this time handwritten and addressed to the home minister, Lal Bahadur Shastri. It was mostly a repetition of her previous letter, but contained her views on China's attack on India, which she decried as an assault on 'our motherland'. It also had her complaining about enquiries from the intelligence sleuths.

~

It is only the next year, in January 1963, that the central government formulated its initial response to Wilayat's request, after the Kashmir government and the IB had sent their responses. It is worth quoting in full.

> On this file, we are dealing with the representation from Mrs Wilayat Butt for permission to settle down permanently in Jammu and Kashmir State. The J and K government who were consulted have no objection to her request being granted. According to information available with I.B. Mrs. Wilayat Butt or her late husband had no immovable property in village Nanibug, Tehsil Kulgam as claimed by Mrs Wilayat Butt in her representation. I.B. have, therefore, expressed the view that there is no reasonable justification in her claim for seeking resettlement facilities on that account. Mrs Wilayat Butt or her late husband, however, did not come to their adverse notice.

2. The non-possession of any immovable property in J&K State cannot perhaps be considered as a disqualification for permanent resettlement facilities in the state. Since there is nothing adverse against her, and the J&K government has no objection to her remaining in the State permanently, we may agree to her request. A draft reply to Mrs Wilayat Butt is put up. A draft letter to the government of Jammu and Kashmir is also put up. I.C. Section may please see before the file is shown to ministry of external affairs.'

(I.C. stands for the Indian Citizenship section in the home ministry.)

The government's stance seems curious. Wilayat's claims to have an association with Kashmir through property ownership and her husband's claim to belong to Kulgam were both dismissed by the IB. It said fairly categorically that there was no 'reasonable justification' for her demand to be settled in Kashmir. The only thing in her favour was that there was nothing 'adverse' against her. That was hardly any ground for allowing any ordinary returnee from Pakistan to be allowed to settle permanently in a politically sensitive region such as Kashmir.

The home ministry, however, waived off the IB's objections and focused on the lack of any 'adverse' notice about her or her family in Kashmir and used it as the basis to grant her request. Handwritten comments under this note by an official suggest that if permanent resettlement facilities were to be granted, then she would become eligible for grant of Indian citizenship under the Indian Citizenship Act passed in 1955 'under sec 5 (1) (a)', through registering herself as one.

The joint secretary dealing with the issue, however, had a different idea. He noted that as a Pakistani national, Wilayat would be eligible for staying in India on a 'year-to-year basis' if it could be shown that she was dependent on her relatives, having lost her husband, or could maintain herself only in India.

Officialdom remained divided on the issue. Another note from the F. III section, dealing with issues related to foreign nationals, which had taken over the matter, once again pointed out that Wilayat had no real reasons or grounds to seek permanent resettlement in India. But then contradicting its own stance, the note mentioned that she may still be granted residence on 'humanitarian grounds' since she was a widow and was being 'persecuted' for her views on Kashmir in Pakistan. The note observed that regardless of what her activities in Pakistan were, if they were not 'prejudicial' to India or 'anti-Indian', she may be allowed to stay in India on a 'year-to year' basis, subject to 'good behaviour'.

~

Bhola Nath Mullik, chief of the IB at the time, has more details on the period in his memoir, *My Years with Nehru*, especially about the role of the IB in managing the conflict in Kashmir. It also sheds light on the attitude the IB must have taken regarding Wilayat's case. Mullik writes, about the second half of 1949:

> The slow infiltration back of Kashmiri and Jammu Muslims, who had fled to Pakistan at the time of the partition, had also started and our information was that many of them were being deliberately sent back after being trained in subversion and propaganda. At that time the Kashmir government showed no anxiety about this process of infiltration and did not take any steps to stop it on the plausible ground that all refugees from the State had the right to come back and should be allowed to do so. Pandit Nehru, when he heard about the various attempts at subversion by Pakistan, urged us to improve our coverage further.[5]

The return of Kashmiris was a special case. While Kashmiris in Pakistan continued to be in limbo, almost stateless, in India they were considered Indian citizens as per the Delhi Agreement of 1952 between the governments of New Delhi and the state of Jammu and Kashmir. According to this agreement, the State legislature was empowered to make laws for so-called State Subjects, or Kashmiris, who had gone to Pakistan 'on account of the disturbances of 1947', if they would return to Kashmir.[6] Perhaps this is why Wilayat tried to convince the Indian government of her Kashmiri identity, and that her move to Pakistan had followed violence against her husband—which would make the move 'on account of the disturbances of 1947'.

~

The latter is, in fact, not likely. Lucknow, where Inayatullah Butt was serving as the registrar of Lucknow University, was not known for large-scale Partition violence. 'There was no riot in Lucknow,' says Amir Mohammad Khan, who has the title of Raja of Mahmudabad and is a well-known aristocrat of Lucknow.[7] We meet him in Lucknow, hoping he may have known Wilayat. He did not, but shares that two of his great-grandfathers died 'fighting the British under Hazrat Mahal' and did not believe that Wilayat was her descendant. He then provided some insight into what may have influenced the Butts's decision to move to Pakistan, as his own family lived through this highly divisive time.

The Rajas of Mahmudabad were taluqdars, a class of aristocrats with large landholdings in erstwhile Awadh, who had supported the 1857 Revolt, but later joined the British and became important partners in the colonial administration. We meet Khan in his family's house in Lucknow, a dilapidated mansion with a few large, scarcely furnished halls and a cosy living room, where he serves us chai and snacks. His was one of the families that was divided over Partition, his father being active in the Muslim League and his mother being a Hindu queen, who would never move. His father, therefore, did not immediately move either. He was mostly abroad, but ultimately took Pakistani citizenship in the 1950s, shocking the entire family.

Though Khan was born just a few years before Partition, he is aware of what happened in Lucknow. Nearing his eighties, he speaks in an upper-class English accent.

'People may have been worried about what had happened in other places. You could not be sure that there would not be a riot.' But it did not occur in Lucknow, he says, and mostly people were motivated by opportunities in Pakistan. 'The best civil servants, the best police officers, the best lawyers, the best educationists, you name it, the intelligentsia ... they went immediately,' he says.

Ishtiaq Ahmed writes the same in his biography of Jinnah:

> The prospects of a separate state for Muslims opened vistas of opportunities, which hitherto had excited only intellectuals and the intelligentsia. But with the contours of a Pakistan now associated with geography, it began to assume a tangible form. It appealed widely across the class structure to all Muslims.[8]

Citing the economist Naureen Talha and her study of economic factors behind people opting for Pakistan, he says that in Pakistan, Muslims of India saw opportunities that had so far been denied to them. Especially for army personnel and civil servants, his book suggests, Pakistan offered possibilities of faster growth in their careers.[9]

So it is likely that, even if Inayatullah experienced a personal attack, there would have been other, more compelling reasons for his move to Pakistan: for instance, the career opportunities the new state offered to well-educated Muslims. This reality would not have improved Wilayat's chances for resettlement in Kashmir. It was important to convince the Indian authorities that it had been not a choice, but a compulsion due to violence. Even then, it was not a given that her request would be approved.

We can clearly note two crucial things from Mullik's narration: one, that the IB did not support the resettlement of Kashmiri refugees, especially Muslims, who had gone to Pakistan during Partition back into Kashmir; secondly, it did not appreciate the Jammu and Kashmir government's support for the returnees. Both these factors would go on to play a role in the events surrounding Wilayat's application to resettle in Kashmir and her stay there.

In the J&K State Archives we find documents that throw more light on the situation. Confidential reports submitted to the J&K government of the time show that the local intelligence department was keeping a close eye on organizations such as the Praja Parishad (PP), which was vocal in protesting the resettlement of Pakistani Muslims back in Kashmir.

~

The Praja Parishad (PP), established in 1947, was a conservative party seeking to protect the interests of the minority Hindus in Jammu and Kashmir. It was allied with the Rashtriya Swayamsevak Sangh (RSS) and later merged with the Bharatiya Jana Sangh, an earlier incarnation of the Bharatiya Janata Party. The PP was particularly active in the Jammu region. In fact, the removal of Article 370—which gave Kashmir a special status—by the BJP government in New Delhi in August 2019 can be traced to the original demand for the same by the PP.[10]

A report submitted in the first fortnight of December 1960 noted:

> The Praja Parishad held public meetings ... wherein Shri Sahdev Singh, M.L.A., said that the government need not allow resettlement of Muslims who had migrated to Pakistan for that might prove harmful.[11]

Another report from October 1960 said:

> Shri Ram Nath, advocate, while addressing a public meeting organised by the Praja Parishad ... alleged that refugees belonging to the state have not been settled on whereas people coming from Pakistan were being allotted land.[12]

The next year, it was reported that 'thirty members of the Working Committee of the All India Bharatiya Jana Sangh arrived at Jammu on 25.8.1961, and were received by about 400 PP workers near the residence of Pt. Prem Nath Dogra'. Prem Nath Dogra was the president of PP and its best-known leader in the state. Among these members of the Bharatiya Jana Sangh who had come to Jammu was a young Atal Bihari Vajpayee, later to become India's Prime Minister. The delegation also included Balraj Madhok, who is credited with establishing the presence of the RSS in the state.

Both delivered speeches—the report noted—'complaining ... that the infiltrators from Pak were being unauthorisedly resettled'.[13]

In fact, that same month, Balraj Madhok raised a question in the Lok Sabha and asked the Ministry of Home Affairs about people from Pakistan who had been allowed to settle in J&K, especially in the past one year. He asked under what law had 'these illegal emigrants and infiltrators been allowed to stay in J & K,' and further added: 'Whether it is a fact that many of them have been acting as Pakistani agents and spies in that state?'

The J&K government responded that:

> 398 persons crossed over the Cease Fire Line from Pakistan Occupied Kashmir unauthorisedly during the period from 1st January to end of August 1961. Out of these, 15 persons were pushed back, 10 allowed to stay on, 14 prosecuted, and the cases of the remaining 359 persons are under examination.[14]

The response added:

> None of the persons mentioned above have been allowed to settle in the state permanently. It is not a fact that the persons allowed to stay on temporarily are acting as Pakistani spies.[15]

Similar questions were raised by Prakash Vir Shastri, an independent MP in the Lok Sabha, with ties to the Arya Samaj and Jana Sangh. Shastri raised concerns about alleged 'anti-national activities' of Pakistani nationals in India staying without a passport. He also contended that Pakistani nationals staying in India without passports were a source of danger to India and that they had a role to play in communal disturbances.

The government told Shastri in response to his queries that 5,687 Pakistani Muslims were residing in India without a passport according to data available till September 1960. The government admitted that a few of them had been found to be involved in 'anti-national' activities. As far as action against those 'illegally' residing in India was concerned, the government said it would go by the provisions of the Foreigners Act in this regard.

After receiving the response from the government, Shastri gave a notice to hold a discussion on the issue in the Lok Sabha. He argued that 'several thousands ton' of gunpowder had been recovered from some such Pakistani Muslims living in Uttar Pradesh and that these individuals were responsible for riots in the country.

Further contending that relations between India and Pakistan had been 'deteriorating', he wondered why such individuals were being allowed in the first place to reside in India, calling the practice 'very strange'.[16]

Among all the other concerns he had, Shastri was right about one thing. The relations between India and Pakistan were 'deteriorating', especially over Kashmir—and rather than a safe homecoming of some kind, which she may have hoped for, it was yet another place where Wilayat would be perceived as suspicious. Only this time, it would be in India, a country where she belonged to a religious minority.

The political situation in Kashmir was going through a particularly turbulent phase. Several political outfits with contrasting agenda were active in the state. One such outfit was the Plebiscite Front (PF). It was formed a couple of years after Sheikh Abdullah was arrested and jailed in 1953 by Nehru. Headed by his close aide Mirza Afzal Beg, the party demanded a plebiscite in the state.

Former civil servant Khalid Bashir Ahmad, in an article for the journalistic website Countercurrents.org, writes about the plebiscite movement:

> For two decades, beginning 1955, the people of Kashmir ran an organized, vigorous and sustained mass movement for holding of a plebiscite ... In the subsequent years, however, a rigid stand of both India and Pakistan on the withdrawal of their armed forces from Jammu & Kashmir prior to holding of a referendum blocked the implementation of the UN resolution on plebiscite.[17]

Aware of the movement's power, the intelligence department kept an eye on the activities of the PF, we noticed in the State Archives.

In August 1962, for example, it reported that the PF was raising funds for the defence of Sheikh Abdullah in the Kashmir Conspiracy Case. The Kashmir Conspiracy Case was based on allegations made against Abdullah that he had conspired with Pakistan over Kashmir. The charges were vague and were dropped in 1964.

We can see that the PF was at one end of the spectrum of public opinion in Kashmir, while the PP was at another end. The PP, other than its opposition to Muslims from Pakistan being settled in the state, opposed Article 370 and wanted it abrogated. It also wanted the state's Prime Minister to be called chief minister instead, since the country already had a Prime Minister, it reasoned. It agitated against the state having a separate Constitution and flag. All of these things would slowly come to pass, although it would take decades to ultimately amend the citizenship laws and abrogate Article 370.

Another organization active in this period was the Kashmir Political Conference (KPC), which was founded by Ghulam Mohiuddin Karra, a former associate of Sheikh Abdullah who later fell out with him. The government kept a watch on its activities too.

Both the PF and the KPC were pro-plebiscite parties. Interestingly, they were also both part of a committee formed to search for a Holy Relic that had gone missing in 1963.[18]

~

The Holy Relic incident, though overtly religious, was a landmark in Kashmiri politics.

A decade had passed since Sheikh Abdullah's dismissal from power by Nehru. After Abdullah, Bakshi Ghulam Mohammad came to power as the Prime Minister of Kashmir. Although he is credited with some lasting measures, especially in the field of education, and for his hands-on style of administration, his regime became tainted with charges of corruption.

By 1963, he had lost his popularity. The Valley was seeking a change and it came about through a scandal that shook the entire apparatus of state administration.

When the Indian–American writer Ved Mehta travelled to Kashmir a few years later, he found there was still unrest about the strange developments.

The Hazratbal Shrine in Srinagar has had special relevance for Kashmiri Muslims, writes Mehta, 'since it had been the repository of a strand of Mohammad's hair since the beginning of the eighteenth century, when the strand was brought to Kashmir.'[19]

In 1963, this relic was mysteriously stolen from the mosque. 'The news swept through Srinagar. All offices and shops, schools and colleges were closed. The streets were cleared of all buses, taxis, tongas, rickshaws, and bicycles, and the waterways of all boats. In every house and every hut the hearth fire was extinguished, as at a death in the family,' Mehta writes. People came out in the streets and spontaneous protests started. The anger of the public against Bakshi, who as a National Conference leader was pro-India, was expressed through the burning and looting of his properties, including those that belonged to his relatives. At the time the protests began, Bakshi had already resigned and a protégé of his, Khwaja Shamsuddin, had taken over, but the public did not think it made much difference.

Mullik, in his memoir, gives a detailed account of the episode. Under a lot of pressure, Mullik somehow succeeded in bringing the Holy Relic back, which was approved as authentic by Kashmir's most well-regarded saint, Fakir Mirak Shah. The entire agitation over the Holy Relic was analysed by many as essentially political.

Khalid Bashir Ahmad, in his article for Countercurrents.org, argues:

> The Plebiscite Front leadership successfully turned a massive public outburst over the theft of the Holy Relic from the Hazratbal Shrine in December 1963 into a mass agitation for the release of Abdullah from jail.[20]

Historian Hafsa Kanjwal, in her dissertation, writes that the movement that followed the theft can itself be seen as support for the demand for the plebiscite, considering the involvement of the pro-plebiscite parties.[21]

The root cause was the people's anger against Bakshi's corrupt and repressive regime, and Shamsuddin was widely seen as his man, so he had to be replaced. The person who took over was G.M. Sadiq, a key lieutenant of Sheikh Abdullah. He had formed his own leftist party, the Democratic National Conference, along with Durga Prasad Dhar. It was a splinter group that had broken away from the National Conference. Both its main leaders later rejoined the National Conference and Sadiq joined Nehru's Indian National Congress in 1961. In 1964, Sadiq became Prime Minister of the state, a position which was renamed as chief minister in 1965.

Sadiq, a communist, was no less pro-India than Bakshi and Shamsuddin, so the argument that Indian rule itself was anathema to the public would not be entirely accurate. Even if Sadiq was not as popular as Sheikh Abdullah, he was certainly not as despised as Bakshi, and he managed to hold on to power till 1971, when he died. In his years in power, he moved Kashmir closer to India.

∼

All this while, the government's Kashmir Bureau of Information was following the reactions in Pakistan, especially in Pakistan-administered Kashmir, over developments in Kashmir. It was doing this by following the newspapers in Pakistan, such as *Dawn* and *Pakistan Times*,[22] among other measures.[23]

Sardar Ibrahim, one of the founders of the Muslim Conference, was reported to have made a speech during this period in which he said 'after a democratic government had been established in the Pak-held area, a struggle should be launched for liberation of the State on the lines of the Algerian Freedom movement'.

Interestingly, Sardar Ibrahim added that 'Pakistan should repudiate the military alliances if her allies did not support her Kashmir policy'.[24]

The reference to the 'military alliances' suggests treaties such as the South East Asia Treaty Organization (SEATO) and the Mutual Defense Agreement Pact that Pakistan had signed with the United States. Perhaps he was also aware that these treaties had made the plebiscite a difficult if not impossible proposition. It is also likely such statements would not have been taken kindly by the Pakistani authorities as the treaties concerned the security of the entire country, of which the region Azad Kashmir was a part.

Another note citing a report from the same period quotes Ayub Khan, the army general who ruled Pakistan as President from 1959 to 1968, after the military coup of 1958. He described the Indian position on Kashmir, post Pakistan's signing of military alliances with the US, as 'hypocrisy', since 'India had been dishonouring her commitments about Kashmir much before Pakistan got into these pacts'.[25]

The confidential papers also report on angry reactions by the Pakistan and Azad Kashmir governments to a statement made by Nehru that, 'Plebiscite had become a joke'.[26]

Meanwhile, approaches were being made to Sheikh Abdullah, while he was in jail, through Mridula Sarabhai, who was in touch with him on behalf of Nehru. In *Pakistan Times*, a report published that: 'Pandit Nehru had expressed his readiness to even consider the formula of loose federation of Jammu and Kashmir State with India should the Sheikh give up his demand for plebiscite in the State'.[27]

～

Despite the worsening relationship between India and Pakistan over Kashmir, and the strong objections some sections of civil society, politics and the IB had against Muslims from Pakistan resettling in Kashmir, Wilayat managed to convince the authorities to allow her to do that. However, she could not prove any connection to the state.

The IB's note to the government categorically states that Wilayat and her husband owned no properties in Kulgam. It adds that her husband had tried, 'long before Partition', to get the Butt families of Nanibug village to back him up in attempts to get a certificate of domicile from the state government, but had failed in his endeavour.[28] This could have meant that Inayatullah, like many who supported the

Muslim League—and since Wilayat was an office bearer of the party in Pakistan, it is quite possible they were associated with the party in India too—thought Kashmir would go to Pakistan.

The IB note, hence, concludes that while there were no adverse reports against them as such, there were no 'reasonable grounds' on which to recommend their continued stay in Kashmir, as they had no actual connection to Kashmir and that the husband's claims to belong to the state were not corroborated.

This is where the matter should have ended. But it did not. The IB's note, which contradicted Wilayat's claims, was ignored and the government proceeded to take Wilayat on face value, not even bothering to investigate her self-disclosed links with the All Jammu and Kashmir Muslim Conference whose politics were not by any stretch favourable to India.

The government seems to have proceeded on the assumption that just because Wilayat had political differences with the Government of Pakistan, she was sympathetic to India's position on Kashmir. It may seem so on a superficial level because she was in favour of a plebiscite. That was her party's position and India too wanted a plebiscite, at least till 1954. But Wilayat's party wanted a plebiscite hoping that as a result Kashmir would either merge with Pakistan or become independent. An outcome that would favour India did not figure in her party's plans.

The central government did have a few queries, and they were sent to the government in J&K for a response in the beginning of the month of March in 1963. The central government wanted to know how Wilayat had maintained herself after the death of her husband; why she did not apply for Indian citizenship earlier; how she planned to maintain herself in India and whether her claims about having relatives in Kashmir were true. It also asked the state government to confirm whether Wilayat could not continue to stay in Pakistan instead of seeking settlement in Kashmir.

The state government sent its reply a couple of months later. Its response more or less repeated what Wilayat herself had stated in her letters. It said that Wilayat had maintained herself in Pakistan after the death of her husband by selling her ornaments. On the issue of why she did not seek Indian citizenship earlier, the letter contended that she tried to leave Pakistan, but was not allowed by the Pakistani authorities 'owing to her political differences with that government'. It added that she had some relatives in Pakistan, but was 'unaware if they are alive or dead'. It then repeated her assertion, denied by the IB, that she had some land and relatives in Kulgam, and Bijbehara, and even an orchard in Ganderbal. It mentions that she had a son, who was a matriculate, and she hoped he could find a job in Kashmir. Finally, the letter stated that it would be difficult for her to maintain herself in Kashmir. This last bit was probably a hint that she should be given a monetary allowance.

Following the response from the state government, the central government decided to allow Wilayat to 'stay on in India as Pakistani nationals by granting them extensions of stay on a year-to-year basis, subject to good behaviour'. It added, 'This will not make them eligible to apply for the grant of Indian citizenship under the Citizenship Act, 1955.'

Curiously, the government changed its position soon after. In another letter to Wilayat, it 'advised' her 'to take steps to acquire Indian Citizenship by applying for registration under section 5(1) of the Indian Citizenship Act, 1955'. The same position was also conveyed to the state government of Jammu and Kashmir.[29]

From then onwards, Wilayat and her children spent close to a decade in Kashmir, leaving the state in the first half of the 1970s.

Transformation

From the 1940s to the 1980s, Wilayat underwent multiple transformations. In Lucknow, she had been known as the wife of Mr Butt. In Karachi, she became Begum Wilayat Butt, a political and Kashmiri activist in her own right. And in Delhi, she was Wilayat Mahal, Queen of Awadh. In between, there were about thirteen years in Kashmir. Who had she been there? And why did the Indian government allow her to resettle in Kashmir? To this, we still don't have a clear answer.

We start our investigation in the place where Inayatullah had tried and failed to get domicile status—even though the IB had dismissed Wilayat's claims of owning land there. The village Nanibug, in Kulgam district, is around 100 kilometres away from Srinagar.

Nanibug turns out to be the name of a village and a tehsil or a block, with several villages falling under it. In the village, no one has heard of Inayatullah Butt or anyone from his family, including the elderly whom we spoke to. But they say nearby there is a village with many Butt families, Kanipora or Nasirabad.

We spend some time in this village, and after some asking around we meet Nisar Bhat, who tells us that all the Butt or Bhat[1] families of the village we have arrived at are members of the same larger clan, divided in four sub-clans—Lone, Dar, Paddar, Bhat—and that they are all Ahmadi Muslims.[2]

Nisar Bhat's father, Abdul Qadir Bhat, used to be a contractor and the family now runs a school in the area. Abdul Qadir Bhat is also an amateur historian, we find out, and he has painstakingly archived the details of all the Butt families in the area since 1794, which is the year they came to settle here. Earlier, they were in another nearby village called Sryundoo. The total population of the Butt clan in the area is 1,500. All of them belong to the thirteen families that first settled here. The entire land used to be owned by a Dogra landlord till 1953, we are told. In 1953, land reforms were initiated by Sheikh Abdullah as part of his New Kashmir manifesto, and that was when the feudal system of landowning was finally dismantled in Kashmir.

According to Nisar Bhat, the village boasts of '100 per cent education' with most people engaged in government jobs. 'We have 35 PhD scholars in the village. Around 200 have qualifications up to MA and MSc. Many are doctors and engineers. Some are based in America.' He claims that Dr Abdus Salam, the Pakistani scientist who won the Nobel Prize in physics in 1979, belonged to their community. 'I met him in 1981 in Kadian,' says his father.

However, we are unable to link Inayatullah Butt to the village, as no record exists in the archive maintained by Abdul Qadir Bhat which, according to him, consisted of government records he had collected over the years. This leaves us with two options: one, the IB was correct to say that Inayatullah did not belong to this village regardless of his claims; and two, even if he did belong to Nanibug, since his family migrated from Kashmir there are no records to prove his connection to this village—especially since we do not know what his parents or grandparents were called.

From the National Archives papers we discussed in the previous chapter, it became clear that Wilayat's application for resettlement was mostly supported by the J&K government. The IB saw 'no reasonable justification' for it and the central government ultimately allowed it based on the advice of the J&K government alone.[3]

The person who was in power in the state for almost the entire period Wilayat lived there was G.M. Sadiq, the politician who had been close to Sheikh Abdullah and who took over as Prime Minister of J&K in 1964. He had just joined Nehru's party, Indian National Congress, when Wilayat applied for resettlement, and his stock was rising. To understand why his government supported Wilayat's resettlement despite IB opposition, we seek out his grandson, Iftekhar Sadiq.

It proves a difficult task to meet him in the first few days of our arrival in Kashmir. We do not have his address to start with, or any contact number. Online, a list of those who are protected by security forces in Srinagar includes him, but his address is not specified beyond stating the name of the colony. It lies near the Dal Lake, but without a specific address we do not know how to find him.

It is the start of June when we arrive, the peak of the tourist season. It has been peaceful so far, but tension is brewing. For one, the controversial film *Kashmir Files* has just been released and is receiving a lot of attention all over the country. Violence and hate speech triggered by the film have also been reported from some places.[4,5] The film has been criticized as a work of propaganda, which demonizes left-wing activists and the Kashmiri Muslim community over the exodus of the Hindu Kashmiri Pandit community during the early 1990s, when an insurgency against the Indian state began.[6,7] People in Kashmir are also talking about it.

Another issue that concerns Kashmiris is the arrest and trial of Yasin Malik for an act of terror committed in the 1990s.[8] Malik is a leader of the JKLF, which was earlier involved in armed insurrection, but has now given it up. Malik has been courted by the powers-that-be in Delhi over the years, so his arrest after so many years is being resented. During the same period, the Valley is on edge because of a series of targeted murders of Kashmiri Pandits and other Hindus. The month we visit, a thirty-six-year-old man had been shot dead in his house by militants.[9]

We ask those we know in Srinagar for Iftekhar Sadiq's address or contact number, but no one seems to have any idea. We know that he has been associated with the BJP, so we consider going to the BJP office to find out. But we are spared the effort as we end up meeting a playwright who is well-connected and gets us his address. We are told that the residence is heavily guarded.

The next day, we set out to find it. After walking for almost half an hour in the bylanes of colonies that lie behind the numerous ghats of the Dal Lake, under a gentle sun, with roses blooming in the balconies of many beautiful, old houses—and stopping on our way to sample local Kashmiri bread from a bakery—we find the house.

It is indeed barricaded and covered with barbed wire. An armed sentry guards the main door. We produce our identification papers. The guard takes them inside. We wait.

He comes out and says Iftekhar Sadiq cannot meet us, but he is willing to speak over the phone. We agree and share a mobile number.

We soon receive a call. The voice on the other end is gentle, with the trace of an upper-class English accent. He asks about our purpose behind seeking him out.

Satisfied when we tell him, he apologizes for not meeting in person. He is worried about Covid-19, he says, and complains about the lax attitude of people about it. He believes it is still a potent threat.

Before meeting him, we had looked him up online. We had found one article in the *Telegraph* in which he was interviewed on the removal of Article 370, which granted special status to Kashmir, almost three years earlier. The article mentioned that his father, Rafiq Sadiq, and grandfather, G.M. Sadiq, were both pro-India and so was he. Iftikhar himself was quoted as saying the roots of Indian democracy were 'very strong and deep' in Kashmir. He had expressed his displeasure with the special status being abrogated, as it was not doing any harm, and desired the return of statehood, which had also been taken away, turning Kashmir into a Union Territory along with Jammu, while Ladakh became a separate Union Territory.[10]

A fifty-three-year-old doctor-turned-businessman, Iftekhar Sadiq was born during Wilayat's stay and is too young to remember her and her children, but he came to know about them through discussions that took place at home, at times at the dinner table. 'Politics was discussed at home all the time.'

He tells us that his grandfather was very popular as a politician in Ganderbal—which explains that Wilayat was staying here, while waiting for the response to her application for resettlement.

Wilayat, Inayatullah and Sadiq went way back, reveals Iftekhar. Lahore is where they first met before Independence. Sadiq visited this city regularly and stayed there from 1942 onwards, to avoid arrest in the turbulent years before Independence.

∼

Lahore was known for its educational institutes, says Iftekhar. 'The best doctors of Srinagar were all educated in Lahore, at the Lahore Medical College. Some of the old actors, like Dilip Kumar and Dev Anand, were educated in Lahore. All the well-to-do people used to go to Lahore to study.'

Other than that, Lahore was a centre of Kashmiri nationalism. 'The movement was predominantly run from the other side, as it could have had ramifications on this side of the border,' says

Iftekhar. The latter part was especially true for the years after the 1930s, with newspapers based there writing in favour of Kashmiri Muslims, political organizations working for them and a supportive intelligentsia.

In 1938, when the Muslim Conference changed its name to the National Conference, Sadiq, who was close to Sheikh Abdullah, presided over the session. Abdullah, in his memoir, explains the reason behind having Sadiq chair the session:

> On 10 and 11 June 1938 the Muslim Conference held a special session at Shahi Masjid, under the chairmanship of Sadiq. His elders had been associated with the movement right from the beginning. While he was still a student at Aligarh University, I had sent him and Beg telegrams inviting them to come to contest election as the Muslim Conference candidates. Like every human being, Sadiq had many failings but he had firm conviction in secular politics, and in the long debate carried out in this regard, he had evinced his emancipation as well as his steadfastness. He represented a forward-looking new generation.[11]

From the late 1930s, communists began to exert a greater influence on Kashmiri politics. Just like Lahore became a centre of Kashmiri nationalism and its proponents, Srinagar too began to see intellectuals from Lahore arriving there and mixing with the local leadership. Intellectuals and artistes such as Faiz, Mulk Raj Anand and Balraj Sahni were attracted by the left turn of Kashmiri politics, writes historian and journalist Andrew Whitehead, who has worked extensively on communism and Kashmir.[12] Part of this same group was the couple B.P.L. Bedi and his English wife, Freda Bedi, who went on to have a long and deep association with Kashmir.

It left its mark on Srinagar of today, says Iftekhar Sadiq, referring to the name of the well-known central square of the old city: Lal Chowk, which means Red Square. 'Lal Chowk was selected as a name as a tribute to the Bolshevik revolution. It was in consultation with Balraj Sahni, B.P.L. Bedi and I.K. Gujral. It was a unanimous decision.'[13]

The Bedis were quite active in the Indian freedom struggle when they lived in Lahore, a decade or so before Partition. Both husband and wife had studied in Oxford where they were part of a group of students with Marxist leanings. Indeed, one of their contemporaries at Oxford in the early 1930s was Sajjad Zaheer—the noted communist from Lucknow who would later move to Pakistan and be arrested in the Rawalpindi Conspiracy Case, before moving back to India again. Zaheer had a short affair with a friend of Freda Bedi's, Olive Shapley, while in Oxford, Andrew Whitehead writes in his biography of Freda Bedi.[14]

According to Whitehead, the Bedis started to become more and more involved in Kashmiri nationalism through their friendships with Sheikh Abdullah and G.M. Sadiq. B.P.L. Bedi is credited to have put together the New Kashmir manifesto, which formed the basis for Abdullah's rule following Partition. The document that advocated measures such as Land to the Tiller and led to comprehensive land reforms later in the state, and championed the rights of women, has always been considered to have been essentially a communist initiative.

Freda Bedi was also active in the women's militia, another novel initiative undertaken in Kashmir before Partition, with Begum Zainab, the sister of Sadiq, as one of its principal recruits.

In 1946, the Quit Kashmir movement was launched by Sheikh Abdullah against the Maharaja. While Abdullah himself was arrested as the Maharaja clamped down on the agitation, leaders like Sadiq escaped to Lahore. Activists in Lahore, especially the Bedis, remained in touch with them, with Freda even acting as a courier at times, delivering messages.

After Independence, the Bedis rose to prominence in Kashmiri politics, as advisors to Abdullah, but since the Communist Party of India changed its stance on allying with 'bourgeois' parties such as Abdullah's National Conference, they were mostly operating on their own. After 1953, when Abdullah's government was dismissed, they lost their main source of political patronage and left the state. Freda, who knew Jawaharlal Nehru personally, became involved with editing a magazine published by the Planning Commission and later became a Buddhist nun. B.P.L. turned to the occult and did not do anything particularly politically noteworthy afterwards.[15]

~

Iftekhar Sadiq makes a stunning revelation. According to him, Wilayat was once part of the same leftist Kashmiri nationalist group as Sadiq and the Bedis in Lahore. After three phone calls and probing him on this question, Sadiq remains insistent: 'Your lady was part of this group.' Most likely, her husband would have known them as well, which raises the question of whether he had leftist leanings, too. Inayatullah knowing some of the Rawalpindi conspirators closely would provide another clue as to why he may have been rumoured to be part of the Liaquat assassination. Faiz was part of the group and Sajjad Zaheer, like Inayatullah, had come to Pakistan from Lucknow. It is very possible the two families knew each other in Pakistan, as they were from a similar social milieu and had moved there from the same place. In fact, when Wilayat returned to Lucknow, she insisted on meeting a brother of Sajjad Zaheer: Ali Zaheer, India's first ambassador to Iran who served as law minister in the Uttar Pradesh government.

This new information makes Wilayat's transformation even more remarkable. How could she have changed so radically from a leftist activist to the royalist she became later in life? The last phase of this transformation happened in Kashmir.

~

Wilayat, Asad, Ali Raza and Sakina started their stay in Ganderbal, which we learnt was a stronghold of Sadiq, who was a cabinet minister at that time. In one of her letters to the government, appealing for the adoption of Indian nationality on 11 August 1962, she wrote down as her address: Rest House, Ganderbal. During our first visit, we couldn't find it. But then we get more information from an unexpected source. The son of Raja Mahmudabad, whom we had met in Lucknow, texted us on WhatsApp. Ali Khan Mahmudabad is a historian and social scientist and first responded to a message of Alim Jafri, a Lucknow-based journalist who had been assisting us in our research. 'Salaam. She was from Kashmir, actually. One theory is that her husband was involved in the assassination of Liaquat Ali Khan.' When we contacted Ali after that, he texted: 'I'm in Srinagar. You should make a trip here, because people remember her from when she was at school! My wife's aunt I think was in school with her.'

Through Facebook we contact Khan's father-in-law, Iftikhar Drabu, an engineer who worked in Ganderbal with the Kashmir government's Public Works Department (PWD) in the 1980s. He lives in Ghaziabad, near Delhi, these days and we speak to him over the phone. Wilayat lived in the PWD guesthouse, he says. 'From the caretaker of the guesthouse I heard a story of a lady who had come from Pakistan in the '60s and had been put up in the guesthouse by the government,' he says. Sadly, the caretaker of that time passed away just a few months before we speak. 'I remember he told me she had dogs, for her security,' Drabu says.

Later, coincidentally, Drabu married a former neighbour of the family, in Brein, Srinagar, where Wilayat and her children were housed after Ganderbal. Brein lies behind the terraced Mughal garden Nishat Bagh, east from the Dal Lake. Drabu's wife and sister-in-law lived in the same street at the time. We call the sister-in-law, Sabia Rashid, now in her sixties and a doctor, who is still based in Srinagar. She says she was a small child when Wilayat lived there and does not remember much. 'I only saw them from a distance.' But she gives us the address, Water Works Road, and says that the house is now a government school.

Drabu also shares the phone number of one of his cousins, Nighat Shafi. She had recognized Sakina in a photo one day, as a former classmate. She still lives in Srinagar.

Encouraged by all this new information, we decide it's time for another trip to Kashmir, starting with Ganderbal.

~

Ganderbal is a small town close to Srinagar. The famous Amarnath Cave, a pilgrimage site for Hindus, is located here, as well as the Kheer Bhawani temple. Nearby are two tourist-favoured sites, Sonmarg and the Manasbal Lake. The town used to be a part of Srinagar, but it was carved into a new district with a separate administration in 2007.[16]

Following Drabu's directions, we find the PWD guesthouse located across the bridge that divides the town into two parts. It has been converted into the block medical officer's (BMO) office. It is a two-storey structure, designed in the old style with a sloping roof and has wooden furnishing. It takes some effort to find it.

The entrance to the building is covered with water, as it has been raining for the past few days. We go inside by walking around it, stepping on bricks and stones placed at its edge.

On the ground floor, we find an office running out of a largish hall, with computers and other paraphernalia. But the two employees working there have no clue about the antecedents of the building.

The BMO, a middle-aged woman, tells us she joined recently and does not know anything about the building's history or who lived there before. A wooden board inside her office shows that it had officers serving as BMO for short terms of one or two years since 2012.

We come out, slightly disappointed, and decide to ask around in the shops that flank the old guesthouse, with a park in front of it called Qamariya Park.

In a stationery shop, we find a retired X-ray technician called Ali Mohammad Dar. To our surprise, Dar instantly recognizes the family when we tell him about them. He offers us tea in his small shop, which has a printer taking up one-third of the space and stationery items for sale. 'I am retired now from all work. This shop is just to pass time and to receive guests.' Dar worked for over three decades at the Sri Maharaja Hari Singh hospital. He is now in his seventies.

As we sit down, he begins to tell us what he remembers from the time when Wilayat and her children lived next door to his family.

Dar was at the cusp of teenage when they came to live in the PWD guesthouse, he tells us. His family had five children—two sisters and three brothers—including him; he is the eldest. Today, his own children are grown up and working. His two sons work as a dental technician and as a lecturer in a college, respectively. His only daughter is married and has three children.

He remembers that Ali Raza and Sakina, who was then called Zohra, studied in a government school in Ganderbal. Dar's family owned a small factory, where they made rotis to sell in bulk on a tandoor. He would at times go inside their home to deliver rotis. 'They had very good Persian carpets with them ... They were quite amiable in their interactions with others. They were Shias but they celebrated and participated in all the festivals. They would invite my parents home as well during these festivals. They visited our home too. Our families had good relations. They were good-natured people,' he told us, occasionally stopping to sell a pen or some other item to a student.

He praised Wilayat for being kind and affable. 'She always spoke nicely to us. She treated me like a son. She had requested my parents to watch out for her children. Their sister [Sakina] was also very nice.'

As he narrates a specific incident, his face contorts, as if he is trying to check an overflow of emotions: 'After they left, she [Wilayat] called us to Brein. I accompanied my father, and a few of us from here went to meet her. The meeting made her emotional and she started to cry. She said she missed our company. What can I tell you about her?! She was a very nice person,' he says, his voice choking as he tries not to cry. 'I remember them at times.'

His wife arrives with the tea. 'Even she remembers them,' he says. 'I have told my children about them.'

As we talk, vehicles pass through the busy street, honking loudly. During Muharram, they would bring sherbet and halwa, says Dar. 'She would always consult my mother before taking any initiatives or decisions.'

He has memories of playing cricket with the brothers. Asad was the captain of the area's local team, he said. They would at times play matches with other local teams of the area. While Asad was a spinner, Ali Raza bowled fast. 'Initially, she told us she would be staying for five to six months. But they stayed on for two to three years.' Based on what she wrote in her letters to Nehru, we ask him if they owned any orchards or any kind of property in Ganderbal, but Dar said he was not aware of any such thing.

Suddenly, he shouts out to an acquaintance passing by for the number of a friend he wishes us to speak to. The excitement in his voice is palpable.

The carpets the family possessed caught the eye of locals. According to Dar, people used to come from Srinagar to buy carpets from them. 'Once, an uncle of mine came to buy, but it did not work out.' Dar's mother negotiated on behalf of his uncle, but the latter was not offering the kind of money Wilayat expected.

Dar remembers the family having one small dog back then. He has memories of the children riding bicycles. 'To go to Srinagar, they would take a bus.' In those days, a bus service ran between Ganderbal and Srinagar twice daily.

According to Dar, the family enjoyed a good reputation in Ganderbal. 'People used to respect them. The family members were also respectful to others,' he said.

After we finish our tea, we once again visit the guesthouse with Dar. According to him, after the family left, tourists started staying at the guesthouse. In 1992, he says the CRPF took over the building. Some years later, it finally ended up with the health department, which started operating it as a health centre.

Dar says in those days there was no boundary wall, like there is today. After crossing a lawn, we enter the building. He shows us the living quarters of the family on the first floor, where there are three small rooms. Wilayat and the children lived separately, but Sakina slept with her mother. The family lived in two rooms and used one room as a kitchen. The hall on the ground floor where there are computers today was where they kept their things. Behind the house was a well, from which they drew water. It is difficult to locate it now as the backyard of the building is overgrown with wild vegetation.

Dar tells us Wilayat was fond of sitting in the balcony that faced the street outside. 'She would sit and sometimes talk to visitors who approached her from here.'

The family had trunks to keep their things and little else in terms of furniture, except the carpets. 'They bought kitchen utensils from the market here,' Dar says.

After we come out of the building and take a few pictures, we ask Dar if he wants to see any pictures of the family that we have saved on our phone. He agrees, so we show him some photos. He recognizes everyone instantly. When he sees Sakina's picture, he is more moved than with pictures of other family members. He presses the screen to his lips, as soon as he sees her photo and kisses her, his eyes closed in ecstasy and perhaps agony, too.

Later, Dar asks us if anyone from the family is still alive. We tell him the bad news. He seems heartbroken. 'Had they been alive, I would have travelled with you to Delhi to meet them,' he says, his voice heavy with regret.

~

On our second trip to Ganderbal, Dar introduces us to his friend Ghulam Ahmad, a retired machine operator. A wizened old man now, he was around eight years old when the family came to live in the guesthouse. 'Ali, Raza and Zohra!' he exclaims, when reminded by Dar of the family—referring to Asad as Ali, indicating that he, too, went by different names.

'They used to feed us and give us sherbet on their Big Day,' he says, with evident relish, referring to Muharram, which the family used to commemorate.

The other memory he has is of Wilayat swimming in the river. 'She was a formidable swimmer!'

He offers to show us a tree in the park where the children had carved out names of personages holy to Shias, among them Fatima, Hassan and Hussain. We walk with him to it.

It is a tall chinar tree, with a thick hide and heavy boughs. The names once scratched on its bark have faded, and nothing can be seen anymore. 'It has been such a long time,' Ahmad says ruefully, by way of explanation.

He remembers both the brothers as star cricketers. He did not play with them as he was quite young and competitive matches featured older players, but he would watch. 'Teams from Srinagar used to come to play with local teams here. Both the brothers were deadly bowlers. We used to feel very happy whenever they played on our side,' he recounts.

We have walked to the edge of the park, from where we can see the river flowing underneath, a small beach leading up to it; its expanse is quite wide. 'She could swim across the river and then back, which is not easy. There used to be strong currents in the water.' She did not swim every day, he says. When she did, she was always wearing a sari.

He remembers Wilayat as being stocky of build and tall. 'Ali, Raza, Zohra, all of them were tall.'

It is time for the azan and the air is filled with its sounds, emanating from a nearby mosque. Ahmad had no idea, he tells us, where the family was from. 'They were not Kashmiris, although Bibiji [which is what they used to call Wilayat] spoke a little bit of Kashmiri.'

Across the river is a government school from those days. Ahmad remembers the principal of the school becoming extremely happy whenever Ali would turn up to play for the school team against visiting teams from Srinagar.

Like Ali Mohammad Dar, he too used to visit their house on Muharram. 'They would catch hold of us and take us inside to feed us. She used to love us children a lot.'

~

Till now, we have not been able to get a clear answer to the question of how old Wilayat and her children were when they arrived in Kashmir.

In 1975, *Hindustan Times* reported Wilayat to be forty-five, Asad twenty, Sakina nineteen and Raza seventeen.[17]

In one letter from 1962 that is part of the MHA file, Wilayat writes that her younger children are thirteen, seventeen and nineteen.[18] Her own age was reported to be forty-five in one of the *Dawn* articles of 1954.[19] Either this was wrong, or she must have looked very young for her age for the *HT* reporter not to notice the twenty-year discrepancy in 1975. In any case, *HT* could have been wrong about the children's ages, as they must have been born before Inayatullah's death in 1951. Unless, of course, they were not his children, which is not a theory for which we have found any evidence.

To get a closer idea, we ask Sakina's former classmate, Drabu's cousin. Nighat Shafi belongs to an old politically connected family in Kashmir. Her maternal grandfather, Ghulam Ahmad Ashai, was the first registrar of Kashmir University and close to Sheikh Abdullah. We speak on the phone, because she is supposed to leave for the US the next day and is busy arranging her travel.

She went to school with Sakina at Presentation Convent, a Christian missionary school located in Raj Bagh, an affluent locality in Srinagar; the school was founded before Independence.

'She was in my class for about one or two years,' Shafi tells us. Shafi was born in 1950 and estimates that Sakina was the same age as her when they were classmates. 'Her name was Marzia Ali,' Shafi remembers. Asked if she used the surname Butt, Shafi affirms: 'Yes, her name was Butt.'

By this account, Sakina and Ali Raza must both have been born in Karachi, shortly after one another and shortly before, or in Ali Raza's case possibly even after, their father's death. They were preteens when they reached Ganderbal and young teenagers when they moved to Srinagar, and Sakina changed her name from Zohra to Marzia.

'There were fewer Muslim girls at the school and more girls from other countries, especially those whose parents were working for the United Nations,' reminisces Shafi, who runs a well-known NGO called HELP Foundation, under which a range of social activities such as education for underprivileged children, counselling and economic support for women are undertaken.

Shafi remembers Sakina as being 'aloof' at school—quite the change from when she lived in Ganderbal, where she is till today remembered so fondly by Dar and Ahmad. 'She used to say she was neither from Kashmir nor from India, so we assumed she must have been from Pakistan or Iran. We found it very strange that she had managed to arrive in Srinagar from Pakistan. Children would talk about her among themselves and speculate if she were a princess.'

According to Shafi, Sakina hardly interacted with the other students. They did not know about her family or whether she had brothers. Other children used to maintain some distance from Sakina due to her mysterious background; her connection to Pakistan was something that made other children wary, as such a thing was frowned upon in those days in Kashmir, as an indication of treasonous behaviour. 'We did not want to get into trouble as the nuns were quite strict about these things.' As historian Hafsa Kanjwal has shown in her dissertation, even uttering the word 'Pakistan' could land you in trouble in that period, when successive governments of Jammu and Kashmir, especially those that came to power after 1953, were trying their best to move Kashmir closer to India.[20]

'What was even more difficult to understand was that how she could have received an Indian passport, despite having come from Pakistan, and been allowed to settle in Kashmir. My grandmother, for example, had been denied a passport since we had relatives on the other side of the border; three of her sons had moved to Pakistan after Partition and we were branded as Pakistani agents. We used to be tracked by spies. Even visiting the Pakistan embassy was considered treason.'

Her own family, despite being from Kashmir, were harassed by the Bakshi regime for their links to Pakistan, she says. 'Every regime branded people. Since my maternal grandfather was close to Sheikh Abdullah, he was arrested and tortured. My uncles, too, were arrested and my cousins had to flee in order to save their lives.'

Speculating why they may have been given the right to stay in India, Shafi's cousin Drabu, in another phone call, brings up the Liaquat assassination rumour. 'It was said that her husband had been part of an Indian government ploy in the conspiracy to kill Liaquat Ali Khan, and that this was the reason the Indian government gave them refuge.' Having seen her appeal to the Indian government for resettlement, and the fact that she came more than a decade after Khan's murder, this theory is very unlikely, and Drabu does not believe it anymore. He is convinced that Wilayat had connections in leftist Kashmiri nationalist circles. 'The communist link must have been there. Because of the kind of support she was getting during Sadiq's time.'

In order to understand better how Sadiq could have supported Wilayat, despite the political climate of suspicion against Muslims from Pakistan, we contact Vijay Dhar, son of Durga Prasad Dhar, a close associate of G.M. Sadiq. D.P. Dhar died in 1975, but his son Vijay has been based in Srinagar throughout. Born in 1941, he was in his early twenties when Wilayat arrived on the scene.

Our first attempt to meet Dhar is unsuccessful; we reach the private school in Srinagar that he runs, but he is unexpectedly busy with an official inspection. However, the same evening he invites us to his residence on the posh Gupkar Road in Srinagar.

An armed guard seeks our identification at the gate and asks us to write down our names in a register, after which we are allowed to proceed. We go down a winding path lined with trees including a red maple tree, and a Krishna statue in black marble. The house looks big and spacious from the outside; the veranda has a few chairs and a table, with many photos in black and white on the walls. A servant asks us to sit in the portico.

Vijay Dhar joins us after a few minutes. We tell him the purpose of our visit. He tells us he did not know Wilayat in Kashmir, and heard of her only after she shifted to the railway station in

Delhi. He used to be an informal advisor to Rajiv Gandhi, who became Prime Minister after his mother, Indira Gandhi, was assassinated in 1984—and that was when Dhar first came to know of Wilayat.

Dhar remembers the early 1960s, when Wilayat resettled in Kashmir, as a tumultuous period. 'The Moi-e-Muqqadas [Holy Relic] agitation was the worst in the history of Kashmir. India had lost Kashmir. No less than a lakh people came out on the streets to agitate. The tide turned against Bakshi.'

It was around this time that Sadiq again fell out with Bakshi. The next year he became chief minister of the state. Soon after, war broke out between India and Pakistan in 1965. He says his father, D.P. Dhar, had dreamt of a war just before. 'A general called my father before the war broke out to inform him that something was afoot. It was afternoon and he was asleep. I was asked to wake him as the general said on the telephone it was something urgent. When my father woke up, he said he was dreaming of an armed uprising like the Algerian one taking place in Kashmir.'

In the years leading up to the war, there had been talks over the Kashmir issue between Nehru and the Pakistani President, Ayub Khan, but nothing concrete had materialized. In 1964, Abdullah was released from jail and the talks continued, but once again there was little agreement on any formula to resolve the issue. Nehru passed away on 27 May 1964. Abdullah was once again arrested in 1965. The situation had reached a dead end when war broke out.

Lal Bahadur Shastri became the Prime Minister after Nehru's death. In his book on Shastri, C.P. Srivastava says Shastri's decision to send troops towards Lahore, after Pakistan opened a front in Kashmir, was seen as an act of aggression by the Western powers, who then, along with the Soviet Union, forced Indian and Pakistani heads of state to meet for a talk in Tashkent, the capital of the Soviet republic of Uzbekistan.[21] A declaration, in an attempt to achieve permanent peace, was signed there in January 1966. Shastri died there, in odd circumstances—some believe that the mystery of his death has never been cleared up. As far as Kashmir was concerned, writes Victoria Schofield: 'While the Tashkent declaration noted the existence of the Kashmir dispute, it effectively put the issue in cold storage.'[22]

We ask Dhar how come Wilayat, despite her sympathies for Pakistan, was allowed to resettle in Kashmir. He says it could have been due to government department and intelligence agencies working on their own with little communication between them. 'Perhaps their case just slipped through the cracks. There were six intelligence agencies operating in Kashmir then, on behalf of central and state governments. Even during Sadiq Sahab's time, the government departments did not talk to each other. I remember once my father Sadiq Sahab and Mir Qasim, who was the number two in the government, had a dinner to clear their misunderstandings, which had arisen due to lack of communication.'

According to Iftekhar Sadiq, it was not as simple as a misunderstanding—at least not when it came to the thinking of the state government, which he says transcended the India–Pakistan division. He says there used to be a policy of the state government to allow those, like Wilayat, who had a love for Kashmir to settle here—even if they had favoured Pakistan, including the accession of Kashmir to Pakistan, at one point of time. 'My father extended all help to their family. It was not because of any Kashmiri roots, but because the J&K administration felt they loved Kashmir, so they were allowed to settle out of goodwill. Even Shammi Kapoor's ashes are immersed in the Dal Lake. Indira Gandhi was also fond of Kashmir, and used to come to seek blessings at the Dargah of Makhdoom Sahib.'

He mentions the fire in Wilayat's house, which Sakina had also referred to in her book. It happened in 1971, the year his father died. 'They left after my father's demise.'

A few days after our last conversation, Iftekhar Sadiq calls back. He has remembered a detail. 'There was a theft in their house once. Precious family heirlooms were stolen. The police followed up on the case. The heirlooms were recovered and returned to the family,' he tells us. He also says it was a kind of government safe house, where they stayed.

∼

We look up Water Works Road, the address Sabia Rashid, the former neighbour, gave us, on Google Maps. It is in the Brein area, behind Nishat Garden, which faces the eastern side of Dal Lake. Sakina, in her book, called their home the Nishat Bagh Palace. We find that there is only one government school in the street, and decide to visit the place.

It is a narrow, steep road leading up from a busy market square. The school is behind a high gate and consists of two buildings: a newly constructed structure stands alongside a heritage building and together they serve as the school premises. A small lawn encircles both; on its sides are other houses. In its front, a road climbs up from the chowk, busy with its small market.

The school authorities say that they had to make some changes to the old building made of red bricks and stone and with a sloping roof, in order to preserve it. The roof was tiled and paint has been applied to some parts. It is a two-storey building: on the ground floor there are offices for school administration and a classroom—we spot a poster for a poetry competition on one of the walls. On the first floor, there are staff rooms. The staircase between the two floors is made entirely of wood.

The school authorities are clueless about the identity of the original owners. We are asked to check at the custodian department, which owns it now and collects the rent paid by the education department.

At the custodian department, we are told that the owner of the building, Qazi Salahuddin, migrated to Pakistan after Partition. The department acquired it in the late 1960s—like many such buildings all over the state after Partition, as records in the Srinagar State Archives show—and leased it to the education department in the 1980s.

Hoping to find records confirming who rented the building in the 1960s and '70s, we visit the office of a local patwari near the Dalgate area. He directs us to another patwari for records for the Brein area. As we are about to leave, disappointed with the dead end, a man approaches us. He introduces himself as Abdul Aziz, a retired tailor. By a pure coincidence, he was among the many petitioners in the patwari's office where he overheard us asking about Wilayat and her family. To our surprise, he says he knew them reasonably well and offers to tell us what he remembers.

Aziz, a short-statured man with a round face, was a teenager when the family lived in Brein, the area where he grew up. He remembers them well, in particular Ali Raza's 'short-tempered' nature. He also remembers that they had a dog of which the local residents were afraid. 'Ali Raza used to say that they were Pathans and could fight with ten people at a time. Their dog once fought with a neighbour's dog. Ali Raza even took out a knife in a fight with someone.'

In fact, he claims that the entire family was short-tempered, except Asad—echoing both Sakina and Kasim, who had described Asad as 'different' from the other family members. Aziz knows that the family used to receive an allowance from the state government. He also remembers the fire in the old building. And he mentions a rumour, that Asad was not Wilayat's own son.

He tells us about Ashraf Naqshbandi and Bimala Kaul, two neighbours of Wilayat, with whom she and her children had contact. 'Ashraf Sahab had a lot of land in this area. He helped Asad during his last days.' According to Aziz, who has lived in the area for decades, Asad fell sick and died in the same house. 'He had fallen into poverty, and lived here alone for a few years.'

We run into Aziz again at the market square in Brein, where he walks us up the slope, past the shops for readymade garments, hotels and a gym to a small lane, at the end of which is a large gate. Behind the gate is the house of the Naqshbandi family.

The Naqshbandis are an old and well-known family of Kashmir. Their ancestor Khwaja Bahauddin came to Kashmir from Tashkent in Central Asia during the Mughal period to spread Islam, and from him comes the Sufi Sunni order called the Naqshbandi. His shrine is in Khanyar in Srinagar and he is honoured with the appellation of Mushkil-kusha, the 'one who resolves difficulties'.

As we enter the house, which is surrounded by a spacious lawn with several labourers at work in its different corners, we are invited inside by an old man who appears to be in his seventies. He is tall and stocky, with a balding head. He introduces himself as Salim Naqshbandi.

He offers us seats around a plastic table, and asks if we would like some tea. When we say yes, he goes inside to have it prepared, then comes out and sits down.

He remembers Wilayat and her family well. There were very few families living in the area those days, he says. His father, Ashraf Naqshbandi, was one of the first doctors to practise in Kashmir. 'This whole area was Naqshbandi land,' he says. Over time, his father sold off parts of the land and a colony came up. 'There used to be paddy fields all over. Everything was yellow and it looked beautiful,' he gestures towards the surrounding houses.

According to his wife, Imtiaz, who has joined us with the tea, and who also knew the family, there was not even a medicine shop in the area in the 1960s and '70s. The first school, in Wilayat's old house, came up only in the '80s, after a request was made to Governor Jagmohan, who was visiting the area. For transportation, local buses plied twice daily.

Both Salim and Imtiaz are soft-spoken, speaking in measured tones; they are both retired professors. Imtiaz's father used to work in the police department.

Both of them remember Asad more than the other family members as he lived in the area for a longer period and was a frequent visitor to their house. He was also older to the other two children, and a bit more social. 'They were a decent family, but could not mix up with others. Begum Wilayat liked to be alone; she had no social touch. But Asad would come to our house.'

Again, this is quite the change from Ganderbal, where Wilayat is remembered as someone who liked to sit in her balcony and chat with people passing by. According to Iftekhar Sadiq, Wilayat did manage to build a social life and she moved among some elite families of Srinagar. 'She was free to go around and attended family functions. But she did not play a role in the local politics,' he told us. Iftekhar said she was good friends with a British woman living in Kashmir, who was called 'Strawberry Mem'—Mem being the Raj-era honorific for a White woman living in India.

Salim and Imtiaz Naqshbandi have never heard of any British lady by this name, but Imtiaz does remember English people coming to live in the area for long periods. The houses in Brein were not separated by boundary walls then, like they are now. Imtiaz says they could see Wilayat's house from their own; the distance between the two houses is hardly a few metres.

The family maintained that they were royals, Salim said, although they never explained their ancestry. 'They always kept their distance.

We never knew of their Kashmir connection. None of them spoke Kashmiri.' Imtiaz remembers Wilayat in black clothes on Muharram, standing outside her house. Salim adds that she looked 'graceful' in her black attire, hoisting the Shia flag with the hand symbol. According to both, the family seemed 'isolated' and there seemed to be something 'suspicious' about them.

Nevertheless, he also remembers the two brothers as 'good cricketers'. They used to play with Salim's nephews, all of whom are now settled abroad. He says that the family had contacts with Bimala Kaul, the other neighbour Aziz had mentioned. 'Her son-in-law, R.C. Sharma, became the director of CBI later,' says Salim.

Imtiaz remembers Sakina too, as they studied together in the Women's College on MA Road. In particular, she recalls one episode at the college that caused Sakina, then known as Marzia, great distress. 'Someone mentioned to her the rumour about her family being involved in the assassination of Liaquat Ali Khan. She was furious. I heard her shouting at the person.'

They remember the fire of 1971 too. 'We tried to douse it with the help of water pipes. One portion of the house was totally burnt down,' Salim reminisced.

After Wilayat, Ali Raza and Sakina left for Delhi, Asad stayed with the Naqshbandis for a month. 'He was very well-mannered and would often bring cakes from Ahdoos [a famous bakery in Srinagar]. He went to see the family in Delhi and came back,' Salim said, confirming what Kasim told us about Asad going back and forth between the two cities.

It was his brother-in-law, who is now no more, who discovered Asad's corpse, along with Ahmed Ali Punjabi, another neighbour, and a servant of the latter. 'They contacted Abbas Ansari, a Shia preacher and on his recommendation, the body was buried at a Shia graveyard.'

Salim said the body was found on the stairs of the house. 'He was living alone and his health was in a bad condition.'

According to the couple, Asad died in 1980, which corresponds with the year of his death Sakina had recorded in her book. It means that Asad must have stayed on in Srinagar for about five years after Wilayat left for Delhi. Salim and Imtiaz remember his death well, as their four-year-old son died the same year, a painful memory for them; even mentioning it makes them palpably sad. 'He used to play with Asad. He liked to tap on his balding head,' Imtiaz said.

∼

The Naqshbandis point us towards more people who remember Wilayat. Imtiaz says she was known to many prominent Shia families of that time, which included, among others, the family of the famous Kashmiri–American poet Agha Shahid Ali. But Shahid is no more; his parents have passed away too. Another person is Sadiq Wani, who owns the famous boutique shop in Srinagar selling handicrafts and other items called 'Suffering Moses'. But Wani had a stroke, according to his son, Muzaffar Wani, and we cannot speak to him.

Next, we go to meet Fahmida Shah, Imtiaz's sister-in-law and Wani's cousin. Fahmida runs a guest house in Raj Bagh. She is surprised to see us at first and calls Imtiaz. Once reassured, she invites us to a shop in the front part of the guesthouse, selling shawls and other garments. She is dressed in Western clothes and wears glasses. She has an air of authority about her.

Fahmida was in class seven or eight when she first came across Wilayat during a Muharram procession. 'You could not miss her. She was tall and slim and during mourning her black hair used to cover her entire face. They said they were Iranians,' she tells us. She describes the route of the procession: from Hussainabad to Zadibal in downtown, the older part of the city. 'My father was the right-hand man of Agha Sahab who was our religious head. My father used to organize the procession.'

The Muharram procession in Kashmir includes a horse called Julzanah, after the horse of Hussain, who was martyred at Karbala. The horse goes through the entire route earmarked for the procession, followed by mourners. 'It would go through Hawal and then arrive at Sazgaripora where women assembled with children to mourn. It was a largish hall where we assembled. The children would crawl under the Julzanah. We would all pay obeisance. There used to be curiosity about Wilayat. She would dress in a black robe, had large eyes and a penetrating and intimidating gaze. Her hair was also totally black and she cut a very impressive figure. All the women would start crying when the Julzanah arrived. She used to mourn very intensely. Marzia would stand apart from her,' Fahmida tells us.

She remembers seeing Wilayat a few times during the processions; other than that, she has no memories of her, as their families were not on social terms. But she insists, again, that the image of Wilayat with her dark hair covering her face, in intense mourning, has stayed with her over the years.

∼

Ahmed Ali Punjabi, the neighbour who found Asad's body, is no more, but we meet his son, Fahim. His father was an entomologist and they lived just across the street. Being a Shia family, they got along well with Wilayat and her children.

Fahim Ali, in his late fifties and now deputy superintendent of police posted at Ganderbal, was eight years old when his family came to live opposite Wilayat's house in 1969. We meet in his spacious living room, panelled all over with wood. It is sparsely decorated. There is just one calendar on the walls. On the centre table, there is an ornate flower vase.

He has a vivid memory of falling off a cherry tree in his childhood, having spotted Wilayat. He remembers her as having a fearsome personality, tall with long, black hair. 'I was afraid of her. She did not keep purdah. They were a modern family,' he told us. He broke a bone as a result of the fall and he remembers Sakina coming to visit him. 'We were close due to our being Shias. We sent food to their house and they used to do the same.' He too mentions the rumour that Asad was not Wilayat's own son, and adds that Asad would even say so sometimes himself.

He remembers the family had a red Volkswagen, which was brought to them from Delhi. 'A truck brought other things, many of which were imported.' Perhaps it had taken all these years for their possessions to arrive from Pakistan.

Fahim had heard the rumour that they were from Iran and were involved in an assassination there—which sounds like a fresh spin on the Liaquat rumour. What gave the rumoured Iranian roots more credence to Fahim was that the family was fair-complexioned with sharp features, as well as their language skills. He remembers Asad as tall and well-built. 'Asad spoke good Persian. Marzia was lean and attractive. They were a classy family and their way of being was sophisticated. They seemed to be a family of intellectuals,' he tells us.

There is a black-and-white photo of Sakina from around this time, among the documents at the Alkazi Collection of Photography. She is wearing a checked, knee-length skirt, a dark blouse and over that a short, white layover that is knotted over the abdomen. Around her wrists are a watch and a bangle, on her right little finger a ring with a dark stone. Her hair is cut in a short bob and her cheeks are round—compared to the hollower cheeks she had in the photos that were taken of her at the railway station. She looks much younger than in those photos, too, perhaps in her late teens. Looking away from the camera, she does not seem particularly happy.

Fahim remembers them as being largely aloof and uninvolved in politics of any kind. Nevertheless, he says that they were under surveillance by the CID, the intelligence wing of the J&K police. 'CID officers used to come to our house and ask my father about Wilayat and her family.'

This calls to mind the article by Swiss journalist Bernard Imhasly, who described Ali Raza's later fear of being followed by the secret service, when he lived in Malcha Mahal in the late 1980s, as a symptom of anxiety. Perhaps, this fear was not so strange, after all.

~

The reason the family was under surveillance lies in the political situation at the time. As Pakistani Muslims, they were suspect in the eyes of the security establishment as potential spies or saboteurs. In the previous chapter, we have written about the objections from the IB to the family, as relayed to Nehru and the central government. The excerpts cited from B.N. Mullik's book, *My Years with Nehru*, give a wider perspective regarding the IB's position vis-a-vis Pakistani Muslims being allowed to settle in Kashmir, as do the archived government notes on parties such as the Hindu right-wing PP, which was fiercely opposed to it.

Clearly, the conservative opinion in India was unhappy with Pakistani Muslims being settled in India, especially in Kashmir, and was taking up the issue through every means possible. The IB also shared this opinion. However, the central government and J&K government acted contrary to their warnings and continued to allow Muslims from Pakistan, including Wilayat, to settle in India and in Kashmir.

Even so, the objections from conservative groups must have made the governments cautious and perhaps that is why Wilayat and her family members were put under surveillance in Srinagar.

By then, Indira Gandhi had come to power in Delhi, succeeding Lal Bahadur Shastri in 1966. She went on to split the Congress and under her India became a socialist republic. Banks were nationalized. Towards the end of the '60s, the government moved to abolish the Privy Purse, which was awarded to former royalty; it consisted of a sum of money and certain privileges. Any respect or deference to former royalty was no longer a part of the new socialist state's agenda.

The Kashmir issue started to recede to the background. In 1968, Sheikh Abdullah was released again, but he did not make much of an impact or headway in resolving it. In 1970, an Indian plane was hijacked by two young Kashmiri men and taken to Lahore, which created a buzz; however, it did not last.

Sadiq's pro-India stance continued and so did the status quo over Kashmir that had come into being after the war in 1965. This became even more pronounced after India defeated Pakistan comprehensively in the next war, of 1971, forcing the West Pakistan army to surrender in Dhaka, and helping Bangladesh liberate itself.

The same year, G.M. Sadiq passed away. During his eight years in power, Indian and Kashmiri politics had changed irrevocably.

Vijay Dhar remembers that this was when even the most pro-Pakistan Kashmiris began to accept the status quo. 'In 1973, we were students and collecting money for defence personnel. There was a businessman who was known to be pro-Pakistan. My friends said: don't go to him, but I still did. He signed a check for Rs 1,500. I asked him why he was donating such a big amount when he was pro-Pakistan. He said that the Pakistan story was over for Kashmir. He had waited for twenty-five years to see Kashmir secede to Pakistan but had given up on his dream.'

In 1972, the two countries met at Shimla and decided that the Line of Control would effectively be the border that both sides would respect. There was no mention of a plebiscite. The issue, one could say, had been resolved without there being a big publicity campaign about it, which suited both sides. India effectively gave up its claim on Azad Kashmir and Pakistan on the Indian side of Kashmir. Although Bhutto kept up with claims of supporting Kashmiris in the quest or struggle for self-determination, the issue was no longer as pressing as it had been before.

Schofield writes: 'Despite Bhutto's rhetoric, from what Farooq Abdullah heard during his visit to Pakistan in 1974, he also concluded that the Kashmir issue was resolved.'[23]

In 1975, a *New York Times* article suggested that the Kashmir issue was nothing more than an 'academic' one.[24] This meant that Kashmir was not going to see any change in its status quo and the politics had moved away from previous positions, such as the demand for a plebiscite, which could have allowed it to secede to Pakistan.

All the things that we suspect Wilayat might have banked upon when she applied for resettlement in Kashmir, such as the whole of J&K one day seceding to Pakistan—came to naught.

~

Fahim Ali's brother, Salim, joins us in the living room. He is an orthopaedic surgeon based in London, visiting his family in Srinagar. He is elder to Fahim and remembers more about the family. 'The cops used to come more frequently during the period of 1974 to 1975,' he tells us, referring to the period in which Wilayat decided to move to the New Delhi Railway Station, and Asad deciding to stay behind.

Salim remembers Asad as a 'thorough gentleman', apart from being 'pious'. He remembers the family as being 'intellectually inclined' but 'isolated'. 'My father went out of his way to help them because he was altruistic by nature,' he says. 'They used to bring meetha chawal for us on Muharram. They used to go to Dalgate for the entire period of Muharram and return after the Majlis on the tenth day. Their house was called Wilayat Manzil and we used to call her Begum Wilayat.'

Their maternal uncle studied in Srinagar's S.P. College and was friends with Ali Raza. 'Ali Raza was handsome, but short-tempered. He talked like an introvert, but his language was posh.' He remembers Marzia 'used to wear shirts', which made her look modern.

The brothers remember their neighbour Mohammad Amin Pandit, who was a government servant in the department of information and public relations. 'His daughter Idrissa Pandit was older than us. She is now a professor based in Canada,' says Fahim.

Salim also remembers 1980 being the year of Asad's death. 'I passed my tenth-standard exams in 1980 and I remember that was the same year. He was ill for quite some time. Dad took him to the hospital once. He was poorly and getting frailer and frailer … Initially, he was in good shape, but slowly his condition deteriorated. I cannot be sure how he managed in his last days. We sent food for him on some days.'

Salim added that Wilayat did have a reputation of being 'mad'. 'You could hear her shout sometimes.'

It was the Punjabis's servant, Ghulam Hassan, who would take food to Asad and this is how he discovered his dead body, Salim tells us. 'The body had begun to decompose when he found it. The door was locked from inside and it had to be broken. The body was smeared with urine and faeces. It had been twelve or thirteen days since it had been in that position. It was found on the stairs of the house. Uneaten meetha chawal was lying around.'

They say that they had no way of contacting Wilayat, and are not sure how she found out about Asad's death. Salim's father contacted Abbas Ansari, a Shia cleric, in order to facilitate Asad's burial. 'He was buried at Chhatbal, a Shia locality, in the graveyard for travellers.'

Some years later, on a visit to Delhi, Fahim Ali Punjabi accompanied Bimala Kaul to Malcha Mahal. Bimala Kaul was married to a senior officer in the Indian Army and 'was everyone's caretaker' in Nishat during those days, according to Fahim. 'Film stars such as Waheeda Rehman and Amitabh Bachchan used to visit her when they came to Kashmir for shoots.'

He says that the Kaul family was also on good terms with L.K. Jha, the bureaucrat who served as Kashmir's governor for two terms and whom Kasim remembered visiting with Asad in his Delhi office.

Later on, Bimala Kaul moved to Delhi and she kept in touch with Wilayat and her children. When Fahim visited them in Malcha Mahal along with Kaul on one occasion, after Wilayat's death, Ali Raza did not recognize him. 'But Sakina did. She tried to explain to Ali Raza, that I was the son of "Punjabi Saab", as my father was close to their mother.' The siblings had changed a lot, he said. "They were more aggressive, started to breed large dogs and keeping people away from them. Maybe they feared hostilities from the outside world. This was not necessary in the area where they lived in Kashmir, in Brein. It was like a village in those days.'

∼

At the Chhatbal locality, we reach in time for Friday prayers. We wait outside the mosque while our Kashmiri colleague Nasir Hasan, a student of fine arts at Kashmir University, speaks to the locals. We are told that the mosque committee keeps a record of all the burials and we should be able to find out if Asad was buried here. Abbas Ansari is no more, but his son is now the preacher and we are told he would know.

A large crowd, all men and young boys, comes out of the mosque after the prayers are finished. Yellow rice is distributed by a few volunteers, which everyone collects in their scooped palms. Ansari's son, Masroor Abbas Ansari, comes out at the end. He is wearing a turban and a tunic and looks regal in his attire, with his close-cropped beard adding to the impression. We ask him if he remembers any burials that took place in 1980 but he says he was too young then; born in 1975, he was five years old.

He refers us to a young man, Showkat Ahmad Dar, who says he can help us with our search. He works as a volunteer at the mosque and has an uncle who was actively involved with community affairs in those days. About the graveyard for wayfarers, he says it is mostly out of use now. Then it was mostly for Shias from Kargil, a border town 200 kilometres uphill from Srinagar, reached through steep, narrow, winding mountain roads. 'Back then, the roads between Srinagar and Kargil used to be closed for months during winters,' Dar explains. 'So if anyone passed away, they were buried here because taking the body back to Kargil for burial was impossible. The Shia community from Kargil was not well-to-do in those days and this was the only graveyard they could access. Now they have another graveyard in Srinagar and the road situation is also better, so this graveyard has fallen into disuse.'

He invites us to his house for tea, as his uncle is not home at the moment. It is next to the traveller's graveyard, so he offers to show it to us first.

It is a small patch of land; the door to it is locked before we enter. Wild grass has grown all over the place. Only a few graves are marked. 'The last burial was of the father of a professor from Hyderabad during Covid-19, a couple of years ago,' Dar says.

At his house, we sit on the floor on a carpet, with pillows to support our backs as we lean against the wall. He brings tea in a flask, with several bowls of savouries and cookies. A couple of neighbours have also joined us. We notice a photograph of Abbas Ansari on the wall with an in-built glass closet. The discussion turns to him; he died in 2022, just a few months before our visit. 'He had dementia so even if you had come earlier, you might not have learnt much,' Showkat says. Ansari was a prominent leader of Kashmir, and not just

Shias, we are told; he was also a member of the separatist Hurriyat Conference. He was even jailed at the infamous Tihar Jail in Delhi. 'He was a part of the Moi-Muqqadas [Holy Relic] agitation in 1963.' He passes a copy of an autobiography written by Ansari to us, but it is in Urdu and we cannot read it.

After some time, his uncle, Ghulam Ahmad, arrives. He used to be the store-keeper at the mosque, but retired in 1985. He is a tall and lean man, now seventy-three years old. As he sits down, Showkat tells him the objective of our visit. After mulling it over for a while, he says he remembers participating in the burial. 'The body had shrunk and become rigid; the knees were …' He lifts his knees up till his ribcage to show us what the corpse looked like. 'We washed the corpse. He was buried like everyone else, with full dignity. All the rituals were followed. We read Fatiha over the grave for three consecutive days.'

In between, Showkat interrupts him. Perhaps incredulous himself that his uncle remembers the details of a burial that happened so long ago, he insists it must be another burial, of a servant of a family in the area who was from Pakistan, which happened a few years ago at the traveller's graveyard. But Ghulam Ahmad insists that he remembers the burial from 1980, in which a body from Nishat was buried. We ask about the person who cleaned the body but he says that the person has passed away.

Suddenly, Showkat asks us to go upstairs with him, where his ailing father is resting; he is elder to Ghulam Hasan and might remember something. His father used to work as an artisan who made Pashmina shawls.

His father, frail and emaciated, is lying in bed when we enter. His name is Ali Mohammad. We tell him about Asad and his burial and ask him if he can corroborate his brother's story.

Like his brother, Ali Mohammad too remembers the burial that took place forty-odd years ago. 'The death had taken place in Nishat. Being Shias, we hoist a black flag called an alam. There was such a flag in their house. As he got ill and his condition progressively deteriorated, he realized that he was going to die and so he wrapped that flag all around himself. After a few days, people came to know that he died. Maulvi Sahib [Abbas Ansari] was approached and he asked the president of the mosque, Haji Ghulam Abbas—he has passed away—to arrange for the burial. We gave the corpse a wash, as the body had been lying unattended for a few days. Afterwards, it was wrapped in a shroud. Other than that, we don't know who he was or where he had come from.'

Showkat speaks to him in Kashmiri and tells us that Asad's grave is next to where the professor's father has been buried, but since bodies have been buried on top of each other over the years due to paucity of space, it is way down in the ground and impossible to identify, as there is no headstone to mark it.

In order to further corroborate the circumstances of Asad's demise, we trace the whereabouts of the servant, Ghulam Hassan, who used to work at Fahim Ali Punjabi's house in the 1960s and '70s.

Fahim told us the area in which he lives now, having left their service at the end of 1980. Nasir manages to track him down through a contact from the same area.

The area where Hassan lives is on the outskirts of Srinagar, near Budgam. We reach his house by seeking directions from his son on the mobile phone. An unpaved road takes us to his place, after we stop on the main road and let our taxi go, as the streets have become too narrow to drive in.

Ghulam Hassan is now an old man in his seventies. His daughter-in-law is home, and she serves us tea. We sit in his sparsely furnished living room and discuss events that transpired when he was in his twenties. He wants to speak first to Fahim Ali Punjabi and since he does not have a mobile phone, we make the call for him. After Fahim Ali Punjabi reassures him that it is safe to talk to us, he begins to slowly open up.

'I used to play with Asad, with the ball,' he starts off. 'Asad used to practise by himself as well by bowling on to the wall.' Asad, being a bowler, would make him bat.

He would go to their house with food, he says. 'On special occasions such as Bada Din (Eid), they would invite me for the feast.' We show him the pictures that we have of the family and he is able to identify the family members.

'The children [Sakina and Ali Raza] would go out during the day and come only during evenings as they would go to study. Asad would stay back and he was the one who would be cooking. At times, even he would leave for some time and then come back. He used to go to Srinagar and bring back rotis from a bakery.'

Ghulam Hassan, like others, remembers their beautiful carpets. 'During Muharram, they would stay in Srinagar and come only after the tenth day. Afterwards they would distribute sweets.'

Considering that Wilayat used the last name Butt, which is a known to be a Sunni name, we ask whether he is sure they were Shia. He insists they were. 'They had the Shia flag in their house. They were not afraid of hoisting it. They would all dress in black during Muharram.'

Wilayat treated him kindly, he says. 'She would always ask me to sit down, have some tea whenever I visited their house. She would also give me Eidi.' He refutes the suggestion that she was short-tempered.

After the family left for Delhi, Asad lived by himself. 'At times, I would take food for him. He would always acknowledge me if he saw me, even from afar. He would approach me and hug me.'

He remembers Asad complaining to him of headaches. 'But he did not wish to see a doctor.' He also remembers Asad receiving money from the government which he would collect from Mohammad Amin Pandit, his neighbour. 'I even asked Asad why he did not accompany his family to Delhi but he gave me no answer. At times, he would disappear for a week or so, but he never told me he had gone to Delhi or elsewhere.'

He also remembers the fire at their house. 'The government gave them a tent to live in. They had lost a lot in the fire. All the carpets and furniture were destroyed.' According to him, the family lived in the tent for around three months till the house was repaired.

Regarding the circumstances around Asad's death, he remembers going to check in on him as he had not seen him for four or five days. 'The door to the house was locked from within so I went and informed Fahim Ali Punjabi's father.' They had to force the door open to enter the house.

They saw the body, wrapped in a flag on the stairs, near the door. After that, the police came. 'The body was taken in an ambulance for burial.' But Hassan did not go to Chhatbal for the burial. 'Fahim Ali's father had gone. He was also questioned by the police. I took food for him to the police station.'

About a month after Asad's death, Ali Raza showed up in Brein. Idrissa Pandit, Mohammad Amin Pandit's daughter who now lives in Canada, remembers he came 'to supposedly claim Asad's body'. We request Drabu for her phone number—the Pandits are also related to his wife—and he shares it. She replies via WhatsApp.

Ali Raza returned to Delhi without the body, she confirms. 'The elders' better sense prevailed and they did not let him disturb the remains,' she says. 'Fahim's father, Mr Ali Punjabi, was involved in all the proceedings after Asad's death. As he was the only Shia neighbour, he arranged a proper Shia burial for Asad. It was good to have him as a witness, otherwise there could have been issues,' she says, referring to Ali Raza's attempt to claim the body. Idrissa says Asad had cholera, and died from that. She thinks it was most likely her father who contacted Wilayat after Asad's death. 'He must have tracked them down through the railway authorities,' she says, but adds that she is not sure about it.

Idrissa has memories of Ali Raza and Marzia driving with her and her parents in their car, probably to college. 'They used to engage us as kids. Raza played cricket with my cousins. He was a vivacious personality with a huge presence; Marzia was strange and not too outgoing, but very nice to us children. Asad was a very pious person, always devoted to prayer, a very kind demeanour, so different from the rest. He would always be busy with chores, almost like a servant. We later heard that he was not Wilayat's biological son, hence, not treated well.'

She does not recollect Asad or any of the others ever coming to their house to collect an allowance. 'I never heard about that. But it is quite possible that they used our address. People used our phone as well, as we were the only ones with a phone line, and address, if they did not know how to get mail.'

Idrissa's memory of Wilayat is that of a 'ghost-like creature'. She recalls moving to the house next door much after the family started living there. By then, Wilayat was apparently not the same woman who liked to sit on her balcony in Ganderbal, chatting with passersby. Her interactions may have been limited to the Shia families, and necessary occasions. 'I do not think their mother spoke to us, or invited us into the house, so their life was a mystery. As kids, we built scary stories around her personality, a red-haired woman always dressed in a black robe, an unwelcoming and a mysterious presence.' Most people remember Wilayat being black-haired, but Idrissa insists it was always red; the kind of red one may get from dyeing the hair with henna.[25] 'Her hair was never tied or covered, quite unusual in a place like Kashmir.'

After they got a dog, Wilayat would be outside the house more often, Idrissa says, recalling that they did not keep a dog initially. 'It's an uncommon practice in homes of Kashmir.' Dogs are generally disliked in Kashmir, where they are seen as impure from an Islamic perspective. Wilayat may have taken a dog for reasons of safety. Iftekhar Sadiq told us that she had experienced a theft in their home, and there was also the surveillance she was under. But Idrissa, as a child, thought that, by keeping the dog, Wilayat 'was trying to scare us all'.

The family's move to Delhi came as a big surprise. 'So sudden, leaving behind Asad, without any communication. Overnight, they were gone, with most if not all their belongings. Who transported them and how, was all so mysterious. The next thing we knew was that she had occupied a place at the New Delhi Railway Station.'

As we are rounding up our chat, she says: 'It is a very intriguing tale. Sometimes I feel like I knew folks from a mystery novel!'

~

In her book, Sakina blames the security agencies and Sadiq for the burning of their house in 1971. She mentions G.M. Sadiq, but says that he never really liked them and merely tolerated them. She also writes that Wilayat had not originally wanted to go to Kashmir but was forced to stay there by Prime Minister Nehru. Sakina claims that Wilayat had little interest in Kashmir, except for the fact that the family vacationed there. 'In 1963 Pt. J.L. Nehru had counselled Rs 15000 for Princess Wilayat Mahal and assured for enhancement with a house in Srinagar Nishat Bagh,' writes Sakina. She says Wilayat 'insisted' upon the return of two ancestral properties in

Lucknow: Chattar Manzil and Kothi Farhat Baksh. Sakina says the money was under the allowances provided to former royalty.

She says in contravention of what Nehru suggested—for which we have no proof—they were issued only Rs 500 by the J&K government. 'Princess resented the decision of Pandit Nehru. H.H. never wanted to have that state as abode,' Sakina writes.[26]

About Sadiq, she writes: 'The chief minister of that state did not like the Indian decision to have this royal house of Oudh there considered as white elephants.'[27]

This does not match what the papers from the National Archives show, nor what Iftekhar Sadiq told us. Did Wilayat not tell her children that it was she who had claimed that the family had property in Kashmir and that she had specifically requested to be settled there? Or did she abandon Kashmir in an emotional sense after a bitter experience there? There is no way of knowing anymore. But from the testimonies of those who knew them, we can gather some insights into how things transpired for Wilayat and her children in their 'ancestral' land.

Initially, they seem to have been well-disposed towards their new bearings and situation. From what we learnt in Ganderbal, they were perhaps hopeful of a better future. They were making a new start; they had an influential patron in Sadiq; they were in the beautiful valley of Kashmir to which Wilayat claimed a familial association. This is borne out from their interactions with others in Ganderbal. Everyone we spoke to attested to Wilayat's 'good nature' and how she and her children were part of the community.

In Nishat, at least in the early days, things seemed to have been all right. They mingled with the Shia families of Srinagar, and their regular participation in Muharram rituals shows that they had started to become involved in Kashmir's society. Wilayat attended family functions and even had a close friend, as per Iftekhar Sadiq. So they had not given up on their hopes of starting a new life. The children continued to pursue their studies at local colleges, so that is another indication of their intentions.

But slowly, they were described as growing increasingly 'isolated' and 'aloof'. Perhaps among people of a higher social standing, Wilayat and her children felt more self-conscious; rumours were afoot about their involvement in a political conspiracy, including some who were aware that it was linked to the assassination of Liaquat Ali Khan. This could have led to Wilayat becoming more reserved in Srinagar. It was this rumour, she told *Hindustan Times* in 1975, that had made it difficult for her to stay on in Kashmir. In the later Nishat years, we also hear more of Sakina and Ali Raza losing their tempers, especially in the latter's case.

The local political situation would have played a role, too. When they arrived in Kashmir, the agitation over the missing hair of the Prophet was in full swing. As has been noted, it was a pro-plebiscite agitation disguised as a social protest. This must have given Wilayat some hope that Kashmir still had a chance to secede to Pakistan. However, things transpired differently. The 1965 war, another attempt by Pakistan to 'liberate' Kashmir, failed. Sadiq, as a pro-Indian politician, moved the state closer to India in the years that followed. After the 1971 war, India was in a far stronger position and the feeling in the Valley was that Kashmir had little to no chance of seceding to Pakistan anymore.

Though Sadiq's nationalistic politics cannot have been a surprise for Wilayat, given their decades-old connection, perhaps she resented him more for it because of her own disappointment. The once-strong hope for the plebiscite, which she had also fought for in Pakistan in the early 1950s, had died out.

Wilayat's disillusionment was possibly exacerbated by her personal troubles, when in 1971 her house burnt down. Following that incident, and Sadiq's death, things seem to have gone downhill swiftly for the family. Wilayat was even described as 'mad', screaming for seemingly no reason.

By 1974, when Wilayat finally decided to move out, she was by some neighbouring children already seen in a dehumanized manner—ghost-like, as Idrissa Pandit described her, and 'un-Kashmiri' with her dog and uncovered hair—we could say she was 'othered'.

At the station in New Delhi, the family went on to live a much-degraded existence as compared to their stay in Kashmir. They stopped trying to have a social life, rather rejected it, by placing themselves on what can be seen as the edge of the city, a place of transition rather than community: the New Delhi Railway Station. They started playing the role of royals from another time, even as Asad's health deteriorated in Kashmir. This is when Sakina, after having lived as Zohra and Marzia Ali in Kashmir, became Princess Sakina. Ali Raza, a cricket-loving schoolboy, became Prince Cyrus. Their mother was now Queen of Awadh.

With Asad's death in 1980, their Kashmir connection finally snapped and they seemed to have given up on the place completely, to the extent of disowning any connection to it, as Sakina does in her book. Perhaps their final reactions to Kashmir demonstrate the great pain Wilayat must have felt at a long-cherished dream that turned completely sour.

Their 'new identity', however, was not just a performance at the railway station. Though later questioned by several authorities, it seems to have been accepted initially since government documents from the year 1974 and 1975 acknowledge Wilayat as a descendant of Begum Hazrat Mahal, referring to her as 'Wilayat Mahal' and the 'Begum of Oudh'. It is part of the correspondence between the central government and the J&K home department, as per a letter sent to the home address of Mohammad Amin Pandit, Wilayat's neighbour who was an information officer, and from whom Asad was said to collect a government allowance. A copy of it was sent to Wilayat and kept in Malcha Mahal, until it made its way to the Alkazi Collection of Photography in Delhi. As per the correspondence, the officials were working out the modalities to pay the family an allowance, and for this purpose discussed the opening of a bank account where this money could be transferred. Later, a handwritten note on a copy of the typed letter mentions the bank account number and the Connaught Place branch in Delhi of the J&K Bank. The money came from the J&K government, the letter says: 'The allowances are directly drawn from Srinagar Treasury.'

Hoping to get more information, we visit the bank. But the exercise turns out to be useless. The account number has only three numbers—and all numbers were converted to sixteen digits later. There is no way of knowing what the new account number would be, the manager tells us. And if the account was closed when the account holder died, all information would be with the RBI.

An application under RTI to the concerned government departments is unhelpful, too. 'The information regarding subject in the RTI is not under the purview of undersigned,' the standard reply reads after the request is passed around between different departments. At the same time, it gives a suggestion regarding the pension Wilayat might have received. 'FFR Division under MHA administers Swatantrata Sainik Samman Yojana (SSSY).' FFR stands for Freedom Fighter and Rehabilitation, and the SSSY is a pension for freedom fighters, such as Hazrat Mahal, and their descendants.

Royal After All?

'You are from India? I'm so jealous of you!'

The frail-looking lady asks us to come sit close to her on her sofa in a small living room in Karachi. Alia Imam, a scholar of Urdu, settled in Pakistan after Partition. She is in her nineties now, but has not forgotten her hometown. It's the first thing she tells us: 'I'm from Lucknow!'

Her persistent love for Lucknow is not the only thing she has in common with Wilayat. 'It was my husband who decided we had to move to Pakistan,' Alia says. She was married to Kasim Imam, the brother of the then Raja of Mahmudabad—the father of the one we met in Lucknow. 'It was because his brother made the move that we had no choice. It is so sad that I don't even want to recall it. All my siblings remained in India.'

She then bursts into a song, delivering the Indian national anthem word for word, without hesitation, shedding a tear at the end.

With Wilayat, she never crossed paths. Alia Imam and her husband both had international careers, she in academics and he in diplomacy, and started living in Karachi only in the 1970s. But her spirit and love for Lucknow somehow make us feel they could have been friends. Had Wilayat never left Karachi, if her life had gone differently, perhaps the two of them would have shared memories of their beloved city over a cup or more of tea.

~

We meet Alia Imam as part of a wild-goose chase. Searching for Wilayat in today's Karachi is like trying to grasp a shadow of the past. With hardly any leads, anybody above the age of ninety could be a possible source. The landmarks that feature in her story are hard to recognize today. About sixty years after she left for Kashmir, Karachi is transformed into a mega city. Unions are organizing street protests against unaffordable electricity bills,[1] while the young and wealthy flock to air-conditioned malls, cafés and oceanside restaurants. High-rise towers block the view of the ocean, while the beach has an old-world charm with vendors offering camel rides and shooting games.

Our search starts at the obvious places: first, at Jahangir Park, where Wilayat Butt interrupted Bogra's speech in 1954. It's a medium-sized park and not particularly special. Children play with life-size dinosaur statues and families watch birds in an aviary. An amphitheatre can be seen too.

'Was it here that you heckled Bogra?' we wonder.

Just outside the park is the nineteenth-century indoor Empress Market buzzing with hawkers and shoppers.

'Did you come here for your groceries?'

The area is populated by migrants from India; Karachi is known as a stronghold of muhajirs—the Urdu word for 'immigrant' that refers to the diverse mix of Muslim migrants from all parts of undivided India—as opposed to the Sindhis who were native to Karachi but became a minority post-Partition. Burns Road is nearby, famous for its street food from decades-old shops such as Delhi Rabri and Delhi Nihari House—nihari being a famous meat dish from Lucknow and Delhi.

We try to imagine what life was like for Wilayat in the years immediately after Partition. A young woman who followed her husband over a new, violent border to a land of opportunities. A mother of multiple children, with a much older husband who was busy working a prominent job, settling into a strange new city in a new country.

Wilayat must have been a remarkable woman who despite her circumstances, threw herself into the women's movement of the new Islamic state. The previously mentioned book by Sarah Ansari and William Gould that mentions Wilayat Butt sheds some light on this movement. It had a large social component, taking care of the stream of refugees into the new country, while debating political questions on matters such as the veil, polygamy and women's rights to work and education.

Wilayat was very much a part of this movement, having the position of treasurer in the Women's Muslim League. This probably meant that she belonged to a small, elite group, explains Ansari, who is an authority on the contemporary history of Karachi, Pakistan's capital until it shifted to Islamabad in the 1960s. Ansari is based in London, and over the phone she paints us a picture of the Karachi of the early 1950s.

'When we think of Karachi today, it is a mega port city with more than 20 million people. But at the time of Partition, it was a small place. Particularly people who were politicized or active operated in a relatively small world. The connections and networks were probably very intimate, in a way.'

Women played a special part in the shaping of Pakistan's identity, with the wife of the first Prime Minister, Ra'ana Liaquat Ali Khan, at the forefront. As Ansari and Gould point out in their book:

On the one hand, the status of women had to be enhanced to enable Pakistan to claim to be a modern Muslim state. On the other hand, women's rights had to be articulated in ways that would not undermine the 'Muslim-ness', or Islamic identity, of the new state, since this had been the basis on which its creation had been supported and sanctioned.[2]

Ansari, in our phone conversation, describes the Karachi of those days as an 'unsettled' and 'emotionally charged' place. 'Particularly among the refugees, who experienced and lived through Partition, there was an awful lot of expectation, lobbying, pushing their case.' And: 'At least a certain class of women wanted their voices heard.'

Wilayat was such a woman. That she was active with the Women's Muslim League rather than one of the women's organizations dealing with charity work, for example, indicates that she had strong political ambitions. And though the Muslim League was no longer the single dominant party in the country after its founder and Pakistan's 'Father of the Nation' Muhammad Ali Jinnah died in 1948, its name did continue to carry authority.

The articles we find in *Dawn* provide clues that imply Wilayat was part of the elite circles of Karachi. Her placing a message in an English-language newspaper after her husband's death indicates that she had an extensive social circle. The name of the lawyer who represented her relatives in 1954 is another indication. 'Mr Manzar-i-Alam, Advocate, made the application before the City Magistrate on behalf of the relatives of Begum Butt,' the newspaper reported on 30 August of that year. The name of Manzar-i-Alam comes up in a few research papers when we search for it online. One is a dissertation about the Pakistan movement in Aligarh Muslim University, which mentions the lawyer as actively recruiting and training students in close association with Jinnah.[3] Another is a book chapter on a landmark court case in Pakistan around the dismissal of the First constituent assembly of Pakistan in 1954. A petition challenging the dismissal was filed on 7 November 1954 by Maulvi Tamizuddin Khan, president of the assembly. 'The affidavit was signed by Manzir-i-Alam as the identifying advocate.'[4] Clearly, Wilayat's family had access to the same lawyer as some of the governing elites of the country.

Ansari, in our phone call, concludes: 'Being the treasurer of the woman's branch of the League in Karachi would have heightened Wilayat's profile. She would have been known to others in those circles. It testifies that she was not an anonymous housewife, getting on with life behind the scenes.'

～

Let's revisit the question of Wilayat's age and children here. If she was a teenage bride who was born in 1931 and was only sixteen years old at the time of Partition, it would make her political position all the more remarkable, and perhaps impossible. It's likelier that *Dawn* was correct when it reported her to be forty-five years old in 1954.

As discussed in Chapter 8, Sakina and Ali Raza were most probably born in Karachi, shortly after moving there, and were still quite young when her husband died. In a letter dated 1962, that is part of the MHA file, she mentions four children: one daughter and three sons, the eldest being twenty years old.

She ended up travelling to India with only three children—in the letters kept by the MHA, she listed only four visa numbers, out of which one must have been hers. So the fourth child mentioned in the letter might have been Shahid—the son who told *New York Times* in 2019 that he ran away from home and ended up in England. It is a bit of a mystery, however, why Wilayat would mention Shahid in these letters, as his presence in 1962 does not correspond with other reported events. Shahid for one, told the *New York Times* he ran away from home at the age of fourteen, long before this. His gravestone, a picture of which was shared by Camellia, his English widow, on social media, says his year of birth was 1940. This would mean he left in the year of Wilayat's arrest, rather than shortly before her move to India. Of course, a gravestone is no definite proof of his year of birth. For those South Asians born before Partition, birth information is often an estimation. The age at which he claimed he ran away does somehow match Sakina's mention of her brother 'Prince Mehdi', who according to her died at age fourteen. The story of his death may have been Wilayat's way of expressing the loss she felt when Shahid ran away. Shahid died shortly after his interview with *New York Times*. We tried to contact Camellia, who also spoke to *New York Times* several times, but she did not reply to us.

There were adult children as well at the time of Wilayat's arrest in the 1950s. The newspapers reporting the 1954 episode mentioned an adult daughter. When Wilayat was released on 31 August 1954, the *Daily Jang* reported that this was done on the personal surety of her daughter, Yasmeen Butt. 'Yasmeen Butt has appealed the court to release her mother who has been kept in jail and said that her detention is "illegal".'

In another letter from the MHA file, Wilayat mentions a fourth son, who died in an Air Force crash around 1953. He would have been an adult and a trained pilot at the time—which is another indication that Wilayat must have been older than she said she was in India.

And then there was Zahid, the eldest son. We learnt about him in the 2019 *New York Times* article, where he is introduced by Shahid, the brother in England. Zahid had an Air Force career and later migrated to the US, where he died in 2017. We contact his family through a friend of the Butt family in Lahore, Zahid Husain, who via Facebook tells us that his father had been an Air Force colleague of Zahid Butt. Through him we hear that Zahid's widow, Salma, suffers from dementia. Their daughter, Sameena, said she has no more information about her father and grandparents' background.

Royal After All?

We find Zahid's name in a book that was published by the Pakistan Air Force Book Club called *Sentinels in the Sky*.[5] Group Captain Salahuddin Zahid Butt, awarded with the medal of honour, Sitara-e-Jurut, features among forty-six heroes of the 1965 war against India. A photo shows a serious-looking man with neatly cut hair and a small moustache. A five-page biography mostly goes into details of his war efforts—so valuable that a road has been named after him in the cantonment area of Rawalpindi, a 'rare honour'— and introduces him as being born on 17 May 1928 in 'a traditional family of Lucknow'. His father Inayatullah Butt is described as a government officer with 'unprecedented repute in Lucknow'—though interestingly there is no mention of his brief career in Pakistan. His mother's name is not mentioned.

At this stage, we wonder if it is possible that Wilayat's older children were stepchildren. Considering that Inayatullah was reportedly much older to her and Asad himself had told neighbours that Wilayat was not his biological mother, it is a possibility. Shahid had also identified himself as a half-brother of Ali Raza and Sakina in receipts for Western Union transfers found in Malcha Mahal by the *New York Times* reporter Ellen Barry.[6] Moreover, the age difference between Zahid, born in 1928, and Ali Raza, likely born in 1951 or 1952, is significant—even if there were four siblings in between. Yasmeen, given her age in 1954, could not have been Sakina with another name. Perhaps Yasmeen was a stepdaughter or a daughter-in-law, married to one of Wilayat's adult sons.

Hoping to find more clarity, we visit the Registrar of Birth and Death in Lucknow. We are directed to the Nagar Nigam, or the Municipal Corporation headquarters, a historical white building. The library is at the top of a narrow, spiralling staircase, past a room where old furniture is piled up till the ceiling and through a large, dark hall with tall bookshelves lining the walls. The librarian is happy to look for Zahid's recorded date of birth, 17 May 1928. Lucknow was divided into eight wards at the time, she says. We ask her to first try the area of the old mansion in the slum we visited on the directions of Mir Abdullah. It's not there. But in the fifth book she tries, it is written in neat Urdu handwriting: on 17 May 1928, Inayatullah Butt had a child; no mother's name; no name of the child. There is one piece of new information, however: a residential area. Khandari Bazar. It's nearby, the librarian says.

Encouraged, we ask her if we can go through more books of the same ward for the subsequent years. Perhaps we can find out, at least, in which years the other children were born. She declines, strictly. She is willing to search only if we have a date of birth. Can we search ourselves if we bring an Urdu reader along? The answer remains a clear no. Can we take a picture of the page with Inayatullah Butt's name? No.

At Khandari Bazar, there are no further leads. It's a lower-income area full of narrow lanes and newly constructed buildings of two or three floors. We ask around if there are any older parts, any houses that have been around for a century or so. The inhabitants have no idea. This is all new, they say.

Without access to records, there is still no conclusive answer to Wilayat's age and those of her children, and we must imagine their family life in Karachi with the best guess we can make.

∼

Wilayat and Inayatullah moved from Lucknow to Karachi with two adult sons (Zahid and his brother), a teenage son (Shahid) and a younger son (Asad). As discussed earlier, we suspect that it was likely not Partition violence that made them leave, but the promises of opportunity in the new country of Pakistan. In Karachi, we can imagine that feelings of optimism and embarking upon a new life contributed to them having two more children. The elder two sons joined the Air Force as young officers—Zahid, according to his biography in the earlier mentioned book about war heroes, secured admission at the Royal Pakistan Air Force (RPAF) college in Risalpur in 1948 and earned his wings in December 1949.

Inayatullah joined Pakistan Aviation Ltd, an organization we cannot find much about. To understand more about his position in society, we meet a historian and aviation expert, Waqar Zaidi, at the Lahore University of Management Sciences (LUMS), a large and green campus at the edge of town.

Zaidi is sure he came across Inayatullah's name in his research, he says, though he cannot recall where it was exactly. He explains that Pakistan Aviation was formed in 1948 for the service and maintenance of both civil and military aircrafts. The civil aircrafts at the time were owned by a few private airlines, which made Pakistan Aviation partially privately owned. In 1954 it became part of the new nationalized airline, Pakistan International Airlines (PIA).

Inayatullah's position would have been relatively minor, Zaidi says. On his computer, we look at a few editions of the Who's Who, almanacs of prominent people that used to appear annually. Under aviation, we find the names of the director of civil aviation and the managing director of Orient, the main private airline of that time. 'Those were the big positions.' Inayatullah's position was more anonymous, apparently, but Zaidi thinks it must have been politically challenging. 'The majority of the spare parts and resources were provided by Orient, but the work on military aircrafts was prioritized,' he says. 'He would probably also be the one who was blamed for many plane crashes, and there were quite a few in the early 1950s, usually blamed on either pilot error or poor maintenance.'

Later, in the *Dawn* archives in Karachi, we hardly find any references to Pakistan Aviation Ltd. Curiously, one of very few articles is about the visit of then Prime Minister Khwaja Nazimuddin to the factory. The person accompanying the Prime Minister was one A.T. Naqvi, chairman of the company, not the secretary. The visit took place on 18 December 1951, around the time that Inayatullah must have died.

Speaking about how aviation ran in the family—with two sons in the Air Force and Inayatullah ending up at Pakistan Aviation Ltd—we mention to Zaidi that even Wilayat was said to be a pilot. Kasim, the retainer who stayed with them in Delhi, told us that she flew planes; Sakina says the same in her book.

This gives Zaidi an idea. 'Flying was promoted a lot in the 1940s and '50s by the elites,' he says. 'There were private flying clubs in Karachi in those days. Many elite people used to have their own small planes.'

It turns out to be yet another dead end in our wild-goose chase. The Karachi Aero Club is a relic of old-world charm, with goats roaming on what used to be the landing strip and lawns, now minimally maintained for the occasional wedding party. It was once the place to be for the who's who of Karachi, says Babar Syed, the secretary of the club, who spent his childhood there in the 1960s and became an active member in the 1970s. Asked for old membership lists, he mentions floods and bad weather conditions, but promises to help. The next day, we are invited to look at the archive, which turns out to be a literal truckload of about fifty large jute bags full of files and loose papers arranged in no system whatsoever. We spend hours going over decades of social functions, pilot licenses, meeting minutes, plane crashes and club scandals, but find no mention of Inayatullah Butt, let alone Wilayat. In fact, there seem to have been no female members at all.

Next, we visit the All Pakistan Women Association, which was founded by First Lady Ra'ana Liaquat Ali Khan after Partition. The president mentions she has an aunt who is close to 100 and if anyone would remember Wilayat, it might be her. But the aunt is ill and can't meet us. Later, she travels to relatives in the US. Our request for a video call is also denied.

Without any documentation or witnesses, we can only guess what happened to Wilayat after 1954. From a feisty, outspoken, politically active woman making it to the newspapers more than once, she disappeared from the public eye for years. Having been persecuted, from being declared a lunatic and institutionalized to her car being impounded, must have crushed her to some extent. 'It raises the question of how it was for her as a lone woman, a mother without a partner, operating in that context,' wonders historian Ansari during our phone conversation.

Wilayat continued to live in Karachi after this, but under circumstances she herself described as difficult in a typed letter to the State Bank of Pakistan, which is in the MHA file kept by the National Archives in Delhi. She wrote this letter to request for 'Indian Currency of Rs 15,000 and gold ornaments valued Rs 5,000', a month before she set sail for India, claiming that the money was meant for the marriages of her eldest son and her daughter.

'This innocent family already tortured by the powers as if not human beings, only due to a difference in opinion,' she wrote, and later in the letter: 'There is no need for detail here. God will take revenge.'

The address Wilayat gave on this letter as her postal address, Ansari informs us, was a home allotted to government employees. 'PECHS stands for Pakistan Employees Cooperative Housing Society, which was set up to cater for people working for the new Pakistani administration, from around 1950,' she writes over WhatsApp after we share the address. 'It's located in what is now quite central Karachi, though originally it was on the eastern edge of the city. Like a lot of such housing societies, people got allocated plots and then built houses on them with loans. Gradually, PECHS spread, so there are at least six blocks these days, becoming increasingly commercialized.'

We visit the area exactly sixty years after Wilayat left. The PECHS area has indeed become commercialized, in the absence of the large central administration that moved to Islamabad. But the address remains the same, so we easily find the plot in Block 3 where Wilayat lived in 1962. It is a traditionally planned neighbourhood, with straight streets crossing each other at regular intervals. The roads are wide and the plots large, indicating that this has become an area for wealthier citizens. Wilayat's plot now houses a centre for people with autism, which was set up twenty years ago. None of the neighbours we speak with, or their relatives, have lived in the area for longer than three decades. About the early 1950s and '60s, and who lived there at that time, they have no idea.

At the society office, an officer called Muhammad Afzal says he has no knowledge of any elderly people living nearby. Asked about the plot, he says he needs his superior's permission to give us information of its ownership. We visit a few more times, without any result. Around the corner of the office, we find the PECHS cemetery. Perhaps, we wonder, Inayatullah would have been buried here. But the guards say there are no records of past burials. 'Somebody' took all the records to some government office, they claim. They show us some 'old' graves they know of, but they are from the 1970s. Later, we read in an article by the news agency AFP that the cemetery is run by a kind of 'graveyard mafia'.

> In the teeming metropolis of Karachi, Pakistan's biggest city, graveyards are filling up and the dead are running out of space to rest. For the right price and for the right person, a plot can be 'found' for the body of a loved one by shady crews who demolish old graves to make room for the new.[7]

At night, we meet a group of local journalists at the beautiful Karachi Press Club, which is based in a nineteenth-century Victorian-style bungalow. It is known as Dinshaw House, named after Seth Eduljee

Dinshaw, a self-made Parsi millionaire who was Karachi's largest landowner in colonial times and contributed significantly towards the city's architecture.[8] Our friends, including a journalist with BBC Urdu and a freelance researcher, laugh about our experience at the Karachi Aero Club and the cemetery. Historical records of any kind are a rare find in Karachi, they know from their experiences. We hear about fires, termites and the general callousness of authorities when the capital was moved from Karachi to Islamabad.

Would we have better luck in Lahore, we wonder. This is where Wilayat and Inayatullah spent time before Partition, mingling with famous communists and Kashmiri nationalists of that time. We will be passing through Lahore on our way back to Delhi, as the city is not far from the land border between Pakistan and India. But where to begin? 'You know,' says one of the journalists, 'I know someone who might be able to help you. He is an Urdu journalist in Lahore and a very good researcher. And he knows the Butt community of Lahore well.' We call Sher Ali Khalti the same evening. 'Give me a day,' he says.

∼

We meet Sher in front of his office, that of the Urdu newspaper *Daily Jang*—the same newspaper that had reported Wilayat's arrest in 1954—immediately after landing in Lahore via a PIA flight from Karachi. Still unaware of what he has found, we introduce ourselves and invite him into our cab. He gives the driver an address and then says: 'We are going to meet a man. He is a relative of Wilayat's.'

We can hardly believe it! After a year of travelling around Lucknow, Kashmir and Karachi, meeting people to whom she was a mystery and going through archives where she was either a brief mention or totally absent, here was an unanticipated meeting with someone from her family. It feels anti-climactic, in an ironic sense, and unreal.

The man, let's call him Mr Butt, meets us outside the gate of his house in a relatively new suburb. Around fifty years old, we imagine this is how Ali Raza could have looked like had he lived a healthier and more prosperous life. His fair skin, grey hair and hooked nose are similar, but the person in front of us stands straight and tall. He serves us tea in a small reception area. We have so many questions that we don't know where to start. Before we can make up our mind, he starts questioning us.

'How did you know about me?' he asks. 'Only one other person knows about me: Suhasini Raj.' Raj works for the *New York Times* in Delhi and worked with Barry on the 2019 article and follow-ups. Butt says that the *New York Times* team tried to convince him to be part of a documentary series on Wilayat and her children and offered him a good amount of money to do so, but that it has not materialized. He also says that he has not shared any information with anyone, so far, and then asks us the purpose of our book.

Meanwhile, we try to ask some questions. Where was Wilayat born, and when? How is he related to her? He answers some but keeps criticizing our line of questioning. 'You must start at the beginning. Did she not claim to be part of the Awadh royal family? You have to start there. You have to understand the history. There is a context. What do you know about Shia marriages?' We share our basic knowledge of nikah and mu'tah marriages, and this somehow satisfies him. 'Ellen Barry knew nothing about all this. Her story is full of gaps and mistakes. She won awards for that story!' he says, now in an angry tone, before revealing a bombshell. 'Wilayat was from Lahore. But it is more complicated than that. *She had royal blood.*'

We almost fall off our seats. Wilayat was royal after all?

For a while, he tests our knowledge and intentions, but in the end, Mr Butt agrees to tell us everything he knows, albeit off the record. He says that being employed in the public sector, he is not allowed to speak on the record on anything related to the government, which is part of Wilayat's story.

Some of the information is unique, while other stories are based on old rumours or his own interpretations. He has handwritten notes and photos, passed down to him by older family members who are no more. In a two-hour conversation and many follow-up phone calls and exchanges of chat messages online, we learn more about Wilayat and Inayatullah's families, her link to Awadh and their connections to Kashmir.

~

Wilayat's father was Khwaja Ahmad Deen Butt, a Sunni Muslim from Srinagar. He migrated to Punjab in the nineteenth century along with many Kashmiri Muslims who fled famine, poverty and discrimination by the Dogra regime. It can very well be that he planted the seed of Kashmiri activism in Wilayat's mind. About the Kashmiri migrant community, which had grown to over 177,000 people in Punjab by the turn of the century, historian Ayesha Jalal writes:

> Kashmiris settled in other parts of India, especially Punjab and the NWFP,[9] retained emotional and familiar links with their original homeland. Like most diasporic movements, that of Kashmiri Muslims drew upon the myth of return and the vision of a free and prosperous Kashmir.[10]

Khwaja Ahmad Deen Butt settled in the Akbar Gate area of Lahore's historic walled city, today one of the poorer areas known for its narrow allies, and worked for the British Indian Railways. Perhaps, Butt suggests, it was through her father's railways contacts that Wilayat managed to live at the New Delhi Railway Station for so long.

He was married to a Shia girl who lived in the nearby Bhatti Gate area. The name of this girl, Wilayat's mother, was Zohra Bibi. *Zohra!* Our hearts skip a beat. Zohra, as mentioned before, was the first name adopted by Sakina when they lived in Ganderbal.

Zohra, Wilayat's mother, was from Lucknow and was said to be a grandchild of Wajid Ali Shah and one of his mut'ah wives. So, it turns out, there was truth in both of Wilayat's identities. She had Kashmiri roots, through her father, but she was also connected to the Awadh royalty and believed to be a direct descendant of Wajid Ali Shah, through her mother. What the name of her great-grandmother was, who was said to be a mut'ah wife of the king, the Butt family does not know. They don't know the name of Wilayat's grandparents either.

Wilayat Butt was born around 1910 and grew up in Lahore with three brothers and one sister. The brothers were called Iqbal, Aslam and Jilal and her sister was referred to as 'Aapa'. Meanwhile, Inayatullah Butt, also of Kashmiri descent, had similarly migrated from Srinagar and settled in Gunahor, a village about 60 kilometres from Lahore, just next to the ancient Great Trunk Road that had connected present-day Myanmar with Afghanistan for centuries.

There is a photo of him in the family archive, in black and white. A gentleman wearing a three-piece suit with a tie, a wristwatch and small, round-shaped eyeglasses, slightly balding around the forehead, posing on a chair. He looks confident and serious, but not unfriendly. 'Be careful with it,' Butt warns us after he shares the photo via WhatsApp. 'You are the only ones outside the family who have this photo.'

Inayatullah was born around 1895, he says. He went to school in Lahore, to the well-known Islamia High School at Sheranwala Gate. There, he had a famous school friend, according to Butt: Sheikh Abdullah.

We look up from our notebook and see him smiling. 'Aha! Now it's getting interesting, right?' We nod. Inayatullah was a school friend of Sheikh Abdullah's? This could explain Wilayat's good contacts in Kashmir and all the support she got from the state in her efforts to resettle there. But how is that possible when Inayatullah and Abdullah were over ten years apart in age? Also, Sheikh Abdullah goes into his early education in Kashmir in detail in his autobiography and makes no mention of this school, or any school in Lahore for that matter.[11] Butt shrugs. 'Sheikh Abdullah's official date of birth must be false.' A lot of Kashmiris used to spend summers in Srinagar and winters in Lahore, Butt says. 'Sheikh Abdullah used to stay in Lahore with relatives in Chuna Mandi,' he says, mentioning an area very close to the Islamia High School.

After high school Inayatullah joined the government college in Lahore. Upon graduation, he started living in Gunahor with a cousin, Shahabuddin, who also happened to be his brother-in-law through marriage with his sister. Inayatullah himself got married to a woman named Miraj, with whom he had three daughters. Our source is the grandchild of one of these daughters, he reveals. So he is not a blood relation of Wilayat, but a grandnephew of Ali Raza and Sakina, from their father's side.

It was during a visit to Lahore that Inayatullah met and fell in love with Wilayat. He was already based in Lucknow by then, and took his young bride there, while Miraj and the three daughters stayed in Gunahor. All the children we earlier learnt about, our source says, were Wilayat's own children and not stepchildren. He gives us their real names. Salahuddin Zahid Butt, the eldest son and later war hero, was born in 1928 in Lucknow; Khalid, the son who tragically died in an air force crash; Immadudin Shahid, the son who ran away;[12] Tariq, whom we later came to know as Asad; Arif, known by the family as Mickey, who later went by Prince Cyrus or Ali Raza; and the daughter, Princess Sakina, who in Kashmir used the names Marzia and Zohra. She was actually called Farhad Yasmeen, our source says. But he is puzzled how Yasmeen could have been mentioned by the newspapers in 1954 as, he confirms, she would have been a small child at that time. This mystery remains unsolved.

Our source returns to Gunahor to share more details of far-removed relatives. Inayatullah's cousin and his wife, who was Inayatullah's sister, had one son, he says. His was born in 1916 and named Bashir Dar. He is not alive anymore, but he is the one who passed on a lot of this family history. Bashir Dar was close to Inayatullah and Wilayat, says Butt. Dar went to school in Lucknow, to the well-known Jubilee College. After school, he joined the Indian Military Academy in Dehradun. While enrolled there, he often spent the weekends in Lucknow with his uncle and his wife, says our source. On many occasions he was joined by two academy friends. One was Hamid Nawaz, the father of Punjab's former governor Shahid Hamid. The other was a great-grandson of Wajid Ali Shah and one of his mut'ah wives. Our source does not know the name of this nawab, but he says that besides being an Academy friend of Bashir Dar, he was also a neighbour of Inayatullah and Wilayat in Lucknow. He and Wilayat discussed their mutual ancestry and after that he treated Wilayat as a sister. He even gave her some family jewellery because of that.

'This is where Wilayat's connection to the royal Awadh family begins.'

~

After Partition, Inayatullah decided to move his family to Pakistan. Butt reproduces the family story that Inayatullah was attacked in pre-Partition violence in Lucknow and says that this was the main reason for the move. Though he was given a job in Karachi, he was allotted a plot in Lahore, on Fane Road, a street near the Lahore High Court where lawyers' chambers were situated. This is where another historical figure crossed their path. Salma Tasadduque, a women's activist and Muslim League politician married to a lawyer, had property in Karachi. The two families decided to mutually exchange their properties, our source says. The house they got in return, Butt claims, was not in PECHS, but a prime property just a few houses away from the Prime Minister's house. Liaquat Ali Khan lived on Victoria Road in those days, a central, wide road that is today called Abdullah Haroon Road. Wilayat was good friends with the first lady, Ra'ana Liaquat Ali Khan, Butt claims.

'She was not poor,' he says, again referring with some anger to the 2019 *New York Times* article. 'She belonged to the elite. She had sold her house just before moving to Kashmir. She had money. She had valuables.'

Salma Tasadduque ran a charity from 9, Fane Road, after Partition. Today, the Punjab Bar Council has its office at this address. Our colleague Sher spends a few days at the Revenue Office to get his hands on the no. 9 plot document, which is nowhere in the public domain. Initially, the officer confirms orally that Inayatullah Butt was the first owner of the plot. But when we finally get a copy of the papers, it shows that the government transferred the plot directly to Tasadduque Hussain, Salma's husband. The name Inayatullah or Butt does not feature in the papers. Perhaps, our source says, the transaction was done orally. Perhaps Inayatullah was offered the plot, and passed the offer on to the Tasadduque family.

Coming to the reasons why Wilayat left for Kashmir, Butt brings up the 1954 incident, but with a twist. According to what he heard from his elder relatives, Bogra had tried to harass Wilayat at a social gathering. In response, she had slapped him publicly, a huge embarrassment for Bogra. Declaring her mentally ill was a cover-up, he says, so that her reasons for slapping him would never be fully known. This crushed her to the extent that she wanted to leave. Butt does not know why it took her eight years, but he speculates that it took time for her to make up her mind and sell all her things. Also, her father was still alive, which Butt says explains why she did not immediately want to leave Pakistan. 'She was not crazy,' he says.

Butt has not heard the theory that Inayatullah was poisoned. 'As far as we know, he died of a heart attack.' He narrates how

Inayatullah had been in Lahore, on leave for a one month, when he was called back to Karachi by his office. He took the train, a journey of twenty-two hours in those days. 'As he rushed back, he died shortly after arrival, on the train station of Karachi.'

Butt has also not heard the rumour, about Inayatullah's involvement in the assassination of Liaquat Ali Khan, before. When we ask him about it, he says that his one month leave around the time of the murder, or the fact that he was called back with urgency, with hindsight, could be perceived as 'suspicious'.

∼

Quite a few relatives of Wilayat are still alive, says our source. Shahid's granddaughter, Wilayat's great-granddaughter, lives in the UK. And Zahid's daughter Sameena, Wilayat's granddaughter, lives in the US. None of them reply to our online message requests to speak about Wilayat. Two of Wilayat's cousins named Wahida and Khalida, who are the daughters of her sister, still live in Lahore. Barry of the *New York Times* met them and says they dismissed Wilayat's claim of royalty; her account makes them seem slightly unhinged. There are others. Wilayat's brother Iqbal, for example, married to a daughter of Inayatullah from his first marriage, and the couple had children. A son of Iqbal married a sister of Bashir Dar. One of their sons, a doctor, lives in the US, another in Lahore. 'Most relatives live in Lahore', Butt says.

Over the course of one and a half years, he says he keeps asking them to talk to us, but reports back that they are not willing. 'They feel that the 2019 *New York Times* story damaged the reputation of the family', he explains. There is another, more important reason, our source says: 'Most family members are not sympathetic to Wilayat, because they are Sunni Muslims.'

Wilayat was raised in the Sunni tradition, our source says, as this was her father's religion. But her mother must have been proud of her roots and shared some of her traditions and knowledge with Wilayat. The rest of the family, however, preferred to suppress the Shia roots, according to our source.

'Sunni Muslims don't accept the Shia concept of mut'ah marriage. Wilayat was part of the royal Awadh family through a mut'ah wife of the king. But they think this is illegal. Both her paternal and maternal sides wanted to hide this lineage.'

Most of the family thinks of Wilayat as mentally ill, says Butt. From her admission into a mental hospital in the 1950s to her 'eccentric' behaviour in Delhi and Lucknow in later decades, the image of the 'crazy aunt' has stuck and was adopted even by the present-day generation.

Our source though has a different take: one of an ultra-conservative milieu wearing down a bright woman.

'She was the second wife,' he says, suggesting that such a relationship was already looked down upon. 'She had a progressive approach. She was ambitious. Such ladies are not accepted in our system.'

Beyond Truth and Lies

'Now, a general criterion of truth would be one that is valid for all knowledge, whatever its objects maybe. But it is clear that such a criterion abstracts from all contents of knowledge (reference to its object), while truth concerns these very contents. It is impossible and absurd, therefore, to ask for a sign of the truth of such contents.'
—Immanuel Kant, *Critique of Pure Reason*[1]

What is true? What is false? What is real? What is imaginary? Throughout the period that we worked on this story, we grappled with these questions.

We started out with the intention to hear Wilayat, Sakina and Ali Raza out properly, which we felt had never really been attempted in the true sense. Someone might say that they got the opportunity to narrate their story over the years, to many journalists. But we feel almost everyone who met them and wrote about them focused on certain tropes and stereotypes, and saw them through a particular lens: royalty, imposters, Pakistani, Indian, Muslim, Shia, Sunni, residents of Lucknow or Lahore or Karachi, high class, paupers or some of these categories put together. But not enough was done to situate them in their overall context and judge them based on that. Rarely was any attempt made to draw a trajectory of their entire lives, from the beginning to the end. One could argue that such an approach does not work in journalism where deadlines are short, and the word-limit is less. But we believe that something else also played a part: the unconscious biases of the media, and the changing socio-political circumstances, which coloured its reporting on them.

Perhaps, the Malcha Mahal residents also played to these preconceived notions. Hence, the same picture emerged over and over: of self-proclaimed royals, cut-off from reality, unable to come to terms with a rapidly changing world. At best, harmless eccentrics; at worst, frauds.

Some of this was true. But it was not the entire truth, we realized as we tried to make sense of their lives.

Their story was part of a bigger picture which included Partition of India, Kashmir, treatment of royalty in Independent India, and the position of Muslims in it, especially those with family links in Pakistan.

Wilayat and her family's story has holes and contradictions, we realized soon enough as we followed their lives in pre-Partition Lahore and Lucknow, via Karachi and Kashmir, to Delhi. We found many traces she and her children had left, in the form of newspaper articles, their own writings, archival records, photos and living sources who remembered them at different stages of their lives.

However, some claims remained unverified, some questions went unanswered, not all conflicting memories could be resolved, and some leads reached a dead end.

For instance, how old was Wilayat when she married Inayatullah? Was there any truth to her claim that he was poisoned, or that the death of her son Khalid was part of a larger conspiracy? Was Asad her biological son or not? Did Wilayat meet a distant cousin from the Awadh royal family via her nephew, Bashir Dar, in pre-Partition Lucknow? Could he have been 'Bashir Nawab', whom Kasim had mentioned as the person at whose home Asad and him used to stay during their travels to Lucknow? Did Asad really bring a black cobra into the railway station? What exactly did Ali Raza do in London? How did Sakina die?

We tried different archives. The Islamia School in Lahore had one Inayatullah graduating in the early twentieth century, but no last name is mentioned. No Sheikh Abdullah pops up in the dusty old record books that the current school management showed us—but the books are not complete. At Jubilee College in Lucknow, we don't find any trace of Bashir Dar either, but there are only a few records of the 1920s and '30s; most are missing. The Indian Military Academy in Dehradun refers us to the army headquarters, where we don't get any answer to our request for any archival entry related to him. RTIs to the government regarding missing files and Wilayat's allowance are passed along to different departments before returning to us with inconclusive answers.

Some sources have died, others don't reply to our messages.

There are rumours. One that goes around in Lucknow is that Inayatullah was related to Mehmood Butt, a former administrator of the Uttar Pradesh state service, and an uncle of author Salman Rushdie. We seriously investigate this rumour but find only tenuous links. A nephew of Mehmood Butt in Pakistan initially replies to our email, but when we ask this question, he stops answering.

The search is frustrating at times. But we keep reminding ourselves: this story is not only about recorded facts preserved at the archives; it lies in the gaps and cracks of memory. Different memories, even when contradictory and unverified, are equally valuable parts of this story. They all contribute to the truth.

When archives fail, we feel re-energized to find new sources that remember the family, and there are many, like Kasim in Delhi; Salim and Imtiaz Naqshbandi in Kashmir; and Mr Butt in Lahore. They bring Wilayat, Asad, Sakina and Ali Raza alive.

They remind us that Wilayat was once a girl with ambitions, excited to get out of her parents' house in Lahore. That Sakina was once a young woman whose picture could still make the heart of an old neighbour beat faster. The boys loved cricket and each had their own unique temper and character. They went to school; made plans for their future. And their transition from people with their feet in the real world to eccentric self-proclaimed royals who seemingly lost a sense of reality was gradual. They were not just the characters of a play they wrote themselves.

Behind the façade of arrogant Awadh royalty, they were humans of flesh and blood. But because they had put these previous selves far away, others could no longer see them. No one really tried to search, either; journalists and other visitors became eager spectators to the play that was performed. When Ali Raza died, he and his sister and mother had not been 'real people' in the eyes of society for a long time. Hence, the step towards becoming ghosts in a haunted old castle was a small one.

∼

What was the truth, after all, of their lives? What was real, and what was imaginary about them? And most importantly, were they liars?

Ali Raza gave the answer himself, in a conversation with the *New York Times* journalist Ellen Barry, who wrote that she '*had* to tell *the truth*', and narrated:

'You are just a very mysterious person, because I don't know who you are,' I said once. His response was coy.

'Oh really,' he said, in a singsong voice. 'Well, anyway. Oh, really? If you have said me mysterious, I am just sitting before you.'[2]

It was not an answer Barry could accept, and she declared him a liar later in the article, someone whose lies had offended her.

Of course, we cannot proclaim to know what was in their heart of hearts. But we are convinced it was not a 'lie', in the casual way we generally mean it, because that defines truth and reality in a simplistic way in the context of this story. Wilayat's life was not simple, and neither is memory or identity. Between the truth and lie, lies the abyss of memory.

We can only wonder whether Wilayat's memories, traumas, fascinations and fabulations had mixed together in a new reality that made sense to her, and started to make sense to Ali Raza and Sakina, too.

~

By the time we were close to completing our work on this book, we started listening to a series of podcasts by the Belgium–Dutch audio collective Schik.[3] They specialize in personal stories that are almost stranger than fiction, but at the same time give us insights into relevant social structures and the human mind. One, called *Bob*, is about an elderly woman with dementia who starts remembering a former boyfriend, Bob. He was her neighbour when she was a teenager. When she was fifteen, in the late 1940s, she got pregnant and was sent to a monastery to deliver and forcefully give her child up for adoption. None of her children had ever heard of this Bob, or a possible sibling, and wondered if the story was true.

The podcasters started an investigation. By talking to the old lady, Elize, they quickly figured out that a lot of what she was saying was impossible. That Bob was a pilot who stood on the wings of planes flying by, waving at her, for example. Or that the two of them had nine children. But they decided: 'We try to not cast her aside as that confused old lady, but to see her as someone who is trying to tell a story.'

They went into the archives and found proof that Bob existed and was indeed a neighbour of Elize's. But Bob had passed away; his widow refused to meet the podcasters, and other relatives had never heard of Elize. Bob never worked for the airline Elize said he flew with. At multiple monasteries they found out that there were indeed unmarried pregnant girls in those years and there were even notebooks with names. But the year Elize would have been there seemed to be missing from all the records. The podcasters didn't give up.

'You can't prove every memory you ever had either, right?' they say to each other.

At the same time, they found out that Elize's favourite soap opera on television had a character whose story was remarkably similar to hers. They remarked: 'Did she just take her story from TV? Or did the TV show trigger a memory?'

They considered every theory, from Bob being an imaginary friend to her being a victim of incest who made up the love relationship to cover up her trauma. Despite the lack of 'proof' and living sources, they stayed sympathetic to Elize. 'We don't know any more what we can believe ... But this is what happens to so many women with painful memories. Who believes you if it was a long time ago and all traces have been erased?'

Ultimately, the investigation remained inconclusive and moved from the archives to experts, including a neurologist, who explained that the human brain often mixes up memories. People can have memories of something happening to them when it in fact happened to someone close to them or was even the subject of a news item that made such an impression that they later remembered it as if it was their own life. And the brain mixes such different memories together in a story that makes sense. The podcasters conclude: 'Every human needs a story, without a story, you disappear.'

∽

After hearing *Bob*, we feel reassured that Wilayat's story is important, no matter how much or little recorded evidence we find. Just like Elize, she was a woman with painful memories who was trying to tell a story. 'A delusion is a belief that someone needs to have', explains Salman Akhtar, a renowned Indian-American psychoanalyst who was born in pre-Partition Lucknow. He now lives in the US and is happy to speak to us on the phone. We tell him about Wilayat, and ask him to help us understand her story in the context of what we know about her life, from his insightful perspectives on the concepts of truth and lies.[4]

Akhtar begins by giving multiple examples of things that large numbers of people believe in but that could be considered delusions. 'An atheist would argue that someone who believes in God is delusional,' he says. 'Poetry is also a kind of private, aesthetic delusion that is shared by similarly delusional people. When Pablo Neruda writes, what is "sadder than a train, standing in the rain?", I, who loves poetry, can say: "Wow!" But another person may think it is crazy, that it does not mean anything.' Another example he gives is nationalism. 'India was one country, then it became two countries, then it became three countries. One day we love Lahore; the next day we hate Lahore.'

The reality as experienced by Wilayat and her children has been described by observers as a delusion, one that was initially believed by many; that was increasingly viewed with scepticism as their behaviour grew more eccentric; that continued to intrigue; and finally attracted contempt from people who found their reality to be ultimately suspicious, crazy, and, for all practical purposes totally untrue. Those who still believe in it, such as Kasim and Abrar, are considered less rational and educated, but are also less powerful than those who now, after Ali Raza's death, control the story: the journalists, the writers—us.

We earlier made references to *Madness and Civilization*, the French philosopher Foucault's extraordinarily insightful treatise on reason and un-reason, in which he treats the subject of madness as a sociological one, rather than psychological. The mad, he argues, have a function in society. Superficially, they may seem so different that observing them is merely entertaining. But they show us a mirror as well as a warning, that in a way, they are close to us and if we are not careful, we could become them.[5]

Wilayat Mahal and her children, Sakina and Ali Raza, were certainly outliers to mainstream society when seen from the outside but paradoxically they also represented its dark heart that beats in all of us. They embarrassed us, intrigued us, exasperated us, they simply refused to fit our idea of the modern, democratic, post-colonial world. Their sentimentality was overweening; their self-pity was revoltingly overwrought; their demands outrageous; their lack of any sense of proportion monstrous.

Incidentally, the word 'monster' comes from the Latin root *monstrare*, and *monere*; the first word means 'to show' or 'to demonstrate' and the second means 'to warn'. Monsters, then, are always to be displayed to the public, as warning; human existence has limits when it comes to thought and expression; cross it and you cross into the world of monsters and become a warning to the rest.

Let's return to the word 'delusion'. Like Dr Akhtar argues, we all need delusions in some form or the other to live. He also tells us that lies have many different functions, as do truths. Lies, he explains, can vary from social lies—say a small excuse to get out of dinner with a relative—to sadistic lies to cause hurt on purpose to narcissistic and pathological lies, the latter being not about lying at all, but about being unable to tell the truth. The truth comes in forms that sometimes seem contradictory—for example, what he calls the manufactured truth—to fluid, such as the narrative truth or the poetic truth.

'The line between delusion and truth, and the line between delusion and lie, is very, very thin,' he says. 'There are multiple elements to what we call a delusion. The outsiders' perspective is that it is totally false. The insider's perspective is that it is totally true. But the fact is that it is all true. By focusing only on the outsider's perspective, you overlook the needs of the person or persons who do believe in it. For them it is not false. So, we should be sympathetic to delusions. It is not something to look down upon. We should be sympathetic and we should be curious of what the person who believes in it needs.'

～

What were Wilayat's needs?

We can imagine that Wilayat, when her husband made the decision to move to Pakistan after Partition, *needed* to believe in the purpose of the new country and, therefore, immersed herself in nation-building. Given hers and Inayatullah's shared Kashmiri roots, and their Kashmiri nationalist friends from before Partition, it is not strange that the Kashmir cause came to play a huge part in that belief. We can also imagine that, when her beliefs were silenced in Karachi, the then capital of Pakistan, she became bitter and disappointed in her newly adopted country and *needed* to go somewhere that she imagined to be home. We can also imagine that she *needed* to forget about her more painful experiences, like the death of her son, her stay in a mental asylum and possible sexual harassment.

It also helped her keep her belief in the Kashmir cause alive, though her position as someone who was allowed to resettle with doubts and was under continuous surveillance meant she could not play an active role in politics. This must have frustrated Wilayat, whom we have come to know as an ambitious and modern woman, while the Kashmir cause became more and more 'academic', as discussed in Chapter 9. We can imagine that Wilayat, full of unfulfilled ambitions and crushed hope, developed the *need* to 'be someone', someone who had fulfilled her ambitions, someone with status, someone who would be seen and heard eagerly by those in power.

~

When Wilayat first arrived in New Delhi, the premise of her story—that she was a descendant of Hazrat Mahal and Wajid Ali Shah—was widely believed. Her story clashed with the reality of historical documents, birth records, family trees and existing royal claims. Her response to that was the story of Almas Mahal, a daughter of Hazrat Mahal. She does not exist in any record or in collective memory. Whether she was a figment of Wilayat's imagination, constructed by her brain to make sense of her reality, possibly based on a name of a female ancestor given to her by her mother, or an explanation she consciously came up with—a 'lie' of some sort—is impossible to know. In our efforts to understand her needs, as suggested by Akhtar, we decide that this is irrelevant, as the line between delusion, lie and truth is thin. 'Even in delusions there is always a kernel of truth,' he says. This also applies to Wilayat and her children.

From all angles and sources, it seems unlikely that Wilayat was a descendant of Hazrat Mahal. However, she did have royal lineage. Butt told us that Wilayat's mother was Zohra Bibi, a descendant of Wajid Ali Shah and one of his many mut'ah wives. The family does not know her name so Wilayat probably did not either. But it is likely true, if we consider that there must have been a kernel of truth to the story she told reporters later about her lineage. Having learnt more about Wilayat's life, it makes sense to us that she ended up identifying with Hazrat Mahal rather than one of Wajid Ali Shah's other mut'ah wives. There are many similarities: Wilayat, like Hazrat Mahal, was not her husband's first wife. While Hazrat Mahal was left behind by her exiled husband and ended up a single mother, fighting the might of the East India Company, Wilayat was a widowed mother, up against the Pakistani authorities. Both fought for lost kingdoms in a way—Awadh in the case of Hazrat Mahal, and Kashmir for Wilayat. Both women faced judgement from a conservative environment; and both ultimately lived and died in exile.

~

Alejandra Moreno-Álvarez, in the earlier mentioned article in the introduction, looks at Wilayat from the perspective of literature and women's studies. She notes that in the history of Partition, the voices of women are among those that have been silenced, and believes that Wilayat's ultimate identity was a result of that. She describes it as a coping mechanism. 'Her tale was a narrative which dealt with the paradox of telling what she could not tell, not to herself, not to her children, not to the press, that of Partition.'

She compares Wilayat to a fictional character from a story by Jhumpa Lahiri, Boori Ma, who works as a building manager but tells all residents that she was rich before Partition. The neighbours don't believe her, but the women in the building sympathize with her nevertheless. 'She probably constructs tales as a way of mourning the loss of her family,' one says. When Boori Ma has to leave the building and cannot tell her neighbours anymore about her past 'she loses control of what she is'.[6]

Wilayat had also lived through Partition and had more than one loss to mourn, in a short period of time. Being uprooted from the place where she created her own identity as a young, modern woman. Losing a child, and then another. Being imprisoned and declared mentally ill for being politically outspoken and ambitious, something unbecoming of a widowed mother.

Moreno-Álvarez suspects that Lahiri was inspired by Wilayat when she wrote about Boori Ma. It might be true. Fiction helps us understand deeply felt truths about human existence. We have also found fiction to be helpful in making sense of Wilayat's story. To us, Wilayat shares many similarities with Blanche Dubois, the tragic protagonist of Tennessee Williams's play, *A Streetcar Named Desire*, written in 1947, first staged as a Broadway play and later turned into a film with Marlon Brando playing the antagonist, Stanley Kowalski.

The plot is simple: Blanche, a woman in her thirties, belonging to the American South—which has its own ethics and aesthetics, and, of course, a strict social hierarchy—finds herself afloat in the less solid world of New Orleans, with its jazz music and bowling alleys and intermixing of classes. He sister Stella is married to Stanley, a working-class man with little sophistication, and they live in a small, cramped apartment where Blanche, played by Vivien Leigh in the movie, turns up, having lost her big house in the South to creditors.

It is not difficult to see the obvious similarities: Wilayat turning up in India having lost her support system in Pakistan, which included her family, her husband and her adult son. As Blanche later admits, she was 'played out' in the town where she lived; so was Wilayat. In fact, we learn towards the end of the play that Blanche had been banished by the authorities—similarly to Wilayat who felt harassed by the authorities in Karachi.

Blanche has a complicated relationship with truth; her behaviour and utterances do not correspond to the commonly agreed upon reality. But for Stanley, her elisions and evasions about her past circumstances are unbearable. He digs into them and finds out some uncomfortable 'truths' without any context: that Blanche was thrown out of Lorel; that she had taken multiple lovers; that she even fell for a teenage student of hers following which she lost her job as a schoolteacher.

The role of Stanley has certainly been played by the media—Indian and foreign—in the case of Wilayat which has tried to 'expose' her; the *New York Times* 'exposé' was only the last example.[7] The media was more sympathetic initially, which could be due to the fascination with what remained of the old world of royalty after Independence, which later dwindled. By the time *New York Times* published some forgotten but not completely known facts about their lives in 2019, many journalists ran with those, without any attempt to understand the context. 'They were simply imposters', wrote Nosheen Iqbal in *The Observer*.[8] Exceptions were there, such as the *Indian Express* editorial, which states that '... their tragedy is starker than their lie.'[9] But more often, the tone of articles was one of contempt and ridicule, and in at least one case, with anti-Muslim elements.[10]

In the course of writing this book, trying to make sense of the jigsaw puzzle that Wilayat's life was, and the ones led by Ali Raza and Sakina, trying to corroborate the details of her story, her elisions and evasions, even embellishments—we realized that a thread was running through all of it, like the thread of the three Greek Fates who are said to stitch the fabric of our lives or cut the cloth when our time is up.

The thread was trauma.

It helped us to finally understand that the incoherence, the refusal to own up to certain events, and even perhaps the story about her origins, were all a testimony to the trauma Wilayat had suffered. Wilayat experienced trauma many times over and it affected her in a fundamental way. In the case of Sakina and Ali Raza, other than the traumatic experience they shared with their mother, the latter's death was perhaps the defining trauma for them, which comes across in the book Sakina wrote.

In her MA thesis, Harvard student Krista Carmichael studied Blanche Dubois as a trauma survivor, looking at her actions and utterances in this light. She writes in her first chapter about post-traumatic stress disorder, where she notes that the traumatic incident or incidents take centre stage in the survivor's life, and all their thoughts, dreams and behaviours become connected to it; that it impairs the survivor's ability to create a cohesive life story, that would also be assimilated into the larger collective experience, and finally, that it may even alter their sense of *who they are*.

Carmichael writes further:

> Due to the detached narrative, inability to re-tell a seamless history, survivors are met with skepticism towards the reality of the traumatic occurrence and even the reality of themselves, including circumstances of death and loss ... Thus both narrative memory, the telling of an integrated experience, and traumatic memory become suspect, especially when combined with the proclivity of the survivor to engage in dissociative fantasy to avoid any reminders of the trauma.[11]

It goes without saying that Wilayat and her children faced this all their lives and even after their death. Doubts, mockery and journalistic exposés marked their life from start to end, at least in India.

Carmichael bases her understanding of trauma on the seminal work on the subject by Judith Herman, who theorized it in her book *Trauma and Recovery: The Aftermath of Violence, from Domestic Abuse to Political Terror*.

Herman writes in her introduction to the book:

> The conflict between the will to deny horrible events and the will to proclaim them aloud is the central dialectic of psychological trauma. People who have survived atrocities often tell their stories in a highly emotional, contradictory and fragmented manner which undermines their credibility and

thereby serves the twin imperatives of truth-telling and secrecy ... [T]he story of the traumatic event surfaces not as a verbal narrative but as a symptom.¹²

This is an insight we believe applies to Wilayat's story, too: the story was a symptom of what she experienced. As we can see, suspecting the story of trauma survivors is very much part of the discourse, and especially if it involves women. The history of psychiatry itself is connected to women and their stories, since hysteria was the first psychological ailment to be studied by the pioneers of psychoanalysis, such as Josef Bruer and Sigmund Freud. They uncovered that hysteria in women originated primarily from sexual abuse—a traumatic event—that women had concealed from others; however, Freud himself later disowned his findings as in those days, women were not believed when they spoke of sexual abuse, like they are today, especially if it involved close relatives.

The answers to our questions at the beginning of this chapter are already implicit in this discussion. Was Wilayat a liar? We don't think so, because for trauma survivors, distinctions between truth and lie are not so obvious. The dissociation caused by the traumatic event in their mind and body forces them to latch on to any story that helps them make sense of the event, and often, if not always, they are informed by a kernel of truth. A story that allows them to both hide the truth and be heard.

As far as her being mad is concerned, just like Carmichael refuses to consider Blanche a lunatic, we also refuse to see Wilayat—and Sakina—as mad women, though they exhibit some symptoms of melancholia and delusion. We see them as unconventional women who challenged prevailing norms of society and who tried to tell us their story. Trauma defined their response to society, history and even their own beings. Perhaps with a sympathetic approach, they could have healed to some extent. Instead, their pain and grief spiralled to a point of no return.

And finally, were they frauds? Did they try to defraud the government? Again, we do not think so. If they did, they would have accepted the offered apartment in Lucknow immediately, allowing Ali Raza and Sakina to get married or make a handsome profit of it later in life. In fact, to come back to Foucault and madness, modern society tends to conflate madness with crime, and that is what happened in their case.

Perhaps in response to the *New York Times* story that aimed to expose Wilayat and her children as a regular family, the public felt defrauded, because they had for a long time believed them to be royals. But should our embarrassment not come instead from our failure to really listen and do justice to their story during their lifetime? No one, including us, can claim to know the full story—some of it has been sealed off by the government and lies in classified files in the home ministry—or so-called truth, but we hope to have added important perspectives.

Wilayat, Sakina and Ali Raza lived extraordinary lives. Their story was a symptom of the traumas they were suffering from, and in this way, it was like a symptom of the traumas weighing on our society, too. Their adopted identity served as a medium of protest against mainstream narratives of history and storytelling. Not every story worth remembering is found in archival records. Institutionalized memory is only one small part of the story of who we are. Their identity may not have been true from some angles, but at the same time it was true from quite a few others.

And not to forget, their history is also part of our history.

Epilogue
History Repeats Itself

At some point during the first Covid-19 pandemic lockdown in 2020, Malcha Mahal got a new resident. In a way only life can bring things to a full circle, the similarities with Wilayat, Sakina and Ali Raza were more than one.

We met Chitti Babu in the summer of 2020 during a performance art event in Malcha Mahal. This was organized by Ajay Sharma, whose video we mentioned in the introduction to this book. With his project 'In Process', he had also organized a workshop in the monument in 2019, the same year he shot the video. As he had conducted workshops and done performances in other abandoned monuments before, we had suggested Malcha Mahal to him, and gone along to report on it.[1]

In the months after Ali Raza died, Malcha Mahal was stripped of almost all the possessions of the family by sundry visitors. The dining table disappeared, with all the plates and cutlery; so did the wooden bed and the carpets. Their clothes, books and personal effects also disappeared slowly. Soon, all that was left was the building itself, sparse and bare; the bats continued to live there, perhaps soothed by the perpetual darkness that enveloped the place.

That lockdown summer, we were a small group at Malcha Mahal, with just a few performers. After some time, we noticed a slim, dark-skinned young man lurking in the corner, almost like a shadow.

Despite his dishevelled appearance and shabby clothes, Chitti Babu spoke fluent English. We learnt that he had been living at the monument for a couple of months, all by himself. Amazed, we asked him about his experience. He said he had no trouble staying there; no ghosts had bothered him so far. With no income or money to get on by, Babu told us that he picked up the bananas and other food items some people left for the monkeys. He seemed content with the situation.

He then asked us if we had any books on the occult. Surprised, we told him to visit us at our residence, and we would see what we could find for him. We did not really expect him to come and thought of it as a one-off encounter.

After a few days, Babu turned up at our place. Our cook Durga was not pleased, but she let him in after we intervened.

He behaved politely and courteously, as before. We did not have what he was looking for in our home library, but we got talking anyway, learning in the process that he was from Andhra Pradesh, had studied engineering and was living in the US before dropping everything and returning to India to live the life of a wanderer. Clearly, something had gone wrong in the US for him to drop the American dream.

Intrigued, we received him again when he showed up a few weeks later. As he began to visit regularly, with requests for small amounts of money, or clothes, before setting out on his travels, we learnt more about him. It appeared that in the US, he had a psychotic episode following which he started to write to the US President—Obama at the time—about potential terror threats. This led to his deportation to India. Going by his slightly rambling narrative, he claimed to have been tortured before his deportation.

In between, he would travel to far-off places such as Kashmir, managing to survive by visiting churches for food and succour—he is a Christian—or using his wits to get on by.

At times, he would go home, but he would call us and say that he did not like it there. His parents' disappointment in him must have been crushing; they were poor farmers and to have a son who was an engineer in the US, but chose to live as a hobo, must have been extremely painful. The last time he was home, he told us, his parents wanted him to leave. They could not bear the embarrassment anymore.

In Delhi, he would often eat at the Bangla Sahib Gurudwara, but ended up quarrelling with the caretakers there, too, and so he could not go there anymore.

Malcha Mahal proved a safe haven for him for a long period. 'Whenever I leave Malcha Mahal and come to the city, even the dogs act as if they are better than me,' he once told us.

When the Delhi government took responsibility for the monument, they posted a guard during the daytime. But even then, Chitti Babu managed to live there, having come to an arrangement with the guard. He made the place liveable over time by cleaning it of all the bat faeces and setting up his corner with some personal effects and bedding to sleep on. The surroundings became his backyard.

However, in the course of 2023, the presence of the Delhi government intensified when plans for the Haunted Walks took shape. During one of our visits to the monument, we met three employees from Delhi government's department of archaeology, all women, surveying the monument for the purpose of repairs and conservation. Though they refused to speak on the record, they did say that orders had been received to refurbish the monument. In a newspaper article that appeared around that time, an official of the department said that, apart from felling of trees, it would 'ensure that its premises are protected'.[2]

Chitti Babu left the monument soon after that. His decision to leave was catalysed by a traumatic encounter with a group of drunks, who had come to the monument for a party one night. Babu told us the story on a visit home. He seemed shaken. From what he told us, the men became randy after drinking and tried to force themselves upon him. When he resisted, they thrashed him. He escaped somehow, but decided to leave the monument. It was not his safe haven any longer.

With no other place to go, he shifted inside the forest, closer to the Simon Bolivar Marg, which connects south Delhi to Karol Bagh. It is a long stretch of road where people drop food for monkeys, just like they do on the forest road that leads to Malcha Mahal. Babu managed to get food from there as well, he told us, often competing with the monkeys and dogs. When we visited him, after the attack, he showed us a shrine we had not seen before, other than the one we wrote about in the introduction. This shrine was also a place from where he got food, Babu said. He then took us to see the watchtower, which is close to the army camp, next to the stables and the sports ground where the horses are kept; they come under the President's Estate.

Towards the summer of 2024, we lost touch.

The last time we met Babu, he seemed disenchanted with religion. A church in the area had forbidden him from visiting its premises. We discussed a story from Old Testament, in which God says he would allow a city to stand even if one righteous man lived in it. He was planning to visit Kashmir again, having fallen for the beauty of the place; in this, he was no different than any other human being.

Epilogue

Over the course of a few years, we listened to Chitti Babu's stories and tried to make sense of it. We attempted to help him, but in the end, we could not keep up with it. His last call was a request for some more money, but we told him we could not help him anymore. It was more out of annoyance at his increasingly frequent requests, and we regretted saying so as soon as we did it. But Chitti Babu took it to heart and stopped calling. Since he always called from an acquaintance's phone, we have no way to reach him.

It did strike us that like Wilayat and her family, Chitti Babu is also an outsider to the mainstream society. Like them, he too came down in the world, and finally rejected it altogether. And he ended up at Malcha Mahal, which he found more peaceful than the rest of Delhi, just like Wilayat and her family did. But unlike them, who managed to spend their last years there, he was turned out.

And so, Chitti Babu was—for now—Malcha Mahal's last resident.

Acknowledgements

Some stories are stranger than fiction. We are grateful to have been long-term residents of Delhi, a city where magic hides in the ancient monuments and where history weighs heavy on the present.

It is thanks to many people that this particular story found its way to these pages. First of all, our agent, Kanishka Gupta, and Swati Chopra and Tanima Saha of HarperCollins India, for having faith in our perspective and reporting. Karan Madhok of TheChakkar.com was the first to publish our long feature on Wilayat and her children, encouraging us to pursue this book.

We received essential help during our reporting from: Nasir Hassan in Kashmir; Alim Jafri in Lucknow; Sher Ali Khalti in Lahore; and Zia Rehman and Muhammad Arsalan Bakhtiar in Karachi. The staff at the state archives of Uttar Pradesh and Jammu and Kashmir helped us with access to the cited files, as did the staff at the National Archives of India, the Prime Ministers Museum & Library in New Delhi and Dawn's library in Karachi. We are particularly grateful to the Alkazi Collection of Photography.

Acknowledgements

Rahaab Allana, Jennifer Chowdhry Biswas and Hitanshi Chopra showed interest in our work, gave us access to the family's personal archive multiple times and provided us with the photos published in this book.

Of course, every source cited in this book was indispensable. We want to mention, in particular, Iftikhar Drabu—for helping us with further contacts and showing active interest in our progress; Fahim Ali Punjabi, for being hospitable and patient, no matter how often we called him afterwards to clarify things; Salim and Imtiaz Naqshbandi, for being so welcoming. In Kashmir, Showkat Katju and Gowhar Yakoob's home was our home away from home; Naushad Gayoor and others from the fine arts department of the majestic Kashmir University were also helpful; Inder Salim put us in touch with an important source we spoke to; Raj Bilal and his family of the Yellow Submarine Houseboat accommodated and fed us like a family member—as they have been doing for all our visits to Kashmir since 2009.

Many of our friends have encouraged us and discussed with us our findings throughout the course of our reporting. In no particular order: Arshi Zama, Agnishwar Sinha, Mohammad Ali, Mir Basit Hussain, Jyotsna Singh, B. Ajay Sharma, Rajni Bairiganjan, Harshh Kumar, Khursheed Mushtaq Ali, Hoshang Merchant, Tanya Mendonsa, Dibyajyoti Sarma, Mohammad Yusuf, Tarun Bisht, Sabina Yasmin Rahman, Abhishek Choudhary and so many others. The same goes for our siblings: Shweta Ved, Swati Ved, Snigdha Poonam and Eva André; their partners Rohan Kaler, Gautam Kadian, Mihir Sharma and Martijn Wubbolts. Our parents—Ved Prakash Narayan Singh, Poonam Singh, Lex André and Froukje André—make sure we are always at home, be it in India or in the Netherlands.

At home, we could not have managed our work without the help and care of Durga, Ganga and Pushpa. Lastly, we must thank our children, Milan and Zoya, for keeping us entertained, on our feet, loved and grounded.

Notes

Scan this QR code to access the detailed notes.

Notes

Index

A

Abbas, Chaudhry Ghulam, 183–185
Abbas, Haji Ghulam, 257
Abdullah, Farooq, 252
Abdullah, Jafar Mir, 44–49, 150, 183–185, 198, 216–218, 228–230, 241, 274
Abdullah, Sheikh, 182–186, 191, 194, 197–198, 216–220, 224–225, 228–230, 238–239, 251, 282–283, 291; meeting Nehru, 184; pro-India National Conference, 191, 195; release of, 241; Schofield on, 185
'An Act of Treason?', Munshi, 168
Adityanath, Yogi, xvi, 25, 30
Afza, Meher, 118–119, 122
Afzal, Muhammad, 278

Agra, 9, 27, 29
Ahmad, Ghulam, 236, 256–257
Ahmadi Muslims, 224
Ahmad, Khalid Bashir, 216, 218
Ahmed, Ishtiaq, 190, 212
Akbar, Said, 192–193
Akhlaq, Mohammad, 22
Akhtar, 41, 43–44
Akhtar, Salman, 295–296, 298
Alam, Shah, 166
Alexander, Jeffrey, 55
Ali, Agha Shahid, 248
Alia Imam, 267–268
Ali, Marzia, 238, 247, 249–250, 253, 260, 264
Ali, Mirza Ramzan, 118
Ali, M.M., 171–172
Ali, Mohammad, 181

316   Index

Ali, Roushan, 159, 164
Ali, Salim, 253
Ali, Syed Mansur, 120
Ali, Wajid, 117
Allahabad, 7, 27, 85, 206
All India Kashmir Committee [AIKC], 183
All India Shia Conference, 65, 141, 154
All Jammu and Kashmir Muslim Conference, 182–188, 206–207, 219, 221, 228; Abdullah on, 184; agitation of Abbas, 185; establishing 'Azad Kashmir', 187; Schofield on, 185–186; Begum Wilayat Butt as president of, 194
All Pakistan Women Association, 276
Almas Mahal (great-grandmother), 80, 118, 126, 298; as Zamrud Mahal, 80
Amber, Miya, 119
Amin, Mir Muhammad, 8, 86, 101, 104; demise of, 9
Amir-ud-Daula Library, Kaiserbagh, 121
Anand, Dev, 227
Anglo–French War, 102
Ansari, Abbas, 247, 254–257
Ansari, Masroor Abbas, 255

Ansari, Sarah, 189, 199, 256, 269–271, 277
anti-statue movement, 114
Ara, Husan Begum, Nawab, 172
Ara, Jamal, 152
Ara, Mahtab Begum, 134, 154, 160
Arif, *see* Asad (as Prince Cyrus or Ali Raza), 283
Article 370, 197, 213, 216–217, 226
'Articles of Impeachment', 109
Aru, Asmat, 41–43
Asad, 60–61, 64–67, 79, 85, 231, 234, 236–237, 244, 246–250, 253–255, 257–261, 265, 291–292; black cobra of, 62; death of, 60, 64, 67, 247, 249, 253–254, 258–260, 264; elder son, 31; Kasim on, 64, 66; Sakina on, 64; on Wilayat, 273
Asafi Kothi, 41
Asaf-ud-Daula, Nawab, xvi–xvii, 29, 37, 103, 107–108
Asiatic Society of Bengal, 102
Asiatic Society of India, 148
Awadh: annexation of, xvii, 7, 10–11, 17, 82, 122, 126, 129, 174; demand for restoration of, 11; kingdom of, 27; nawabs of, xvii, 3, 8–10, 101, 166; royal heritage, xiii; royals of, ix

Index

Awadh dynasty, 142
Ayodhya, 27, 120
Azad Kashmir. *See* Pakistan-occupied Kashmir (PoK)
Aziz, Abdul, 244

B

Babu, Chitti, 305–309
Bachchan, Amitabh, 254
Bada Din (Eid), 258
Bahauddin, Khwaja, 245
Bahu Begam, 107, 109
Bahuguna, Hemwati Nandan, 30–31, 33–35; Chandra on, 54
Bahuguna, Vijay, 54
Bahujan Samaj Party, 53
Banaras, revolt at, 108
Bandi, Allah, 53
Banerjee, Mamata, 141
Bara Imambara, Lucknow, 29, 36, 140; Mustafa on, xvi
Barry, Ellen, xii, xv, 20, 78, 181, 273, 280, 286, 292–293
Bashir Nawab, 65, 291
Bawariya tribe, 88
Bedi, B.P.L., 228–230
Bedi, Freda, 228–230
Beg, Mirza Afzal, 184, 216
A Begum and a Rani, Mukherjee, 130

Begum Hazrat Mahal documentary, 137
Begums of Awadh, 56, 81, 95–96, 101–102, 107, 126, 129–130, 265
Begums of Awadh, Santha, 7
Bengal, nawab of, 104–105, 148
Bentham, Jeremy, 111
Besant, Annie, 89
Bharatiya Janata Party (BJP), xvi, 22, 46, 53–54, 213, 226
Bhat, Abdul Qadir, 224
Bhat, Nisar, 224
Bhatt, Ravi, 9, 53, 127
Bhowal, Tiasa, 21
Bhutto, Zulfikar Ali, 241
Bistedari Mahal or Bistedari Malcha, 15
Black Lives Matter movement, 113
Blavatsky, Helena, 89
Bob, 293–295
Bogra, Mohammad Ali, 180, 194–199, 268, 285
Boori Ma, Jhumpa Lahiri, 299–300
Brando, Marlon, 300
Brass, Paul R., 33
Brein, 231, 234, 244–246, 255, 260
British counter-insurgency measures, 133

British East India Company, xvii, 36
British rule, x, 110, 116, 128
Broekstra, Leonie, xiv–xv, 63, 78
Bruer, Josef, 303
Bumiller, Elisabeth, 67
Burhan-ul-Mulk, 101
Burke, Edmund, 109–110, 112
Butalia, Urvashi, xiv
Butt, from Kashmir, xi
Butt, Aslam, 282;
Butt, Immadudin Shahid, 283
Butt, Inayatullah/Butt, I.U., 48–49, 179, 190–191, 193, 207, 211–212, 220, 223–224, 227, 230, 273–276, 278–279, 291; birth of, 282; death of, 242; education of, 283; joining Pakistan Aviation Ltd, 275; Kashmiri origin of, 282; marrying Miraj, 283; meeting Wilayat in Lahore, 283; moving to Pakisan, 284; Zaidi on, 275; death of, 237, 285–286
Butt, Iqbal, 282
Butt, Jilal, 282
Butt, Khalid, 283, 291
Butt, Khwaja Ahmad Deen (father), 281
Butt, Mehmood, 291
Butt, Salahuddin Zahid, 272–274; birth of, 283
Butt, Yasmeen (stepdaughter), 272–273, 283
Buxar, battle of, 106–107

C

Calcutta, 10–11, 102, 104–105, 126–127, 137, 144, 147, 154, 156, 158, 161–162, 166, 171–172; Black Hole incident of, 148; British community in, 112
Calcutta High Court, 164
Cama, Bhikaji Madame, 137
Camellia, 272
Carmichael, Krista, 301–303
Cease Fire Line, 214
Chandra, Atul, 52, 54
Charbagh Railway Station, 32, 34, 55–56
Chatar Manzil Palace, 86
Chattar Manzil, 26, 28, 40, 262; demand for, 35; excavation around, 29; Taqui on, 28
Chehlum meeting, Wilayat disturbing, 188–189
Chhota Imambara, 29, *see also* Bara Imambara
Chinhat, battle at, 131
Clive, Robert, 105–106, 111–112, 114
Colston, Edward, 114

INDEX

communism, 196, 228
Communist Party of India, 16, 32, 230
concubines, 81, 123, 125
Congress Party, 53, 184
Covid-19 pandemic, 25, 58, 61, 226, 256, 305
Criminal Tribes Act of 1871, 88

D

Dalrymple, William, 113
Dar, Ali Mohammad, 233–238
Dar, Bashir, 284, 286, 291
Dar, Showkat Ahmad, 255–258
Datar, B.N., 163, 165
Daulat Khana complex, 37, 40, 47
Dave, Shanti, 15–16
Delhi Durbar, 80
Delhi Earth Station, 5, 16
demands: for palaces in Lucknow, 85–86; for property in Lucknow, 86; for return of jagirs, 163
Democratic National Conference, 219
descendants, xiii, xv–xvi, 46, 134, 153, 156, 163, 167, 170, 172–174, 265–266; African, 42, 121; of Begum Hazrat Mahal, 57, 96, 134, 137; Birjis Qadr, 126, 134, 139; of House of Awadh, xv; Khan on, 39; Wajid Ali Shah, of 57 wasiqa or royal pension to, 36–37
Dhar, D.P., 219, 240–241; death of, 240
Dhar, Vijay, 240, 252
Dilip Kumar, 227
Direct Action Day, 185
Dogra, Prem Nath, 214
Dogra dynasty, 182, 185, 194, 281
dogs, 19, 35, 52, 55–56, 59–62, 70–72, 76, 84, 87–89, 93–94, 307–308; death of, 74–75
Doon-Ghati Nalapani, Ghising, 119
Drabu, Iftikhar, 231–232, 239–240, 260
drug research institute, 13, 28
Dubois, Blanche, 301

E

Earth Station, x, 16, 19, 21, 87
East India Company, 7, 9, 104–106, 108, 111, 113, 120, 166, 299
educational grants/scholarships, 36, 162, 173–174
Edwardes, Michael, 104, 106, 110
1857 Sepoy Mutiny, xiii, xv, 11, 14, 112, 114, 117, 126, 129–131, 134, 136–137, 160, 162–164, 167, 170; revolt in Jhansi in, 132; siege upon Lucknow, 156

Elize, 293–295
Emergency, 32–34, 84–85
An Era of Darkness, Tharoor, 103
eunuchs, 107, 125
exorcisms, 5

F
Faiz, Alys, 191
Faiz, Faiz Ahmad, 191–192, 228, 230
Farhad Hakim, 140
Fatima, Manzilat, 150
Fatima, Talat, 142, 153
female heroism, 81
The First Two Nawabs of Awadh, Srivastava, 101
'Five Year Fuss for "Mogul" in Penury', xiii
Fort William, 105, 113, 128–129, 144, 147–148, 153
Foucault, Michel, 74, 96, 296, 304
Fox, Charles James, 109
French, The, 96, 104, 107, 296
Freud, Sigmund, 94, 303

G
Gadar Ke Phool, Nagar, 119
Ganderbal, 83, 203, 222, 227, 231–236, 238, 246, 249, 261, 263, 281

Gandhi, Indira, 30, 32–34, 39, 51, 61, 66, 68, 85–86, 240, 242, 251
Gandhi, Mahatma, 89
Gandhi, Rajiv, 66
Gandhi, Sanjay, 34
Gautam, Prawash, 134, 141
Gayatri Devi, Maharani, 85, 120
Ghazi-ud-Din, Nawab, 10, 28
Ghaznavi, Ismaeel, Maulana, 183
Ghulam Mohammad, Bakshi, 184, 208, 217–219, 241
Gomti, 28, 64
Gould, William, 189, 269
Gracey, General, 191
Great Calcutta Killings, 185
Gujral, I.K., 229
Gunahor, 282–284
Gupta, Brijen K., 105

H
Habib, Sayyid, 183
Haider, Ghazi-ud-Din, 55, 81
Hamid, Shahid, 284
harem, 125, 127
Hasan, Ghulam, 257
Hasan, Nasir, 255
Hasanov, Behram, 55
Hasnain, Aseem, 52–54
Hassan, Ghulam, 254, 258–259

Hastings, Warren, xviii, 9, 96, 101–114, 116; death of, 110; family of, 103–104; loot of Awadh's begums, 103; to Madras, 104; trial of, 107, 116

'Haunted Walks', 21–22

Havelock, Henry, Gen., 111, 114

Hazratbal Shrine, Srinagar, 217–218

Hazrat Mahal, xi, xiii, xv, 30–31, 51, 80–81, 96, 116–133, 135–139, 152–154, 156–157, 159–161, 167, 173–174, 298–299; Begum, 57, 65, 128, 130, 136–137, 150, 154, 156, 265; Begum of Oudh, 129; death of, 136, 160; grave in Kathmandu, 134; heroism, 81, 96; leaving Lucknow, 133; led army against British, 11; Mehak Pari to, 119; memorials of, 137; as Muhammadi, 119; Nawab Hazrat Mahal Sahiba as, 119, 124; origins of, 120, 138; Queen, 139, 159–160; Sakina on, 129

Herman, 302

Hindu Kashmiri Pandits, exodus of, 225

Holy Relic (Moi-e-Muqqadas), incident of, 217, 217–218, 241, 256

House of Awadh, symbol of, xi

Hurriyat Conference, 256

Husain, Gulam, 118

Husain, Zahid, 272

Husainabad Clock Tower, 29

Husainabad Trust, 35, 37; and Allied Trust, 36

Hussain, Abrar, 43–44, 56, 89, 296; dog trainer, 64

Hussain, Imam, 35, 55–56, 87, 142

Hussain, Inayat, 48, 189

Hussain, Wasif, 142–143, 150

Huzn-e-Akhtar/Huzn-i-Akhtar, Taqi, 127, 129

Hyder, Ghaziudin, battle with British, 81

I

Ibrahim, Sardar, 219

identity, xiii, xv, xviii, 97, 177, 179, 293, 299, 304

Iftikhar-un-Nissa, 123–124

Imhasly, Bernard, 18, 21, 250

Indian citizenship, 203, 205, 209, 221–222

Indian Citizenship Act 1955, 203–204, 209, 222

Indian National Congress, 185, 219, 225

Indian National Trust for Art and Cultural Heritage (INTACH), 5, 15

An Indian Political Life, Brass, 33

India TV, 19–20, 22; and raiding, 19
Indo-China War of 1962, 202
'In Process', 305
Institutionalized memory, 304
Instrument of Accession, 39, 186–187
Iqbal, Allama, 182–183, 282, 286
Iqbal, Nosheen, 301
Indian Space Research Organisation (ISRO), x, 5, 91, 69, 90–91

J

Jaan-e-Alam Aur Mehak Pari, Naheed, 118
Jaddan, 53
Jafar, Mir, 105
Jafri, Alim, 231
Jagmohan, 245
Jalal, Ayesha, 281
Jan, Haider, 53
Jan, Mughal, 53
Jana Sangh, 32, 53, 85, 213–215
Jha, L.K., 66, 254
Jinnah, Mohammad Ali, 183–185, 188, 190, 212, 270
A Journey Through the Kingdom of Oude, Sleeman, 128
'The Jungle Prince of Delhi', xi

K

Kalhan, Promilla, 13, 30–31, 48
Kalidas, S., 16
Kamini, Gulshan Ara, Begum, 171
Kanjwal, Hafsa, 218, 239
Kant, Immanuel, 289
Kapoor, Shammi, 242
Karachi, 194–196, 199, 203, 207, 267–271, 274–279, 284, 286, 290, 297, 300
Karachi Aero Club, 276, 279
Karbala, 35, 47, 55, 87, 143, 164, 248; battle of, 35, 47, 87, 143
Kashmir (and Jammu): xi–xii, 182, 194–195, 198, 210, 225, 237, 252, 281, 283; activism, 281; dispute, 192, 197, 241–242, 251–252; infiltration, 210; Muharram procession in, 248; Muslims, 182, 217, 225, 228, 281; nationalism, 227–229; Pakistan/tribal invasion of, 186, 190, 192–193; Pandits, 226; return to, 210–211; roots, 193, 242, 282, 297
Kashmir Conspiracy Case, 197, 216
Kashmir Martyrs Day, 194
Kashmir Political Conference (KPC), 217
Kasim, Mohammad, 24, 58–61, 64, 66–73, 79, 84–85, 89, 244, 247, 254, 291–292, 296

INDEX

Kasimbazar, 104–105
Kathmandu Dilemma, Rae, 135
Kaul, Bimala, 244, 247, 254
Khalti, Sher Ali, 279, 279–281
Khan, Abid Ali/Dara Nawab, 38, 55
Khan, Akbar, 192
Khan, Ali Vardi, death of, 104
Khan, Amir Mohammad, 211–212
Khan, Amjad Ali, Nawab, 41
Khan, Bihar Ali, 107, 109
'khangi', 122–123
Khan, Hossain Ali, Gulam, 122
Khan, Ibrahim Ali, 37–38, 44–45, 150
Khan, Jowar Ali, 107, 109
Khan, Liaquat Ali, 189, 192–193, 207, 239, 247, 263, 269, 276, 285–286; assassination of, 31, 188–190, 192–193, 230–231, 247, 263, 286; death by Said Akbar, 192; rumours, 250; State trip to US, 191
Khan, Mammoo, 125–127
Khan, Maulvi Tamizuddin, Maulavi, 271
Khan, Mummu, 126
Khan, Ra'ana Liaquat Ali, 269, 276, 285
Khan, Sadat, 8–9, 38, 86, 101, 104; *see also under* Burhan-ul-Mulk
Khan, Sadiq, 114

Khan, Sarbuland, 8
Khan, Sardar Ibrahim, 186
Khanum, Muhammadi, 136
Khosla Commission, 33
Kishwar, Malika (mother of Shah), sailing to London, 10–11, 127–128
Knowland, Senator, 196
Krishen, Pradip, 6, 19, 21
Kud, Birjis, 122

L

Lahiri, Jhumpa, 299–300
Lahore, 7, 80, 180–182, 227–230, 241, 251, 272, 279–286, 290, 292; and Kashmiri nationalism, 227–228
Lakhna, 27
Lakshmibai, Jhansi Rani, 130, 132, 138, 161; Mukherjee on, 131
Lal, Bhure, 66
Lal Baradari/Badshah Bagh, 82
The Last King in India, Llewellyn-Jones, 10, 120
The Life and Times of the Nawabs of Awadh, Bhatt, 9
life story, 118, 120, 302
Line of Control, 252
Llewellyn-Jones, Rosie, 10, 120–121, 127, 129–130, 156
loyalties, 10, 54, 58, 124, 126, 162, 191

Lucknow: Brajesh Pathak for change of name, xvii; city of nawabs, 26; house offering, 63; older parts of, 27; Aishwarya Pandit on, 36; Victoria Park, 136

Lucknow: Fire of Grace, Mishra, 9, 28

M

Madhok, Balraj, 214

Madho, Rana Beni, 130

Madras, 104–105

Mahan, Rhodos, 134

Mahmudabad, Ali Khan, 231

Malcha Mahal, x–xi, 14–15, 27, 51, 68, 70, 273; Dave on, 15; as hunting lodge, 3; Kasim on, 69; to Lalit Kala Akademi, 15; names of, 15; offering to, 68; Parashar on, 14

Malcha Marg, xi, 14

Malcha Patti, 14

Malcha village, 6, 11, 14

Malik, Satya Pal, 34, 54

Malik, Yasin, 225–226

Malla dynasty, 119

Malmal Bibi, Musammat, 193

Manzar-i-Alam, 270–271

Manzilat, 150–151, 153–156, 164, 174

Marathas, 8, 106–107

Marshall, James, 107–108, 110

Marx, Karl, 99

Masani, Zareer, 113, 115

Meerza, Sahibzada Kaukab Quder Sajjad Ali, 159

Meerza, Sahibzada Nayyar Quder Wasif Ali, 137, 141, 150–151, 154–155, 159, 165, 172–173

Mehak Pari, 123; Iftikhar-un-Nissa for, 124; *see also* Nawab Hazrat Mahal Sahiba

Mehdi, 79, 272

Mehta, Ved, 217

Merchant, nanny, 83

Metiaburj, 140, 145–148, 154

Military Alliance Programme (MAP), 196

Mirza, Irfan Ali, 142, 153

Mirza, Kamar Kadr, 166

Mirza, Kamran, 164

Mirza, Meher Quder Zahid Ali, 158–159, 162–163, 165

Mirza, Mohi-ud-Din, 137

Mirza, Moin-ul Ali, 142

Mirza, Yusuf, as King of Oudh, 168–169, 173

Mishra, Amaresh, 9, 28

Mishra, S.G., 84

Mitra, Sudipta, 144

mob-lynching, 22

Modi, 137
Mohammad, Ali, 257
Moreno-Álvarez, Alejandra, xiv, 299–300
Morrow, Ann, 62–63
Mountbatten, Lord, 162
Mughals, 7, 10, 27, 106, 166
Muharram, 35–36, 53–54, 142–143, 234, 236–237, 246, 253, 259; processions, 54, 248; rituals, 263, *see also* Shias
Mukerjee, Shikha, 113–114
Mukherjee, P.B. (J), 164
Mukherjee, Rudrangshu, 130–133, 136, 138
Mullik, B.N., 195, 210, 213, 218, 251
multiculturalism, 113
Munna Jan, 81–82
Munny Begum, 106
Munshi, K.M., 168–169
Murad, Kenizé, 125
Mushtri, 53
Muslim League, 182, 185, 188–189, 211, 221, 270; Schofield on, 185
Mustafa, Kulsum, xvi
mut'ah wife, 174, 282, 287, *see also under* Shias
Mutual Defence Assistance/ Agreement Pact, 196, 219
My Years with Nehru, Mullik, 210, 251

N

Nagar, Amritlal, 119
Naheed, Nusrat, 118, 120–121
Naidu, Sarojini, 169
Najju, 53
Nana Sahab, 136
Naqshbandi, Ashraf, 244–245, 247
Naqshbandi, Imtiaz, 245–248, 292
Naqshbandi, Salim, 245–247, 253–254, 292
Naqvi, A.T., 275
Naqvi, Saeed, 181
Narasimha Rao, P.V., 86
Naseer-ud-Din, 42
Nath, Ram, 214
National Conference (NC), 184–185, 218–219, 228
nationalism, 139, 295
Navroz, 88–89
Nawabi architecture, xv
Nawab Wajid Ali Shah Memorial Hospital, 149
Nawaz, Hamid, 284
Nazimuddin, Khwaja, 275
Nehru, Jawaharlal, 13, 15, 170, 206, 210, 251; Abdullah and, 184–185, 194, 216–217, 220; and Bhutto, 241; death of 241; Freda and, 230; inauguration of drug research institute 28; letter from Wilayat Butt, 201;

Noorani on, 197; and pension to Mirza, 158; and residence for Wilayat, 83; Sakina on, 83, 262; and USSR, 191; visit to Bogra, 195

Nepal, 24, 117, 119, 129–130, 133–134, 137, 141, 143, 154, 157, 160; escape to, 136

Neruda, Pablo, 295

New Delhi Railway Station, x, 12–13, 23–25, 30, 57–58, 60–62, 65, 68, 84–87, 250, 253, 261, 264–265; for eviction, 86; memories of staying in, 84; protest at, 3; and railway authorities, 84, 260

Nishat Bagh, Sri Nagar, 83, 254, 257, 262–263

Nixon, Richard, 33, 196

Noorani, A.G., 197

O

oceanic trade, 105

oil crisis, 33

The Other Side of Silence, Butalia, xiv

Oudh Royal Family Association, Calcutta, 171

Outram, James, 128

P

Pakistan: creation of, 188, (*see also* Partition); administered Kashmir. *See* 'Pakistan-occupied Kashmir' (PoK); army, 186, 190; defence pact with US, 197; Muslims, 215, 251; resettlement of Muslims, 213

Pakistan International Airlines (PIA), 275

'Pakistan-occupied Kashmir' (PoK), 187, 219–220, 252

Pakistan–United States Aid Pact of 1954, 195

Panda, Chitta, 114

Pandit, Aishwarya, 36

Pandit, Idrissa, 260–261, 264

Pandit, Mohammad Amin, 253, 259–260, 265

Pant, Govindvallabh, 169

Parashar, Arpit, 11, 14

Parikhana, 118–119, 122–123, 130

Parikhana, Shah, 153

Partition, x, xiii–xiv, 48, 185, 187, 190–191, 197–198, 210–213, 229, 243–244, 267, 269–272, 284–285, 297, 299; Karachi and 269; refuges, 270; violence, 211, 274

Patel, Sardar Vallabhbhai, 40

Pathak, Brajesh, xvii

Pearl by the River, Mitra, 144

pension, xv, 36–37, 158, 162–163, 165–167, 170, 174, 266

Père Lachaise cemetery, 12

INDEX 327

Persian invasion of Delhi, 7
'Persons of Indian origin,' 205
petition, 63, 159, 161, 164–165, 170–173, 271, (*see* demands); to Buckingham Palace, 63
Picture Gallery, 30, 36
Plassey, battle of, 105–106, 148–149
Plebiscite Front (PF), 216–218
police raids, 19
Praja Parishad (PP), 213–214, 251
"Pride of Purse", 85
Princely states, accession to India, 39, 184, 188
Privy Purse, 39–40, 62, 163, 251; abolishment of, 40
Punjabi, Ahmed Ali, 247, 249
Punjabi, Fahim Ali, 249–250, 253–254, 258, 260

Q

Qadir, Abdul, 182
Qadr, Anjum, xiii, 20, 139, 141–143, 150–151, 154, 159, 164–165, 169, 171; death of, 154
Qadr, Birjis, 123, 125–127, 129, 134, 137, 139, 141–143, 150, 152–153, 156, 159–160, 172, 174; assassination of, 152, 154, 172; British confiscation of, 167; coronation of, 160; descendants of, 172; Gautam on, 134, 141; return to Calcutta, 161; marrying Mahtab Ara, 134
Qasim, Mir, 242
Quder, Mehr (Baba Abba), 143, 154, 157, 161–162, 168–169, 170–173; death of, 162; special pension for, 168
Queen Mother, 11–13, 32; death of, 12; in London, 11, 13
Quder, Kaukab, *See* Meerza, Sahibzada Nayyar Quder Wasif Ali
Quit India movement, 162
Quit Kashmir movement, 229
Qureshi, S.M., 180

R

Rae, Ranjit, 135, 157
Rahim, Abdul, 47
raids, 19, 22
Raj, Suhasini, 280
'Raja Hussain'—King Hussain, 24
Rao, Gangadhar, death of, 132
Rashtriya Swayamsevak Sangh (RSS), 213–214
Rawalpindi Conspiracy Case, 192, 203, 229–230
Ray, B.C., 171
Raza, Ali/Ali Raza Mahal, ix–xii, 3–4, 17–24, 57–60, 62–63, 65–66, 70, 79, 90–94, 233–234,

236–237, 238, 244, 253–254, 259–260, 263–264, 273, 283, 291, 301, 304–305; as artist, 23; Berry on, 292–293; as 'Cyrus Riza', 79; death of, 4, 18, 20–21, 23, 48, 70–71, 78, 151, 292, 296; Kazim meeting, 59–61; as younger son, 31

Raza, Tabrez, 41

Razee-ud-Daula, 124

Rehman, Waheeda, 254

Revolt of 1857, *see* 1857 Sepoy Mutiny

Ridge Forest, 3, 6, 18–19

Right to Information Act, 201

Rizvi, Ammar, 35, 39, 43, 51–52, 54, 65; meeting Wilayat, 31–32;

Rizvi, B.H., 65

Rooprai, Vikramjit Singh, 19–20

Royal Families of Awadh (RFA), 37, 45–46, 49

royalty, xi–xii, 40, 42, 46–48, 62, 85, 131, 138, 251, 286, 290; claim of, 286

'Rulers of Oudh', 4, 38

Rumi Darwaza, 29

Rushdie, Salman, 203, 291

S

Sabaism, 89–90

Sadiq, G.M. 184, 191, 218–219, 225, 227–231, 240–241, 252, 262–264

Sadiq, Iftekhar, 225–228, 230, 242, 246, 252, 261–263; death of, 264

Sadiq, Rafiq, 227

Sadr-un-Nisa, 107

Safdarjung (Safdar Jang), 9, 101, 104, 107; tomb of, 27

Sahiba, Rani, 43, 60–61, 64, 67, 70–72

Sahni, Balraj, 228–229

Sakeena/Sakina/Sakina Mahal (daughter), 14, 17, 22–23, 31, 55, 64, 67, 125, 231, 237, 292, 301: on Asad, 64; book of, 11, 66, 68, 78, 85, 89–90, 95–96; on brother 'Prince Mehdi', (*see also* Mehdi) 272; death of, 20; as Farhad Yasmeen, 283; Hussain on, 44; names as Marzia and Zohra, 283; as Princess, ix–x, 20, 91–92, 264, 283; on Zaheer, 51; as Zohra, 233, 236–238, 264, 281–282

Salahuddin, Qazi, 243

Salam, Abdus, 224

Samajwadi Party, 53, 155

Santha, K.S., 7, 126

Santragachi railway club, 164

Sarabhai, Mridula, 220

Savarkar, V. D., 130–131, 139

Schofield, Victoria, 185–186, 242, 252

Scindia, Vijaya Raje, Maharani, 85
servants, 4, 11–12, 24, 31, 38, 59, 70–71, 240, 247, 257–258, 260
Shafi, Nighat, 232, 238–239
Shahabuddin, 283
Shah, Amjad Ali, 119, 123
Shah, Fahmida, 248–249
Shahid, 63, 181, 248, 271–272, 274; as half-brother of Raza Ali, 273
Shah Jahan, xvi
Shah, Ahmadullah, Maulvi, 136
Shah, Mirwaiz Yusuf, 185
Shah, Mohammad/Muhammad Ali, King, 36, 45
Shah Najaf Imambara, 55–56, *see also* Bara Imambara; Chhota Imambara
Shah, Wajid Ali, x–xi, xiii, 117–120, 122, 124–125, 127, 130–132, 139–148, 152–154, 156–157, 165–168, 170–171, 173–174, 282, 298–299; British imprisonment of, 128; exile to Calcutta, 10, 166; marriage to Hazrat Mahal, 81; thumris of, 10; titles of, 143
Shamsuddin, Khwaja, 218
Sharma, Ajay, 22–23, 305
Sharma, R.C., 247
Sharma, Shankar Dayal, 95
Sharma, Uma, 16

Sharma, Virendra, 114
Shastri, Lal Bahadur, 195, 208, 241, 251; death of, 241
Shastri, Prakash Vir, 215
Sheesh Mahal, 30, 35, 37–38, 42, 44, 48, 55, 140
Sheikhzadas, 9, 47
Sheridan, Richard Brinsley, 109
Shias, 35–36, 46, 48, 53–55, 87–88, 144, 233, 249, 255–257; Day of Ashura and, 35; identity, 55, 190; influence, 47; mut'ah marriages of, 81, 174, 280, 282, 284, 287, 298–299; rituals, 89
Shia–Sunni politics, 52, 54
Shirinov, Agil, 55
Shuja-ud-Daula, Nawab, 104–107, 148; Mishra on, 9
Singh, Amar, (grandson of Gulab Singh), 14
Singh, Chait, 107–109
Singh, Charan, 33–34, 65
Singh, Gulab, as Kaaleghodewala, 11
Singh, Hari (Maharaja), 185–186
Singh, Karan, 85
Singh, Maun, 120
Singh, Kunwar, Raja, 163
Singh, Man, Raja, 130
Singh, Sahdev, 213
Singh, V.P., 85

Siraj-ud-Daula, Nawab. *See* Shuja-ud-Daula

Sirajuddaullah and the East India Company, Gupta, 105

Sleeman, William, 128, 166

Smith, R.V., 6

socialist Janata Party, 32

Som, Sangeet, xvi

South East Asia Treaty Organization (SEATO), 219

Soviet Russia/Soviet Union, 191–192, 241

Srivastava, A.K., 8, 119, 195–196, 241

Srivastava, Ashirbadi Lal, 8

Srivastava, C.P., 195, 241

A Star Shall Fall, 127

A Streetcar Named Desire, Williams, 300

Sultan, Tipu, 163

Sunni names, 48, 259, *see also* Shia-Sunni politics

Swaminathan, Jagdish, 16

Syed, Babar, 276

T

Taj Mahal, xvi; Adityanath on, xvi; Son on, xvi

Talha, Naureen, 212

Tandon, H.K., 170

Taqui, Roshan, 28–29, 46, 119–121, 123, 127, 129

Tasadduque, Salma, 284–285

Tashkent declaration, 241–242

Taylor, P.J.O., 127

'Tea with Nawab', 46

tensions, 52, 54, 202, 225

Tharoor, Shashi, 103, 114–115

The Time and Trial of the Rawalpindi Conspiracy 1951, Zaheer, 190

Tiwari, N.D., 34, 52; job offering to Asad Ali, 60

Tope, Tatya, 130, 161

Transfer of Residence Rules, 207

Trauma and Recovery, Carmichael, 302

trauma survivors, 301, 303

Treaty of Banaras, 106–107

Treaty of Chunar, 108

Tripathi, Kamalapati, 34–35

Tripathi, Sachin, 49

Trudeau, Danielle, 94

Tughlaq, Firoz Shah, 6, 68

U

Umber, 118, 122

U.S.–Pak Aid Pact, 195

Uttar Pradesh, xv–xvi, 22, 25, 27, 29–30, 32, 34, 51, 57, 63, 82, 85, 161

Index

V

Vajpayee, Atal Bihari, 46, 214
Varanasi, 27, 82
Victoria, Queen, 11–12

W

Wani, Muzaffar, 248
Wani, Sadiq, 248
war, of 1971, 252; of 1857, *see* 1857 Revolt
wasiqa or royal pension, 36–37
Watergate scandal, 33
water supply, 5, 19, 87; from the ISRO Earth Station, 69; Sakina on, 87
Wazir, Nawab, 108
Wilayat Butt/Mrs Butt/Inayatullah Begum/Shehzadi Wilayat Mahal/Wilayat Mahal, xi–xii, xiv–xv, xvii, 26–27, 40, 72–73, 79, 86–88, 101–102, 151, 179–181, 190, 200–202, 208–209, 221, 223, 268–270, 292; Abdullah on, 49; arrest of, 188, 199, 272, 279; Atul Chandra on, 52; birth of, 282; born as Taj Bakht Nasr, 80; children of, xiv, xvii, 16–17, 30, 41–44, 66, 69, 231, 233, 262–263, 271–272, 295, 298, 302, 304; claims of, xii, xviii, 13, 51, 126–127, 150, 209; *Dawn* on, 180; death of, 4, 17, 71, 74–77, 80, 92, 95; on death of husband, 207; demand for royal palaces, 175; family of, xvii, 190, 271; husband, xiii, 64, 189–190; Hussain on, 44; identities, xiv, 265, 282; Idrissa Pandit on, 261; for Indian nationality, 200, 231; in Karachi, 277; Kasim on, 61; letter to Nehru, 206; letter to Shastri, 208; letter to Tiwari, 57; Mahanagar Colony house for, 35; marriage of, 83; to mental hospital, 199, 287; Pakistan nationality, 209; protest at New Delhi Railway Station, 3, 12; protest for Awadh, xvii; relatives of, 286; resettling in Kashmir, 203–210, 220–221, 242; Rizvi on, 35, 51; Sakina on, 179; transformation, 230; travelling to India, 271; wife of Wajid Ali Shah, 31; writing history of Awadh, 75
Wilayat Manzil, 253
Williams, Tennessee, 300
Women's Muslim League, 188, 269–270
Writing and Rewriting the Holocaust, Young, xiv

Y

Yadav, Akhilesh, 47, 135, 155
Yadav, Mulayam Singh, 154

Young, James, xiv
Yusuf, Syed Mohammad, 49

Z

Zafar, Bahadur Shah, xiii, 7, 134, 167, 177
'Zafar's Real Descendant Stakes His Claims', xiii
Zaheer, Ali, 36, 51, 230
Zaheer, Sajjad, 191–192, 229–230; Indian citizenship for, 203
Zahid, Salma, 272
Zahid, Sameena, 286
Zaidi, Waqar, 275–276
Zamend Tamkeen Mahal (grandmother), 80
Zamrud Mahal. *See* Almas Mahal
Zohra (Wilayat's mother), 281–282, 298
Zoroastrianism, 89

About the Authors

Aletta André is a Dutch historian and journalist, who has covered South Asia for Dutch and international media since 2009. Her debut youth novel, *Het meisje dat door India fietste* (The girl who cycled through India), about the mass exodus of migrant labourers from Indian cities during the Covid-19 pandemic lockdown, was published in the Netherlands by Luitingh-Sijthoff in 2021. After fifteen years of living in New Delhi, she returned to her native Netherlands in 2024.

Abhimanyu Kumar is an Indian poet and journalist with a wide experience covering politics, arts, culture and minority issues. His poetry collection *Milan and the Sea* was published by Red River in 2017. He has translated Australian poet Robert Wood's poetry collection *Redgate*, also published from Red River in 2020. His long-form reportage on lynchings in India was included in the anthology *Notes from the Hinterland*, published by Aleph Book Company in 2019. He divides his time between New Delhi and Deventer, the Netherlands, with Aletta André and their two kids.

HarperCollins *Publishers* India

At HarperCollins India, we believe in telling the best stories and finding the widest readership for our books in every format possible. We started publishing in 1992; a great deal has changed since then, but what has remained constant is the passion with which our authors write their books, the love with which readers receive them, and the sheer joy and excitement that we as publishers feel in being a part of the publishing process.

Over the years, we've had the pleasure of publishing some of the finest writing from the subcontinent and around the world, including several award-winning titles and some of the biggest bestsellers in India's publishing history. But nothing has meant more to us than the fact that millions of people have read the books we published, and that somewhere, a book of ours might have made a difference.

As we look to the future, we go back to that one word—a word which has been a driving force for us all these years.

Read.